THE IRAQ *I* KNEW

THE IRAQ *I* KNEW

From Saddam Hussein to Weapons of

Mass Destruction to Al Qaeda in Iraq

Book I: *Into the Storm*

Colonel Burl Randolph, Jr., DM
US Army (Retired)

Book I: *Into the Storm*

The Iraq *I* Knew
*From Saddam Hussein to Weapons of Mass Destruction
to Al Qaeda in Iraq*

Copyright © 2024 by Colonel Burl Randolph, Jr., DM,
US Army (Retired)

MyWingman, LLC

Contact Dr. Burl at https://mywingmanllc.com/contact-us.

Or use your cellphone camera to scan the QR Code below:

Published by:
MyWingman, LLC Publishing
Cover Design by Author
Cover Photo courtesy of the Author.

Kindle Direct Publishing

ASIN-10: B0D5WJ3D9Y

ISBN-13: 9798848848533

First Edition

Printed in the United States of America.

DEDICATION

This book is dedicated to the Service Members and their Families who have sacrificed for this country through combat deployments after combat deployments, year after year.

Most Americans will never truly realize and appreciate the sacrifices that were and are made on their behalf. Many people do not grasp that our nation is secured by the one percent who serve to protect the other 99 percent. Or that approximately 350,000 Americans volunteer each year to serve, but only a third are selected. The other two-thirds either change their minds at the last minute or are found unqualified.

Serving our country was a true honor that took many service members to a new level in their lives. It allowed us to discover who we are and, in many cases, who we wanted to be.

"Greater love has no one than this:

To lay down one's life for one's friends."

John, Chapter 15, verse 13

Book I: *Into the Storm*

Table of Contents

DEDICATION...*V*

PREFACE ....*VIII*

INTRODUCTION ....*IX*

PART I: "AND MUCH TO OUR SURPRISE" ....*- 0 -*

CHAPTER 1: "THE LONG, HOT SUMMER"........................*- 1 -*

CHAPTER 2: "AND THE SIMMERING BEGAN"................*- 15 -*

CHAPTER 3: "THE MOMENTS I WAITED FOR" ....*- 29 -*

CHAPTER 4: "THE REAL MIND BLOWER"........................*- 37 -*

CHAPTER 5: "THE GAS CHAMBER OF HORRORS" AND OTHER ODDITIES..*- 45 -*

PART II: DESERT SHIELD: "OUT OF THE FRYING PAN"............*- 53 -*

CHAPTER 6: "IT BEGAN TO SIZZLE" ....*- 56 -*

CHAPTER 7: "THIS AIN'T NO NTC ROTATION"...........*- 62 -*

CHAPTER 8: "THE WAITING GAME".................................*- 77 -*

CHAPTER 9: "A CHANGING OF THE GUARD…" ....*- 90 -*

CHAPTER 10: "GETTING THE QUICK WIN".................*- 101 -*

PART III: DESERT STORM: "INTO A FIREY STORM".............*- 111 -*

CHAPTER 11: "BECOMING THE S2".............................*- 112 -*

CHAPTER 12: "BEFORE THE STORM".............................*- 126 -*

CHAPTER 13: "OUR G-DAY CAME EARLY"...................*- 133 -*

CHAPTER 14: "INTO THE EYE OF THE STORM".........*- 142 -*

CHAPTER 15: "TIME – IT'S ALL RELATIVE"................*- 159 -*

PART IV AFTER THE STORM…I THINK FEB 28, 1991 ....*- 171 -*

CHAPTER 16: "IT'S NOT OVER, TILL IT'S OVER" ......*- 172 -*

CHAPTER 17: "MEDIC!!! MEDIC!!! MEDIC!!!" ....*- 184 -*

CHAPTER 18: "UNCONTROLLED CONTROLLED DETONATIONS "AND OTHER MISCHIEF..*- 192 -*

CHAPTER 19: "A STORM FRONT WAS A BREWIN"....................*- 197 -*

CHAPTER 20: "THE HEROES' HOMECOMING, ACT I"............ *- 209 -*

PART V: HERE COME THE "THE REAL STORMS"...................... *- 223 -*

CHAPTER 21: "THE HEROES HOMECOMING, ACT II"............. *- 224 -*

CHAPTER 22: "RESET – "THE WHIRLWIND NEVER ENDS" ... *- 231 -*

CHAPTER 23: "USING WHAT I LEARNED, PART I"................... *- 242 -*

ACKNOWLEDGEMENTS... *- 252 -*

AUTHOR'S BIOGRAPHY.. *- 253 -*

ADDITIONAL WORKS BY DR. RANDOLPH................... *- 255 -*

EDITING CLIENTS .... *- 256 -*

PEER-REVIEWED WORKS .... *- 259 -*

BUSINESS INFORMATION .... *- 258 -*

ABBREVIATIONS & ACRONYMS....................................... *- 259 -*

NOTES... *- 263 -*

Preface

T hank you so much for taking the time to pick up my book and read part of my story. The Iraq I Knew changed on every deployment. I do not believe two stories about the military, combat deployments, or Iraq are alike, and this is a series of those stories. As the public realized the horrors of War through the burn pit legislation, people need to understand what Soldiers sometimes endured during combat deployments. For us, that was just daily living in Iraq.

You will learn several things from this narrative story. First, you will learn about the stressors of pre-deployment and deployment, and how we took care of ourselves before a shot was fired. How we said our goodbyes, flew thousands of miles away to a foreign land, ate, showered, and how the burn pits came about. Second, after shots were fired, you will learn what it was like to engage in the daily tasks of War, the challenges of self-care, and how we managed to care for each other. Third, you will learn about the aftermath of transitioning back to a peacetime Army, family, and community while your Soldier brain remained on a wartime footing.

Fourth, you will discover how the Iraq I knew differed each time I deployed from experiencing conventional combat operations against Saddam Hussein, his regime, and the Iraqi Army. Then, on the second tour of duty, we searched for Weapons of Mass Destruction (WMD). And on my final deployment, we were fighting a counterinsurgency against Al Qaeda in Iraq (AQI) to regain control of the country. Last, you will understand how and why I changed with each deployment and may have left some of myself in Iraq each time. This may also apply to any combat veteran with multiple deployments, their families with prolonged separations, government civilians supporting military forces, contractors in harm's way, or anyone who faced the strains of War. I hope this helps veterans, families, all those caring for veterans, and the American public better understand wartime deployments.

Colonel Burl Randolph, Jr., DM
US Army (Retired)
Veteran, Operations Desert Shield/Desert Storm
Operation Iraqi Freedom One
Operation Iraqi Freedom 07-09

INTRODUCTION

"There is no such thing as an 'easy' deployment."

Can you imagine going to work on a Friday morning, dreaming about the wonderful weekend ahead, but returning home that Friday evening to prepare for war? That is exactly how Desert Shield began for many of us: An unusual formation on Friday afternoon to be told that we were on alert to deploy somewhere at some time to do something but were not quite sure what that was.

Operation Desert Shield began in early August 1990 after a UN Resolution ordering the Iraqi Army out of Kuwait was ignored by Saddam Hussein. The wheels for deployment were not just turning at Fort Hood, TX, but throughout the Army, and what we discovered later, all over the world. It was decided that a coalition of forces would need to be created to expel Saddam Hussein and the Iraqi Army from Kuwait.

The 'somewhere' for deployment was Saudi Arabia as a staging area, with the 'sometime' defined as ASAP (As Soon As Possible). ASAP turned into 60 days for my 700-man field artillery unit. Our minds were laser-focused on the pending mission and brushed aside deploying to the desert as *'just trading one blazing hot and humid place for another one.'* Boy, were we cocky and wrong. The deserts of Saudi Arabia were not the lush hills surrounding Fort Hood, TX, or the desert floor of the National Training Center (NTC) at Fort Irwin, CA, which is littered with hills and surrounded by mountains. The Saudi desert was a dry, harsh, barren, and unrelenting place where a 110-degree day was cool, and we would live in for an unknown period, and were not visiting for a Field Training Exercise (FTX).

The waiting game extended from a few weeks to a few months and created tension in the ranks, not to mention learning how to live with several sandstorms, SCUD alerts, and possible attacks from Iraq. Those events were between the daily living of using pee tubes, filling burn barrels with human waste, and then burning the feces with particulate matter sure to float into the air. The months of waiting ended in January 1991 as Tomahawk missiles pierced the skies over Iraq.

Operation Desert Shield took us out of the frying pan and into the fire. Still, the failure of diplomacy took us into the storm, Operation Desert Storm – full-scale conventional force-on-force combat operations. We braced daily to enter the storm and were consumed by the preparations necessary to meet our enemy. This effort was a joint operation between all the US Armed Forces and coalition forces from around the world. We prepped the battlefield using air operations, precision targeting, artillery raids, and feints to fool the enemy.

The ground operations only lasted 96 hours, but Soldiers have battled its effects ever since. Between the airborne feces from burn barrels, rooting through unexploded ordnance, and being exposed to unknown elements from controlled detonations of enemy artillery rounds, Gulf War Syndrome was likely born. As redeployment began, it seemed like a year before things returned to normal, but truth be told, they never have. As the night sweats occurred, congenital disabilities abounded, and Soldiers experienced unknown medical maladies, this was just the beginning of The Iraq I Knew.

The Iraq I Knew…

Some summers seem like they never end. What began as a routine summer became one of the longest, hottest summers of many of our lives. Summers in Texas typically began when they began and ended when they ended. Our summer of 1990 felt like it started in April and morphed into something most of us had only seen on television, in the movies, or in the history books: War.

Preparing for what turned out to be the deployment of the entire US Army was no small feat, even if I only had to worry about my responsibilities. Operation Desert Shield was the build-up of US and coalition forces and a prelude to what we could expect from the Iraqi Army. It was a long, hot summer in August 1990 when we received that first deployment alert. And we conducted nearly 24-hour operations through the dog days of October. Then, we departed and landed in the sweltering heat of the Kingdom of Saudi Arabia. That made for a long, hot summer.

Over 120 days later, we crossed the Line of Departure (LD) from Saudi Arabia into Iraq to liberate Kuwait from Iraqi combat forces. For the next 90+ days, we downloaded equipment, moved to base camps, and learned to live in the desert for an extended period. As we continued our training regimen of rock drills and sand table planning, we reacted to incoming SCUDs without firing back. There were also the Thanksgiving, Christmas, and New Year's holidays to contend with, and back then, the most crucial event was the Super Bowl! Operation Desert Storm began in January 1991 when Tomahawk missiles enroute to Iraq were launched from US Navy carriers. It pierced the otherwise quiet sky, starting an operation to liberate Kuwait.

Iraq responded to the Tomahawks by launching SCUDs at a neutral Israel. Once ground combat operations began in February 1991, they were fast, furious, and fleeting. What some do not realize, however, is that lives were lost during that short period, and lives were forever changed. The return home to a hero's welcome in March and April 1991 began a transition for many service members from one reality to another, a transition that has lasted a lifetime for some of us. Those series of events are what led us into and out of the storm.

Chapter 1:
"The Long, Hot Summer"

The heat was like an oven.

Texas is HOT! I had lived in Texas for two years, but the summer of 1990 seemed the hottest I had experienced. Stationed at Fort Hood, Texas (now Fort Cavazos), known in the Army as 'The Great Place,' it seemed more like 'the Hot Place! In 1988, we had a fire ant infestation in my upscale apartment complex. The fire ants were vicious! When I left a basket of clean laundry by my ground-floor window, the scent of the detergent must have lured them in. When the ants were finished chewing through one of my Army t-shirts, it looked like Swiss cheese!

E P I S O D E 1

In 1989, a grasshopper invasion caused a crunching sound with each step as we walked through the motor pool. We had a cricket plague in the summer of 1990, and the crickets never stayed quiet. Unseasonal warmth began in April 1990, and natural heat began in June 1990, with average daily temperatures reaching nearly 100 degrees. With a mild July, we believed the worst of it had passed, but then came August, with another month of average daily temperatures of 100 degrees, one day reaching 108 degrees. That made the outdoors feel like an oven.

It was April 1990, and the President of Iraq, Saddam Hussein, was shaking up the world. I faintly remember the rumblings about oil prices, some advanced weaponry, and Iraq being dubbed *'The fourth largest Army in the world.'* Nothing mattered much to me as I transitioned to a C-level staff position. I was the Firing Battery Platoon Leader, Executive Officer, and Special Weapons Officer (SWO, pronounced Swo) for Bravo Battery, 3rd Battalion, of the 82nd Field Artillery, 1st Cavalry

Division (B BTRY, 3-82 FA, 1CD). A firing platoon consisted of four howitzer artillery guns and 40 personnel, whereas a Firing Battery had two firing platoons and a support platoon for nearly 120 people. SWOs led the tactical nuclear sections for the Firing Batteries, and yes, we had tactical nukes in the early 1990s.

Photo 1. M109A2 155mm Self-Propelled Howitzer under camouflage nets.

Photo provided by the Author.

Also, in the 1990s, Field Artillery was one of the combat arms branches that are now referred to as Maneuver, Fires, and Effects (MFE). MFE units are the units that close with and destroy the enemy directly, with the maneuver branches of infantry, armor, and aviation, or indirectly with Field Artillery and Air Defense Artillery (ADA), which are the fires. The effects are the Corps of Engineers, Chemical Corps, military police, and Cyber.[1] Cyber Warfare did not exist in 1990, but it is now one of the Army's newest branches, based on cyber warfare and terrorism. As an aside, I served 4.5 years in the Corps of Engineers in the Army Reserves and 5.5 years as a Field Artillery Officer, so my first 10 years of service were as a combat arms officer, hence my swagger.

Back then, combat arms units did not have women assigned to them, so imagine a bunch of testosterone-laden,

Type-A personalities that are all vying to be top dogs. That was where I learned my competency, confidence, directness, and gruffness, because success as a combat arms officer depended on them. Under the current system of Brigade Combat Teams (BCTs), women are part of the equation because the unit is self-sustaining, with most military occupational specialties (MOSs) assigned.

In this new C-level position, I was a First Lieutenant assigned to Captain's duties as the Battalion S4 – Logistics and Supply Officer (Vice President for Logistics) for 300+ artillerymen. In the Army, a battalion is considered a corporation of various sizes. Battalion Commanders are Presidents and CEOs selected by a Department of the Army Selection Board at the level. My selection for the C-level staff as a First Lieutenant would have been more significant if I had not been on the captain's promotion lists, slated for promotion in either September or October 1990.

As a First Lieutenant, I had not attended the Officers' Advanced Course, which taught you how to lead as a Captain and function on a C-level staff, so I was literally 'winging it.' I studied extensively to learn about the classes of supply, equipment, supply requisitions and turn-ins, and reports of surveys. Reports of Survey are now referred to as Financial Liability Investigation of Property Loss – FLIPL (pronounced Flipel). I also tracked the status of the Equipment Readiness Codes (ERC) (pronounced 'Irk'). As a platoon leader, I learned why it was pronounced 'irk': If you were not at the top readiness level, someone was constantly on your butt to get there. Hence, it irked you.

All of that seemed simple compared to what was referred to as 'The War on Excess': Lateral Transfers. Lateral Transfers were where one unit swapped excess equipment with another unit that was short but authorized the equipment. Although the transferring unit had excess or unauthorized equipment, they still did not want to release it. You know, more is always better, right? That's what made the process a monster and a war.

It was mostly a paperwork drill until it was time for the equipment swap, and then it became oh-so-real! That is likely why an officer was assigned to oversee it; for my organization, that officer was me. I will not bore you with the details of the constant fighting, bickering, complaining, and general harassment associated with the process, but the job got done, and with good reasons, as we all soon discovered.

Saddam Hussein's Saber-Rattling

The President of Iraq in 1990 was Saddam Hussein, and he was constantly making headlines. Already having boasted about *"the fourth-largest army in the world"* and all the new toys that went along with it, I thought, 'Big deal,' and 'fourth ain't first!' In April 1990, Newsweek published an article in which Hussein bragged about building a rocket gun with a range of 750 kilometers, which gave rise to the term "rocket gun." The typical artillery piece did not have a firing range that far, as those distances were reserved for rockets. The Multiple Launch Rocket System, or MLRS, was the largest rocket in the US Army inventory at the time and was also shipped to Ukraine in 2022 to help defend against the Russian invasion.

Hussein also crowed about something referred to as a SCUD missile. Unlike the Soviet FROG (Free Rocket Over Ground) missile, SCUD was not an acronym. Also, the firing ranges were reported as 150, 300, 450, 650, or 900 kilometers, depending on the type of SCUD and the source. [2] None of this seemed particularly important at the time, and just like the heat in Texas, it was the norm. However, by August 1990, Hussein and the heat would have significant meaning for me, my unit, and the nation.

The Iraq I Knew…

Photo 2. Newsweek Article, April 1990, on Saddam Hussein's Big Gun.

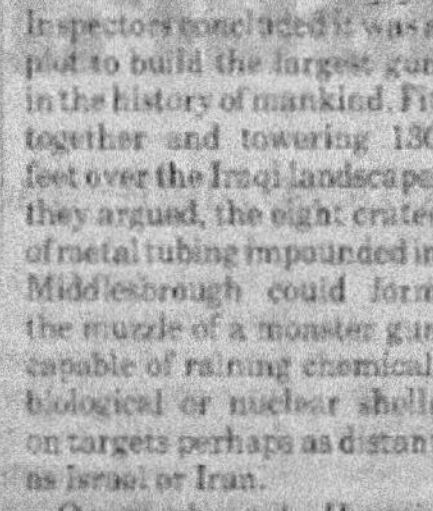

Britain Catches Iraq Again, With a . . . Gun?

Acting on a tip about a consignment of arms bound for the war chest of Iraqi strongman Saddam Hussein, British officials conducted Operation Bertha, a dockside swoop named after the massive German howitzer, Big Bertha. What they found last week was a whole lot of pipe. Inspectors concluded it was a plot to build the largest gun in the history of mankind. Fit together and towering 130 feet over the Iraqi landscape, they argued, the eight crates of metal tubing impounded in Middlesbrough could form the muzzle of a monster gun capable of raining chemical, biological or nuclear shells on targets perhaps as distant as Israel or Iran.

Or, maybe not. Hussein quickly denied the charges. So did the pipe manufacturer, Sheffield Forgemasters, which insisted the tubes were designed for petrochemical purposes. Phillip Wright, the company's chief executive, told officials the pipe contract had been approved even by Britain's Department of Trade and Industry. If it were used for a gun, said Wright, "it would probably blow itself to pieces." Still, some questions lingered. If there were no gun, specialists said, why did Hussein hire Gerald Bull, a Canadian arms expert who previously designed a 120-foot-long gun, to help Iraq perfect its long-range artillery? And who killed Bull last month before his Belgium-based company had completed its work? No one had answers. But by the weekend one part of the mystery had been solved. When officials learned that Sheffield Forgemasters had shipped 44 pieces of pipe to Iraq they conceded it was probably a pipeline, not a deadly weapon.

False charges? *Hussein*

Photo provided by the Author.

Photo 3. Scud B on a launcher used in Desert Storm.

A Sudden Shift

Sometime between May and June 1990, Saddam Hussein rumbled about how Kuwait was still part of Iraq. No one fully realized what he was talking about or how serious he was until, in July 1990, Iraqi tanks began massing on the southern border of Iraq, which was the northern border of Kuwait. Reported by Iraq as 'military exercises' within their sovereign borders, the world watched and monitored the build-up until August 1, 1990, when the Iraqi Army crossed the border into northern Kuwait. 'What was he doing?' the world asked. Once we looked at a map, it became clear what he was doing: Iraq had seized the Rumaila oilfields in northern Kuwait.

There were Rumaila oilfields in southern Iraq and northern Kuwait, but Iraq accused Kuwait of 'slant-drilling': Drilling into an oil well at an angle and pumping the oil out. On the Iraq/Kuwait map I eyeballed, Kuwait had just as many, or more, oil wells in the north as Iraq did. The issue: Hussein's saber-rattling in the previous months was just a pretense to invade Kuwait to seize its oil fields, in my opinion. Remember, the Iraq/Iran war lasted eight years, and although hostilities had ceased in 1988, it ravaged Iraq's natural resources and crippled its infrastructure, especially oil production.

That impeded Iraq's ability to produce and sell its oil at levels that would generate the significant income it was accustomed to. Hussein probably thought, 'Why not just take someone else's oil?' Regardless of the United Nations (UN) Declarations and US sanctions, Iraq refused to withdraw from Kuwait. This left only one option: An invasion by US forces to remove Iraqi troops from Kuwait forcibly.

So Much for The Weekend

Everyone lives for the weekend. No matter how much you love your job, and especially if you don't, the weekend is the respite that recharges, and we all look forward to and crave it all week. So, what if the weekend is filled with honey-dos, children's sports, and yard work? Watching major league sports, attending church, and sleeping longer on Sunday make it all worth it, right? Friday, August 10, 1990, began like any other Friday: searching for ways to leave work early. Physical Training at 0630, work call by 0830, and doing the day's business in anticipation of the weekend. That was until I received a call at 1530 (3:30 pm) from the Battalion S3 Officer (Operations and Training Officer). *"S4, battalion formation, 1600 in the motor pool,"* he said. Nothing like a short, sweet, and to-the-point conversation with a superior officer. The S3 Officer was a Major's position, one of three majors in an artillery battalion, and the second in the line of succession. My response was just as short and sweet, *"Yes, sir."*

As we stood in formation in front of the Battalion, waiting for 1600 (4 pm), I asked the S3, *"What's up, Sir? Why are we here?* His response startled me:

"I have no idea."

I was shocked and dismayed because that was his job: To know every operation occurring in the organization, including formations. If the S3 didn't know, then who did? As the S3 turned and began speaking to me, he noticed I was ignoring him, my eyes fixed on the motor pool entrance.

"Hey, S4," he said, *"I'm talking to you. What the fuck are you looking at?"*

I pointed toward the motor pool entrance. The S3 turned to see our Service Battery, wearing civilian clothes, marching into the motor pool. Field Artillery battalions have batteries rather than companies, like most of the Army. With his mouth gaped open, the S3 response was classic:

"What the fuck's going on?"

Service Battery had a scheduled Organization Day and was supposed to be at Six Flags Over Texas in Arlington, TX. As the

Service Battery took its place in the formation, there was a great deal of head-scratching and questions being asked. The Service Battery Commander walked over to tell us what was happening.

"Look, the Old Man contacted me and said to return here ASAP. With the urgency in his voice, I didn't ask any questions. We just found everyone and put the pedal to the metal to be here by 1600."

Before we could begin speculating, the Battalion Commander, Executive Officer, and Command Sergeant Major entered the motor pool. After the customary reporting procedures, the Battalion Commander walked out into the middle of the formation and said,

"Gentlemen, the 1st Cavalry Division has been alerted for deployment to Southwest Asia."

You could have heard a mouse pee on a cotton ball as he continued.

"All leaves (Paid Time Off), PCS (Permanent Change of Station), and ETS (Expiration Term of Service) are canceled, and we are in Stop Loss status. Battery Commanders and staff, meet us in the conference room ASAP."

Alerted to deploy? Were all the leaves, PCS, and ETS moves really canceled? And what the heck was Stop Loss? What did all this mean? And where was Southwest Asia? We soon found out the answers to most of our questions and thoughts.

It Got Hotter

Most of us were mute as we sat around the conference room table. The typical jokers were quiet, the snoozers were awake, and we fidgeters sat perfectly still. When the commander entered, he told us to keep our seats and began speaking. He explained that the unprovoked invasion by Iraq into Kuwait was tantamount to a declaration of War on another sovereign country. All diplomatic measures had failed to convince Saddam Hussein to withdraw the Iraqi Army from Kuwait. Fast forward to

February 2022. Does this sound familiar? The Battalion Commander explained.

"The United Nations felt all means had been exhausted to convince Hussein to leave Kuwait peacefully. UN Resolution 662 created a coalition force of countries willing to participate in expelling the Iraqi Army from Kuwait." [3]

When, where, and how we were supposed to deploy were still unclear, but the requirements for preparation were clear-cut.

Batter Up

Our commander loved baseball, and I thought this metaphor/cliché was appropriate. As the meeting continued, the battalion commander said,

"S4 (that was me), you need to have the requisitions submitted for all classes of supply to the Division Property Book Officer (PBO) by 0730 tomorrow morning."

Everyone oohed, ah'd, and gasped as they all looked at me. It felt like people were looking at me through the windows, hanging from the ceiling, and looking up through the floor, but of course, that did not happen, but it sure felt like it. What else could I say but "*Yes, sir.*"

I thought, '*How in the world would we complete this humongous task of ordering all our required equipment and supplies by 0730 Saturday morning?*' I needed to get back to my office quickly and nearly began running, but it was about a mile away, and I had walked from the motor pool to the headquarters (HQ). Then I needed to gather my crew of three and explain the mission as I understood it.

As I hurried to my office, my mind raced and my heart fluttered with everything I knew we needed to accomplish as I quickly walked and war-gamed. I needed to call my fiancé to tell her that dinner would probably be late that night. Back then, we did not have the convenience of cell phones, text, or email, so it was not like I could walk and talk. Worse yet, I could not tell her why I was 'working late' because deployment information was and is classified, especially over an unsecured line. Once I reached the office, sweating like crazy, the new situation made it hotter inside the building, and the outside heat became inconsequential.

Photo 4. 1LT Burl Randolph Jr. in the S4 Office of 3-82nd Field Artillery Battalion, Fort Hood, TX, Jun 1990. Photo provided by the Author.

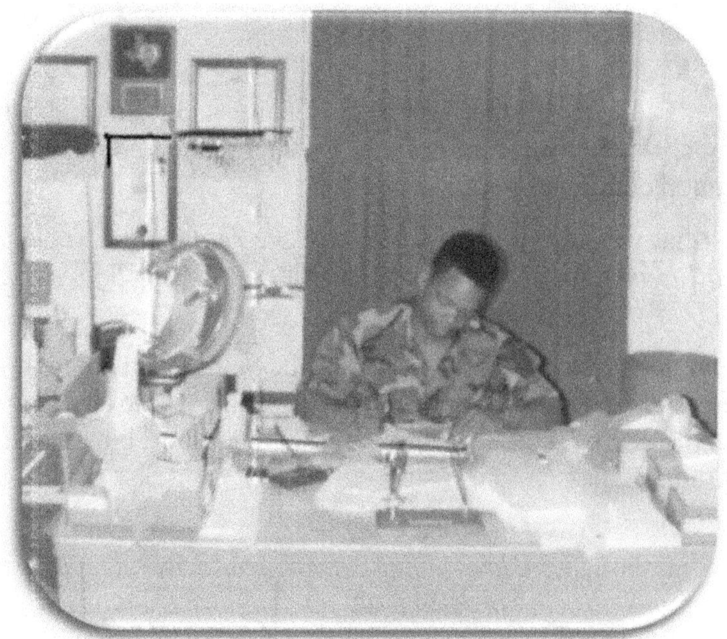

Please recall that this was August 1990, and conveniences like the internet, Google, Wi-Fi, Wikipedia, and Artificial Intelligence (AI) did not exist. This required us to collect information the old-fashioned way: Look in a book, magazine, the library, or phone a friend. The maps on the following pages were the most basic maps I could get my hands on to at least show me what Iraq and Kuwait looked like. I was shocked to see how tiny Kuwait was compared to Iraq. Iraq is the size of Texas, and

The Iraq I Knew...

Kuwait may be the size of Iowa or Ohio. Another interesting fact I observed was that Iraq was entirely landlocked by six other Middle Eastern countries, including Kuwait. We did not expect Iran, Kuwait, Saudi Arabia, or Turkey to help Iraq if a war began, but what about Syria or Jordan?

Inquiring minds wanted to know, and Terry, my fiancé, was one of them. All I could tell her was that we, 1st Cav, were going somewhere at some time to do something, and I had to work on Saturday. I imagined those same conversations occurring across Fort Hood and the adjacent towns of Killeen, Copperas Cove, and Harker Heights. CNN (Cable News Network) suddenly became my new best friend.

My curious mind also wanted to know whether we were fighting to defend another country and what that country looked like. As we scrambled for information, being able to see Kuwait in more detail became vitally important. Also, there was this thing called the Persian Gulf. I knew that Iraq was once called Persia and that the area extended to what is now Kuwait, but that information isn't something people carry around in their minds. And because we likely weren't going directly to Kuwait, I also needed to picture what our new home for a few months might look like.

Photo 5. Map of Iraq with adjacent countries, with Kuwait and the Persian Gulf in the circle. Photo provided by the Author.

The Iraq I Knew…

Photo 6. Detailed map of Kuwait with major cities.

Photo 7. Detailed map of Saudi Arabia with major cities.

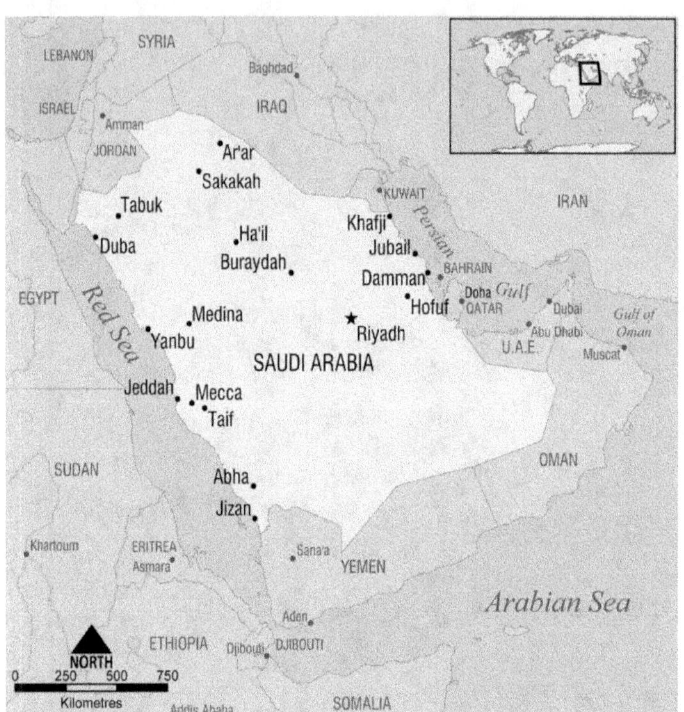

Saudi Arabia was likely where we were deploying, but no one had officially told me. All the maps were at the battalion HQ, and it was not until much later that I saw a complete map of Saudi Arabia. Geographically, Saudi Arabia appeared to be 2-3 times the size of Iraq, meaning twice the desert. Having spent a reasonable amount of time at the National Training Center (NTC) in California, I was very accustomed to the desert and sand and did not like either. To that point in my life, I had never been to a beach, since the Midwest did not offer such luxuries. Just looking at the maps made me feel hotter.

Chapter 2:
"And the Simmering Began"

The heat was so intense I felt like a brisket.

Did I explain I was a trained field artillery officer, not a trained logistician? What about only being in the position for three months? Did I mention I had just gotten engaged? Or that arrangements needed to be canceled for our all-expense-paid three-week trip to Europe to inspect prepositioned equipment? None of that mattered as everything became OBE – Overcome by Events. From one day to the next, we went from being a peacetime Army with us preparing for a fall National Training Center (NTC) rotation at Fort Irwin, CA, to being on a wartime footing. Imagine the amount of confusion, consternation, and stress this placed on everyone: Single Soldiers, married Soldiers, families, leaders, government civilians, and the community. The heat in Texas had become a slow simmer as the frying pan became hotter.

Fortunately, I had a tremendous noncommissioned officer-in-charge (NCOIC) in Sergeant First Class (SFC) E. SFC E was of Puerto Rican descent, and most people could not pronounce his last name. Hence, he had everyone refer to him as SFC E. After telling him about the monumental tasks, SFC E said, *"Sir, we can just use the 1348-1's (back then, an Army requisition form) we already prepared for Europe. We never put in dates, locations, or quantities, so we can use those for all the supplies we need to order."* It made perfect sense to me, but what were the dates and locations? I called the Division PBO, who told me the date was NOW, and the shipping location was our Fort Hood, TX unit. It sounded simple enough.

In the coming days, simplicity went out the door. Our unit was expected to double in size, from 300+ Soldiers to 600+. I have yet to find out where all these Soldiers came from, and they seem to have appeared overnight. We required enough food and supplies for at least seven days of deployment, three desert camouflage uniforms per person, and our basic ammunition load for all weapons systems. Although I had not been on the job long, I was good at it, so I took a calculated risk. That is when you use all your resources and information available to estimate the most adverse outcomes with the least risk to you. My gambling proved great for me and my unit. I directed that we use 700 Soldiers as a planning factor for everything.

"Why 700?" asked SFC E.

"Because, so far," I said, *"not much in my short Army career had been exact. I am 'estimating' that we will end up with more than 600 but less than 700 Soldiers. Either way, we will be covered."*

Why is all this important? Because the American public needs to know the sheer magnitude of what we were asked to accomplish quickly. Also, it took an entire battalion of 600 – 700 Soldiers, not just me and the three I led, to make this happen. There were 10 classes of supplies, and we ordered 9 of 10. In a short example, Class I – Subsistence (food) - we needed to requisition enough Meal, Ready-to-Eat (MRE) for 700 people. The worst-case scenario was three meals per person per day for seven days.

Photo 8. MRE case.   Photo 9. MRE packages.

The Iraq I Knew…

That is 2100 meals per day, with 12 meals per case, for a total of 175 cases per day. Fifty cases per pallet, so 3.5 pallets, right? Multiply 2100 by seven days, which equals 14,700 MREs, 1,225 cases, and 25 pallets. Now, what are MREs? Dehydrated food rations that come in different 'flavors' (and I use the term 'flavored' loosely). They were rehydrated with water and eaten hot or cold. I preferred mine to be hot, but the norm was cold, especially at night when the light from a campfire or the heat signature could alert the enemy to your position. Now, to pick up the MREs. Eight pallets fit on a 5-ton truck, and four pallets fit snuggly on a 2.5-ton truck, also called a Deuce-and-a-Half. If you have ever been to Mission BBQ, you know they use a Deuce-and-a-Half fleet to deliver food for the events they cater.

With only two 5-ton and four 2.5-ton trucks assigned to the supply sergeants, this sounds like an easy task; however, we were also ordering from the other supply classes. We could only imagine the sizes and shapes of the containers holding Desert Combat Uniforms (DCU), petroleum products, sundry packs, ammunition, sandbags, barrier material, and many other supplies. The supplies arrived when they arrived, and we went from a four-man team to supervising 14 to 24 supply sergeants, Soldiers, and NCOs daily. Trust me, I am not a mathematician, but I needed to accurately calculate those quantities without using computer software, cell phone apps, or AI, none of which existed then. The table below is a short example to illustrate the enormity of our task.

Table One. Beans, Bullets, and Uniforms for 700 Soldiers for Seven Days.

Supply Class	Items	Class of Items	Basic load	Totals
I	Subsistence (Beans)	CL C – MREs	Three meals, Seven Days	14,700 meals
II	Clothing (Uniforms)	DCU	Three per Soldier	2,100 uniforms
V	Ammunition (Bullets)	5.56 rounds, 30-round clips	210 rounds per Soldier	Over 1 million rounds

And Now Came the Big Stuff

Ammunition was one of the most consequential items we ordered. This was because we not only procured the primary load for each M-16A1 rifle (in 1990) but also the rounds for the Colt 45 pistols, M203 grenade launchers, M60s, and 50-Cal machine guns. And then there were the artillery rounds for 24 M109A2 155mm self-propelled howitzers (Photos 10 & 11), with 36 93-pound rounds each. I included photos so the reader can better visualize the equipment and the massive undertaking of loading these enormous vehicles with ammunition and supplies. Each howitzer was over 27.5 tons or 55,000 pounds minus the ammo, charges, and primers – another 4,000 pounds, plus the additional equipment, such as camouflage systems, which were also massive and annoying. And there were also different uniforms and personal gear packed on these vehicles, making them even heavier.

Photo 10. M109A2 155mm Self-Propelled Howitzer.

Photo 11. 155 mm Artillery Rounds.

Photo retrieved from the GlobalSecurity.org website.

As you can see, we had a great deal of firepower, and our capacity to carry the ammunition had significantly improved. In May 1990, we acquired 24 M992A2 FAASVs – Field Artillery Ammunition Support Vehicles (pronounced FAS-V). The FAASV replaced the M548, an old tracked supply vehicle used as an ammunition carrier.

Photo 12. M992A2 Field Artillery Ammunition Support Vehicle.

Photo retrieved from https://www.wiki wand.com/en/File: M992A2_FAASV.jpg

The FAASV carried 90-95 artillery rounds and the accompanying powders and primers; it was armored and utilized a hydraulically powered conveyor system to load the ammunition from the FAASV into the M109.[4] This reduced both the wear and tear on the crew.

Photo 13. M90px Loader, M992. Photo retrieved from https://en.wikipedia.org/wiki/M992_ Field_Artillery_Ammunition_Supply_Vehicle.

One of the many outstanding qualities I love about Soldiers and NCOs is their ingenuity. Although the ammo loader was more accessible to the crew, several crews reported that it was not 'better' or quicker, and did not reduce loading time. So, the teams loaded the ammo by hand, putting the units' needs first. We also acquired 24 M977 HEMTTs – Heavy Expanded Mobility Tactical Trucks (pronounced Him-It).

The upgraded HEMTTs were also a considerable improvement. The HEMMTs not only carried ammunition but could also serve as general supply vehicles, reducing the number of trips required to transport equipment from the supply depots. A bonus was a winch on the back that could lift 45-60,050 pounds, depending on the variant, and the sides could fold down to allow easy forklift loading onto pallets. Both acquisitions made the lives of the howitzer crews and supply sergeants much more manageable and improved combat readiness to the highest equipment readiness level. Those events/tasks were only the tip of the iceberg in preparing for deployment.

Photo 14. M977 HEMTT

Photo retrieved from https://en.wikipedia.org/wiki/Heavy_Expanded_ Mobility Tactical_Truck.

Now, visualize packing and loading 24 howitzers onto HETs – Heavy Equipment Transports, and driving to a port four hours away to load onto ships sailing to the Middle East. The HETs belonged to the Main Support Battalion (MSB), and we were mostly on their schedule. Imagine hundreds of M1 Abrams tanks, Bradley Fighting Vehicles (BFV), howitzers, and other oversized vehicles not allowed on Texas highways.

This also required personnel to travel with the equipment on the ship, because there were not only the vehicles listed above, but also all the battalion vehicles. The wheeled vehicles were driven to the port and onto the ships, generally on the same day. This was mainly the driver for the armored vehicles that traveled on the vessel, and NCOICs supervised the drivers and ensured Uncle Sam's investment in the equipment was protected. As the convoys rolled down the road, I thought our job was mainly over for the time being. Boy, was I wrong.

Photo 15. Heavy Equipment Transport (HET).

I Didn't Get It

I thought we were on top of everything logistically. I felt proud of the section, and I was like a peacock strutting my feathers. Those feathers, however, were about to be plucked. We conducted a war game on the essentials for basic survival during the deployment. We had very few Vietnam veterans in our unit, and Vietnam was very different from Iraq. Vietnam – Southwest Asia had foliage, and Iraq – in the Middle East had sand. Additionally, we were deploying to a foreign country with different ethical and environmental rules. Hence, our mindsets had to shift from the strict European scenarios we had trained in for years.

First, what were we going to use for latrines? Latrines are toilets. Because it was a desert, we could not dig deep enough to employ the Army version of a porta-potty: A slit trench dug six feet deep and covered with a wooden support structure with two toilet seats. That concept was from World War II, but hey, it was the only thing I had ever used. The only difference between the ones I used early in my career and those in Photo 16 was that the seats were side-by-side versus back-to-back, which may have been preferable. A heavy canvas cloth surrounded the latrines on the outside. However, as the years passed, a small GP tent was erected over the latrines to provide greater privacy.

Photo 16. WWII-Era Dual Military Field Latrine. Photo retrieved from https://www.pinterest.com/pin/437975132486865946/.

Because the surface in Iraq was sandy, our standard field latrine procedures went out the window. Then, someone said, *"Since we can't bury it, why don't we burn it?"* Yes, *it* was our feces. But how, you ask, would we burn it? Burn barrels. Imagine if you were around in the 1950s, 1960s, and 1970s, when people burned trash in a 55-gallon drum (a burn barrel) in their backyard. I recall watching my dad burn trash like this in our backyard. That was the precursor to the Environmental Protection Agency (EPA) and the Clean Air Act of 1970. Our toilets required something to capture the waste. The 55-gallon drums were cut in half, and the halves with the lids were soldered shut to avoid leakage.

Now, the toilets required housing like in the photo, but there was no time to order those, so we decided to make our own because the 'waste receptacles' needed to fit under the toilet seats. That required the housing to be high enough to place the barrels underneath without requiring a stepladder to sit down. What did all of this have to do with me? The S4 ordered all Class IV construction materials: wood, nails, hinges, screens, toilet seats, and all other supplies. I was curious about who or how would complete the construction; however, that was not my concern. We just ordered the supplies. The finished product is below.

So, the way this worked was that for cleaning, the barrels were removed from the rear of the latrines by opening a horizontal door and pulling them out. I am trying to remember if the door was an original feature. Still, it may have been added after we arrived in the country and discovered how windstorms and creepy crawlies impacted the structures if they were not completely enclosed. I will show pictures and explain the burn pits later. At the time, we were still not done with our needs.

Photo 17.1990 Soldier-Built Field Latrine. Photo provided by the Author.

The Never-Ending Story

We did well with building the latrines, right? Although the latrines were built, what about urination? I don't need to explain the mechanics of this task; just the results of peeing on the soil: smell, pestilence, infestation, and disease. Accordingly, something labeled as a 'piss tube' was devised because pissing our way across Saudi Arabia was not an option. Some scientists or doctors estimated that we would need urine to go down at least three feet into the ground to avoid the consequences. Someone suggested using PVC piping because it was inexpensive, and we would not reuse it, so numerous

amounts were ordered. The pipes were one or two inches in diameter and six feet long, since three feet would be stuck in the sand.

Photo 18. 3" x 10 'PVC Pipe

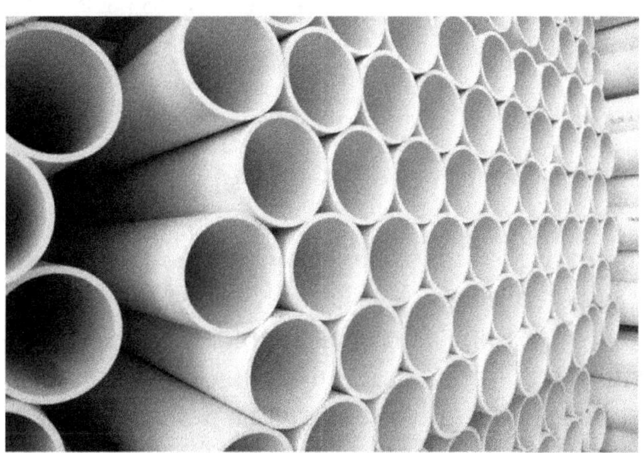

I am sure that discussing soldiers' toilet habits may sound strange, but this is what we endured in the early days of deployments. Also, as I mentioned, we were in a foreign country expecting to go to War, so porta-potties were not readily available or practical. With the toilet business resolved, we focused on keeping ourselves clean. The second order of business was showers. Taking a bath in your helmet was no longer a viable choice. The Army no longer issued 'steel pots' that allowed you to remove the plastic insert, place your water (warm or cold, your choice) into the steel portion, and clean yourself from there. We were issued Kevlar helmets, and although many of us were versed in using them to clean ourselves (this involved inserting a shower cap inside the helmet), nothing replaces a nice, hot shower.

Photo 19. Steel Pot Helmet

Photo 20. Kelvar Helmet

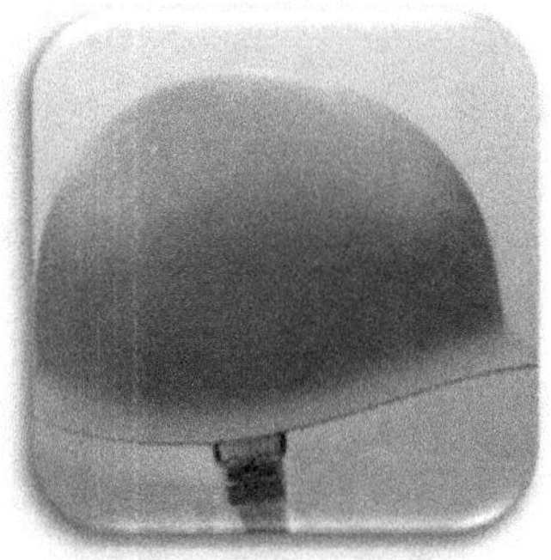

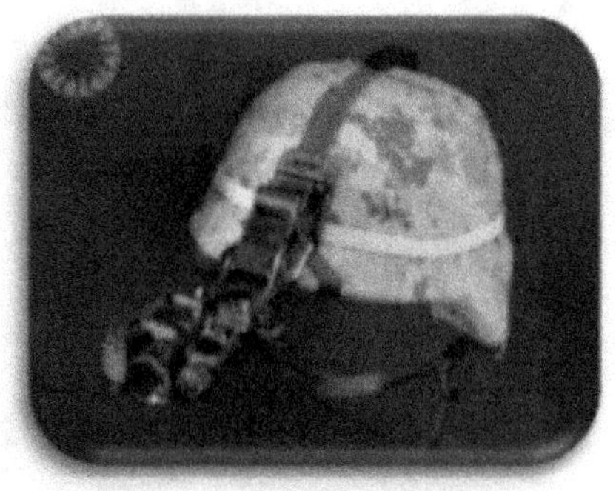

By Graham Sherwood - The Vietnam Database, https://commons.wikimedia. org/w/index.php?curid=218054

Retrieved from Creative Commons. CC BY-SA 3.0,

Although the helmets may not look much different, there is a world of difference. The Kevlar or K-pot was lighter and had greater density against shrapnel fragmentation and stray bullets. Washing up at the 'water buffalo' was also outdated for sanitary reasons, and because we were in a desert, we needed to conserve water. Hence, we designed and built our own showers. Unlike the latrines, which were small enough to be constructed stateside and shipped, the showers were too large for that, as you can see.

Straight from the Army Times, our three-stall showers looked like this. Starting at the bottom, the flooring was pallets, most likely secured from the MREs we had ordered. The frame was made of standard 2-by-12 wood to accommodate taller personnel and provide space for showerheads. So, the showerheads hung about three or four feet, leaving about eight feet of clearance. Yes, I served with some non-basketball players who were anywhere from 6'8 "to 7'2".

Photo 21. 1990 Soldier-Built Showers

Retrieved from Army Times, January 21, 1991.

The compartment on top held the water and, in some cases, had a potbellied stove inside to heat it. The ladder on the back was initially intended to carry the water up, but that required too many trips and people. More about our showering habits later. Now, do you get the picture? I mean, really get the picture. All units were required to be 100 percent self-sufficient. We ordered thousands of pounds of food, clothing, petroleum products, building materials, ammunition, hygiene products, major equipment, medical supplies, and repair parts.

We discovered that what we thought was Class Six – Alcohol, was not just alcohol, but 'personal demand items,' also referred to in the supply system as sundry packs. For the Army, sundry packs were toiletries, male and female. Because it was an all-male unit, we ordered seven packs, each with enough toiletries for 100 men. I had never seen this logistical marvel before, but I would see it again in my next deployment. A peacetime Army operates very constrainedly, whereas in wartime, all the stops are pulled out. Even amidst all this turmoil, several significant things happened for me.

Photo 22. Army and Air Force Field Manual on Hygiene and Sanitation.

Photo 23. Army and Marine Corps Field Manual on Hygiene and Sanitation.

Retrieved from https://archive.org/ services /img/FM21-10_2000/full/pct:200/0

Photo retrieved from https://archive.org/services/img/FM21-10_201212 /default.jpg

Chapter 3:
"The Moments I Waited For"

Patience and waiting are not the same thing.

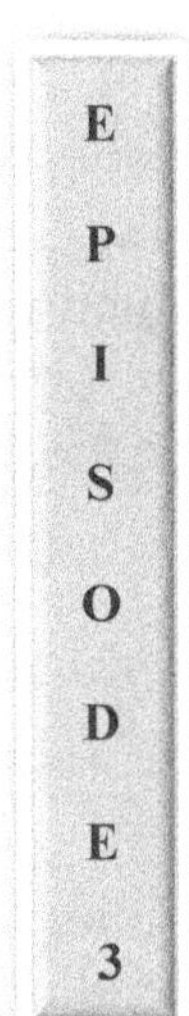

Amidst those fast-moving operations, three other events occurred for me, both personally and professionally. First, I got engaged in early August when the Iraqi Army invaded Kuwait. Second, on August 15, 1990, I managed to get married. I wrote 'managed' because, at our operational tempo (OPTEMPO), sleeping and eating had to be meticulously planned or done on the fly, let alone time to get married. Third, I had waited 18 months for my sequence number to come up, and I was eligible for promotion to Captain on September 1, 1990. Although my promotion sequence number was six, I waited 18 months because the 2,000 to 3,000 names from the previous Captain's promotion list had to be exhausted before my list could be started.

A Wartime Wedding

Getting engaged was easy, but getting married sooner differed from what we had planned. We planned the wedding for May 19, 1991, exactly one year after we met. The wedding would likely occur like any other: Invitations, planning, stress, and the appropriate venue – I am from the Midwest, and she is from the East Coast. None of that occurred. Life changes when significant events occur, so we decided to move the wedding date up. What if something happened before May 1991, like not returning from Iraq?

I do not recall how we chose the date, but it was probably predicated on the uncertainty of the environment. We were told we'd be deploying every day, which stressed everyone out. When I told my boss, the Battalion Executive Officer (XO), that I needed the evening off to take care of some personal business, I received the typical Army response of,

"S4, what could be more important than going to war?"

My response was, *"Getting married, sir."*

Major S was a great boss who genuinely cared about people. He knew the mission was supposed to be first, but he also knew caring for the people would ensure a successful mission. I explained to him that because this was not our original plan, we were keeping it low-key and getting married at our apartment by a Justice of the Peace. Like a little kid, he asked,

"Can we come? Margie and I will make great witnesses!"

"Sure, Sir," I answered. *"We are planning for a 1830 (6:30 pm) start time."*

Well, true to form, things did not go as planned for the evening. Terry had no problem with my boss and his wife attending the wedding, but we didn't plan for the Justice of the Peace (JOP) to arrive at 1800 (6 pm)! It may have even been slightly earlier than that, but all I recall when we asked why he was so early was his Texas drawl,

"I gotta bunch of other weddings to perform and was already in the neighborhood, so let's go!"

Imagine the classic cowboy, except with a Bible rather than a six-gun or a rope. The JOP was a tall, thin man who wore a large cowboy hat and boots, a string tie, and a tan jacket with patch-like pockets. It was just like something out of the movies, except we were not actors; this was reality, not Hollywood.

The wedding may have lasted 15 minutes, and the JOP was off to the next event. I decided to include this short scenario because it was not just my singular story, but as the JOP said,

"I gotta bunch of other weddings to perform…"

Imagine that across the Fort Hood area of Killeen, Copperas Cove, and Harker Heights, TX, Army Soldiers were getting married before deploying to War. Small, intimate, unplanned weddings occurred everywhere, and then, back to work. Consider turning over all your possessions in a noticeably shorter period than you had planned. Do I have the statistics on 'wartime wedding' success? No, because once that war or deployment began, it seemed like they never ended. I was fortunate to have adequate time between deployments, but others were not.

When Major S and Margie arrived at 1830, they were dismayed to find the wedding over but continued as if it were time for a reception. We popped champagne, cut the cake, took pictures, and acted like we were in a crowded room. We thanked them, and they left. We ordered dinner and kept the rest of the evening for ourselves—no wedding march, departure march, big reception, and driving off to a honeymoon. But I did receive a phone call from SFC E, saying the DCUs had arrived and they were picking them up that evening. I returned to work the following morning and prepared for the subsequent events, including my promotion.

Wartime Promotions: The Start of My Trend

Just like the wedding did not occur the way I wanted, neither did my promotion. Of course, September 1, 1990, was on a Saturday, and the Labor Day holiday was the following Monday. So, my promotion ceremony to Captain was on Tuesday, September 4, in front of a 600-man artillery battalion; even though I wanted to be promoted on Friday, August 31, the Battalion Commander overruled me. Although I was good with a small ceremony in the conference room, the Battalion Commander said,

"S4, you may never be promoted again in front of a 600-man formation during a time of war."

Of course, I pouted all weekend, wondering what the big deal was about being promoted in front of a formation. Part of the 'big deal' was that if I were promoted on Friday, that would be one less thing on my plate. Short, sweet, and to the point was my motto back then. Plus, this weekend would be our first weekend off since this ordeal began, and maybe even the first day we had off. The 21 or so days we worked seemed like years. I wanted to savor the moment and get used to the *idea* of 'Captain Randolph.' Because of my transfer from the Army Reserves to Active Duty, I had been a lieutenant for six years, two years longer than the average Active-Duty captain. I was ready.

Although our unit was off for the four-day holiday, not all organizations were. So, in addition to not having the promotion ceremony I wanted, I was tasked with developing a system for my section to capture all messages, such as assigning someone to duty every day over the weekend. I never realized that being an S4 would be so cumbersome. That was until I became the S2 officer (Vice President for Intelligence and Security), but that is later in another episode.

Anyway, that requirement defeated the purpose of having time off. As my last official function as a First Lieutenant, I made the command decision NOT to have anyone on duty. Rebellious, did you say? No, I was just ahead of my time in using technology. I brought in our answering machine from home. I know that is not rebellious but unorthodox, and I changed the message to reflect the organization.

"This is the S4 Section of the 3rd Battalion, 82nd Field Artillery. Please leave your name, number, and a brief message, and we'll get back to you." Beep.

This bought my section a well-deserved weekend off and allowed me to pout privately.

I knew returning to work on Tuesday would feel like a Monday because our unit had taken the Labor Day weekend off.

This meant everything would be a mad dash to get back up to speed for deployment. My first order of business would have been to check into my office to hear a few messages from the answering machine while Terry waited in the car for me before the promotion ceremony. I thought better of it and went in on Saturday, listened to each message, and wrote the pertinent requirements. This allowed me to tape over the previous messages and start over again. With the advent of voicemail and digital answering machines, some readers may need to realize that in the 1990s, answering machines were merely souped-up tape recorders.

Tuesday finally arrived, and I cannot lie; I was giddy with excitement! If you know me, you cannot envision me as giddy. As we ambled to the motor pool for the ceremony, I looked across each Battery. I realized that the Battalion Commander was right – having 600 people watch your promotion was an incredible feeling. Camouflage or chemical uniforms are based on training as far as the eye can see—no conference room, Class A uniform, or cake and punch. We were at War, by God!

I also realized something else that I carried with me for the remainder of my Army career: often, the people who helped you along the way were rarely allowed to participate in recognizing your success. After the ceremony, many of the noncommissioned officers (NCOs) congratulated me profusely and were happy and proud of me. When the African American NCOs congratulated me, they also told me I provided 'proof.' After several had made the same remark, I asked one that I knew well, "*Proof of what?*"

He responded, *"Sir, proof that African Americans can be successful in the Army."*

I was also told that I was,

"A role model for the young African American Soldiers, noncommissioned officers, and lieutenants aspiring to move up

further in the Army hierarchy, but were indecisive on whether that was possible."

Those comments were humbling and enlightening. I was humbled because I never considered myself a role model, and enlightened because I did not realize how other African Americans may have struggled in their careers. I had challenges in my career, but you can read about those struggles in my previous book, **Inspired, Not Retired**: *Leadership Lessons from Father to Son.*

Photo 24. Promotion Ceremony for 1LT Burl Randolph, Jr.

Promotion Ceremony for 1st Lieutenant (1LT) Burl Randolph, Jr. to Captain on September 4, 1990. LTC Kenneth R. Knight officiated, and Randolph's new wife, Terry Randolph, pinned the captain's bars onto his cap as a 600+ artillery battalion watched. Photo provided by the Author.

Some may wonder why I chose to include a racial component to this event, and the answer is simple: that is the circumstance I live with daily. Out of the 56 officers in our Battalion, I became the third African American Captain. Three out of 56, or 5.35 percent. I now occupied one of the 15 captain's positions and was the only African American officer on the C-level staff. Over the next two years, the number of African

American captains did not increase, but it was only a one-for-one swap.

With African Americans comprising 10 percent of the Army officer corps, I thought the numbers for captains would at least reflect that in our unit. I will not attempt to speak for all African Americans, but certain themes have always resonated with me since leaving home in Kansas City, MO. Some of the questions that swirled in my head after I left an environment where 95 percent of my existence was with Black people in a Black community were:

1. Will I be accepted?
2. How will I be accepted?
3. Will I be good enough to accomplish the task?
4. How do I compare myself to my peers?
5. Do I have any haters, and why?

Sometimes, people do not know how good or bad they are because they assume they are just like everyone else. However, once a distinction was made, I questioned my qualifications, acceptance, and detractors. Even today, over 30 years later, those same questions sometimes arise.

In my first draft of this book, I wrote,

"I am uncertain what changed for me after my promotion other than a feeling of accomplishment, the requirement to upgrade all my uniforms to captain's rank, and, of course, the pay."

As I typed the third or so draft, I realized that the thought process was untrue. Since being told I was a role model, I have felt a new sense of responsibility: to mentor. Although I may have been mentoring since I was 14, I never thought of it that way. I was helping people, specifically my peers and coworkers, regardless of race. While helping people was true, the NCOs introduced the concepts of aspiration, *success*, and *hierarchy* into the equation. Those words can help define the mentoring relationship.

I also realized that in a pyramid, space becomes smaller and smaller as you move up. I went from having 20-25 lieutenant peers within my unit to only 15 peers as a captain and only four by position. I wrote 'within my unit' because I was promoted to Army captain, not just to Field Artillery captain. This meant I needed to up my game, and the responsibility was profound. Even though many people would tell you I have no problem being serious, my demeanor paled at what had occurred and what would be required of me next.

The promotion ceremony seemed like just another blip on the radar screen. As some of my new peers congratulated and welcomed me, others ignored and avoided me. Sometimes, you need to look in the closest mirror to determine why people treat you as they do. When I looked in the mirror, I realized that some, if not all, the captains perceived me as brash, confrontational, and disagreeable as a lieutenant and subordinate. I was competent, confident, and determined to accomplish all missions. I needed an 'extreme makeover' from that persona I had created for my new peers. I needed to be more tactful, more of a collaborator, and remove any chips from my shoulders. My shoulders would need to become much broader for the tasks ahead, and chips would only weigh me down.

Chapter 4:
"The Real Mind Blower"

Have you ever even amazed yourself?

Imagine is an inadequate word for the feat we accomplished in 45-60 days without prior notification. This is important because we were not part of the Rapid Deployment Forces (RDF), which can deploy in hours versus days and months. Additionally, we conducted various recertifications concurrently before departure while shipping and receiving equipment and supplies. That training included:

- Weapons Qualification on individual and crew-served weapons, day, and nighttime firing, and in MOPP IV.
- Nuclear, Biological, and Chemical (NBC) Qualifications (which included the Gas Chamber).
- First Aid, both individual and mass casualties.
- Medical Evacuations (Air and Land).
- Training on Night Vision Goggle (NVG) use.
- Full range of immunizations.
- Partial physicals for some.
- Cultural Customs for Saudi Arabia.
- Cultural Customs for the Middle East.
- Prisoner of War (POW) Training - in the event of being captured.
- Enemy Prisoner of War Training (EPW).
- Law of Land Warfare Training.
- Enemy Intelligence Training.
- Situation Reporting (SITREPS).

- Rules of Engagement (ROE) training.
- **S**ubversion **a**nd **E**spionage **D**irected **A**gainst the United States Army (SAEDA).

This was a brief list and changed slightly with each deployment. Everything described to this point occurred between August 10 and October 10, 1990. To recount some of the accomplishments:

- 100 Soldiers deployed as an Advanced Party.
- Hundreds of training hours.
- Hundreds of planning hours.
- Over 300 new personnel were in-processed.
- Over 120 vehicles were shipped.
- Thousands of supplies were ordered, accepted, and packed.
- Thousands of pounds of supplies were shipped in seven cargo containers.
- Over 600 Soldiers were prepared and deployed for combat.

Every day in September, we continued our pickup, pack up, ship out, and train up routine, repeating it. Pick up supplies, pack up equipment, ship out equipment and supplies, train on the previously listed topics, and more, and repeat it every day. During this time, the deployment process threw several curveballs our way that we did not expect.

A Perplexing Pattern

While the flurry of pre-deployment activities occurred, an unexpected trend emerged. We held a Command and Staff meeting daily, and by mid-September, S2 (Intelligence and Security) reported a disturbing set of events. There was a dramatic surge of Soldier indiscipline throughout Fort Hood: Drunkenness, DUI, DWI, fighting, and missed formations. Those offenses were normal but had significantly increased. The S2 validated other events we heard about through the Daily Military Police (MP) Blotter Report. The Blotter Report contained all offenses committed by all Soldiers, regardless of rank, that the

MPs engaged with or were reported by the local police forces and the sheriff's department.

Destructive Disruptions

Soldiers sometimes go AWOL – Absent Without Official Leave, and I had one as a platoon leader, but the S2 reported the numbers were now staggering. My one AWOL Soldier may have been the only one in our battalion, but now there may be several in each battalion. There had also been at least two instances of the fort being locked down because of a Soldier brandishing a weapon and threatening others. Then, there was the new wrinkle in the urinalysis. Apparently, there was a substantial increase in positive pregnancies, and many were considered questionable. And then there was the deluge of patients at the medical clinics and the hospital seeking non-deployable illnesses, and some instances of domestic abuse.

The assessment was that Soldiers were looking for any reason they could become 'nondeployable.' Some of those things were occasionally seen when Soldiers did not want to deploy on Field Training Exercises (FTX), but now the numbers were too huge. We were instructed to check in with our personnel to determine whether any were having problems we were unaware of or had second thoughts about our mission. Spouses were on edge, and with school just beginning, children were distracted as well. If there were enough of those disruptive distractions, an organization could find itself nondeployable. I do not know of any unit that happened to, but I mention this so that people do not mistakenly believe that everyone was gung-ho to deploy. That was just the first thing that surprised us as we prepared to depart.

Blindsided: Pack It All Up!

We believed that everything was going smoothly and according to schedule when we received the surprise order of,

"Pack it all up like you're not coming back because some of you aren't."

Then and now, I thought that saying it was dumber than dog crap, especially since many lives were lost during combat operations. *"Pack it all up"* meant that we had to pack up all the remaining equipment, office items, and personal items from all our buildings. That included the Battalion HQ, the S3 and S4 operations buildings, and the motor pool. All of that seemed inconvenient compared to the major packing event: Packing up the four barracks the single Soldiers were living in!

Of our 600+ personnel (We peaked at 700 and reduced a bit from there), 400 were single Soldiers who lived in the barracks. Some services refer to the barracks as 'dorms,' as if we were on a college campus rather than a military installation. And because we were on a military installation, this was not a supply function but a housing function, or so I thought. Believing we were off the hook, SFC E busted my bubble when he said,

"Sir, the Battery Commanders are signed for all the furniture in the barracks from the Housing PBO. That makes it an S4 function."

I rolled my eyes, felt like a dumbass because I knew that, and said to SFC E,

"Please tell me you're kidding?" SFC E replied, *"I wish, sir,"*.

Now came the daunting task of coordinating with Installation Housing, which could sometimes feel like having a hernia: It only hurts when you move.

Can We At Least Get a Mint on The Pillow?

The mint on the pillow was because it felt like we were getting screwed. Packing up our offices was one thing, but to have the Soldiers living out of duffel bags and one box with some civilian clothes was crappy. To make matters worse, we felt sorry for the housing folks because they were as blindsided as we were. Coordinating with housing was no joy because they were ill-prepared for this massive undertaking of packing our likely 15,000 Soldiers across Fort Hood. Housing had to provide boxes, packing materials, and storage facilities in accordance with wartime deployment rules. Securing high-dollar value items such as TVs, boom boxes, jewelry, and vehicles was the other wrinkle. Yes, Privately Owned Vehicles (POV) were required to be stored.

Of course, the POVs were not being packed away per se, but they were moved to a secure motor pool. And then there were the POWs – Personally Owned Weapons. Those would be stored in an armory. So, each Soldier was issued at least four large boxes for packing their personal belongings from the rooms, each box marked with the Soldier's full name, room #, barracks name, and Social Security number (SSN). Identity theft wasn't quite as prevalent back then, so we used our full SSNs. Different packing materials were used for high-value items, which were also stored in a more secure location. If the Soldier had a POW and a POV, they would need to sign four different receipts for their possessions in addition to maintaining their deployment equipment and doing their day job.

The NCOs had the best idea: Provide copies of all receipts to the rear detachment in the event a Soldier misplaced their copies during the next 6, 12, or 18 months while deployed. This ensured that the Soldiers could retrieve their personal items when we returned. The battery separated the receipts, and Soldiers would need their ID to get their copy back if required. For our offices, we cleared out our personal items, boxed up the files, and stored them in secure areas. And then there were the single NCOs, officers, and families.

The single officers and NCOs had to pack up their living spaces because our return dates were unknown at the time. That meant breaking leases without getting broken, hence, the Soldiers and Sailors Act. This Act allowed service members to break housing leases if they were on deployment orders. Orders? When were we getting our orders? Without the deployment orders, the leases and contracts were legally binding, so the S1 (HR) had to get on the stick with the G1 (Bigger HR) to provide them. We were given something called 'Blanket Orders', but those off-post personnel needed something with their name on it. The S1 officer figured it out, but it was fingernail-biting for those who needed the orders. And then, there was the packing.

If memory serves, the off-post personnel were on their own getting boxes, packing material, and storage facilities. We arranged for their vehicles to be locked in the motor pool, which provided them with some comfort and saved them one less expense. And now, the families. If the families stayed, no problem, but many wanted to pack up the kids and go back home to a better support system. Families went through the same packing process as single NCOs, with the added frustration of travel. It was impractical to keep an empty house or apartment and still pay rent, but Soldiers and their families figured out how to do it.

Most of the time, the deploying Soldier traveled with their family to the new location and then returned. This small example illustrates the complexity of everything we were doing to prepare for our first deployment. Personally, through all of this, I failed to practice what is now known as 'self-care', but the Old Man corrected that.

My First Deployment Faux Pas, I Think…

This blunder was not intentional, but could have been detrimental if things had gone south. I was summoned to the Old Man's office, and he gently read me the riot act. I made sure that I was standing at attention.

With a raised voice, the Old Man asked, *"S4, what are you **DOING**?"*

Perplexed, I responded, *"Just doing my job, sir."*

"So, what makes you exempt from chemical weapons?" he said, and didn't leave me hanging. *"Have you been to the gas chamber yet?"*

"Ah, no, sir," I said. *"I was going to get around to it."*

"Yah, like right now!" he said. As he moved from around the desk, his tone changed.

"'4', you're doing a great job, but you've got to take care of yourself," he said. *"If you don't get your gas mask checked, and it has a leak in it, you don't want to be the test case in Iraq to see if we know what to do during a chemical attack, and if the antidote works,"* he chuckled.

"Yes, sir," I said. *"I'll head over now."*

This is important because the Battalion Commander had about a billion better things to do than chasing a captain down about not going to the gas chamber. Although I was working my butt off, this did not excuse me from conducting the other training, so I am uncertain of why I blew off the gas chamber. I felt even more special, and like a fool when I arrived on site.

I checked in and told them my name and unit. The NCOIC said,

"Sir, you're lucky. This is the last day the chamber is open so that you would have been SOL (Shit-Out-of-Luck) *after today."*

I'm sure I had a stupid look on my face as he continued,

"Someone must really like you because they called to make certain you had a spot."

Although it did not always feel like it, I must have been doing something right for the Old Man to have me tracked down and sent me to receive training that might save my life. A leak in a gas mask in the gas chamber is no big deal. However, the same leak on the battlefield could be lethal. The big picture, however, was that it was more about the over 600 members of the unit who depended on me to do my job.

Photo 25. Prepping a Gas Chamber for participants.

Chapter 5:
"The Gas Chamber of Horrors" and Other Oddities

"Sometimes you forget how easy it is to get killed."

I surmised that my readers may want to know what the gas chamber is. A training gas chamber is in a building, or a perfectly sealed GP medium tent filled with 20-30 Soldiers standing around three tables with a cannister emitting fumes. The fumes were CS gas, also known as riot gas. CS is the symbol for a long chemical compound that I can neither pronounce nor would you remember. We were required to hold our breath, take off our gas mask, and then breathe. Not a big deal, I thought, but I forgot: CS works best with air. When we walked out of the tent one by one, and the air hit our faces, imagine the gagging, screaming, crying, cursing, and even puking that occurred. Not me, of course.

I follow instructions well when my life depends on it. All I recall was the instructor saying,

*"If you do **exactly** as I say, it will not be as painful."*

As painful meant that there would be some pain involved, no matter what you do, hence, the gas chamber of horrors. Outside, a sergeant walked up to me and said,

"I see you listened, huh, Captain?" "Yep," I said.

Tears were running down my face just like everyone else, but thankfully, I was not gagging, screaming, hollering, cursing, or puking. This could have easily gone the other way had I not followed instructions, or, worse yet, if my mask had a leak or was not properly sealed. All in all, an exercise well worth the chewing out I received and the concern.

Photo 26. Participants entered the gas chamber.

Many people ignore the final instruction after "take off your mask…," which was "*…and then breathe.*" In this instance, holding your breath only makes it worse because you cannot hold it indefinitely. If that were the case, we would not need gas masks! You are supposed to breathe normally for about a minute and then walk outside. Many people try to avoid the inevitable: pain, but it was coming! Well, after I finished drying my tears and could see straight, I needed to get moving. Although the gas chamber training seemed mundane, the training monotony would end soon enough, but not before receiving our next 'curve ball': Immediate deployment of the Advanced Party.

Photo 27. Soldier giving the 'thumbs up' in a gas chamber.

SLEEP, WHO NEEDED SLEEP?

Out of the blue in mid-September, we were alerted to deploy our Advanced Party within 96 hours. I do not recall how large our Advanced Party was supposed to be, but we were ordered to deploy 100 people. This primarily fell on Headquarters and Headquarters Battery (HHB), and the HHB Commander was quick to ask for help. He let the Old Man and staff know that his requirements were extensive. The correctly sized uniforms were needed for all deploying personnel, with nametags, patches, rank, etc., sewn onto the uniforms, and some Soldiers still required desert boots. About half the personnel were single, so they needed more packing boxes ASAP to finish packing up their rooms. They also needed to store their POVs.

At first, it seemed like an S4 function, but it quickly became a Battalion-level mission. Uniforms were cross-leveled between batteries. Soldiers needed help packing and storing their personal gear, and the POVs were the last items stored. The reason this is titled "sleep, who needs sleep" is that I believe we worked until at least 1 or 2 am each of those days until the Advanced Party departed.

Taking A Breather

With all the vehicles, equipment, and volunteers who hated flying aboard ships sailing across the ocean, most of the office spaces were packed, and the Advanced Party was deployed. Things slowed down significantly. Most of the training over the next 2-3 weeks was classroom subjects. This included training on the cultural customs and courtesies for Saudi Arabia and the Middle East, Conduct as a Prisoner of War (POW), and Treatment of Enemy Prisoners of War (EPW). Some of the more notable training was the Law of Land Warfare, Rules of Engagement (ROE), and SAEDA – Subversion and Espionage Directed Against the United States Army (now referred to as TARP – Threat Awareness Reporting Program).

The Law of Land Warfare was directly tied to the treatment of EPWs and to what was permissible on the battlefield. SAEDA covered what to do if approached by a foreign agent, regardless of the reason. Rules of Engagement were the most serious because they instruct personnel on how to engage the enemy and the level of force that can be used. For example, we could not use deadly force against enemy personnel attacking without weapons, nor could we shoot at unarmed personnel. There was a list of what we could and could not do, which was reviewed by the Judge Advocate General (JAG) for legal sufficiency.

Mostly, we spent time with our families, ensuring our affairs were in order. Wills, powers of attorney, and updating life insurance policies were the big ones that we conducted in the gyms or other large areas to accommodate several people. There were also applications for new identification (ID) cards for Soldiers, new families, and new children or receiving updated ID cards. Housing leases, finances, and property settlements were all reviewed. As the days ticked by, we were always ready to go, and soon our anticipation came to an end.

Tomorrow, Tomorrow

All our pre-deployment events occurred in about 50ish days, and in a scant nine days later, on October 9, 1990, I received the word for deployment, and the word was given: Tomorrow. Tomorrow was not going to be just another day. With that phone call, what we had dreaded was now coming to fruition: Departure. When my wife returned from running errands, I had to tell her I was leaving the next day. I also needed to call my parents and six siblings to say goodbye. What began as an evening of hilarity and fun quickly turned solemn and somber.

That one phone call impacted me for the remainder of my Army career because *my bags were always packed*. For any assignment after this one that required me to pick up what we referred to as TA-50: personal field training and combat equipment, I asked for a packing list, and my bags were always packed.

What Packed Bags Really Meant

Just as a precursor, most military spouses hate all the equipment we are required to carry because it was generally scattered all over the house or apartment before the deployment. Having your bags packed seems like a small task, but it's a ***monumental feat***. Our bags were two duffel bags and a rucksack. By the time the duffels were fully packed, they weighed 70 pounds or more each. The rucksack easily weighed 50 pounds if it weighed an ounce. The duffel bags contained all our personal and professional equipment and clothing that might be needed for a deployment, while the rucksack served as a 'rapid reaction' bag.

Beyond what we were initially issued, such as a 'pup' tent and a shovel, we were required to pack our personal gear. That was a field jacket, numerous sets of Army t-shirts and underwear, complete physical fitness uniforms (3-6 t-shirts and at least three pairs of shorts, plus the jacket and pants), a pair of running shoes, toiletries, and other miscellaneous but necessary items. We were also issued an entirely new set of clothing for the deployment.

Photo 28. Empty Army Duffel Bag, era 1990s. Photo provided by the Author.

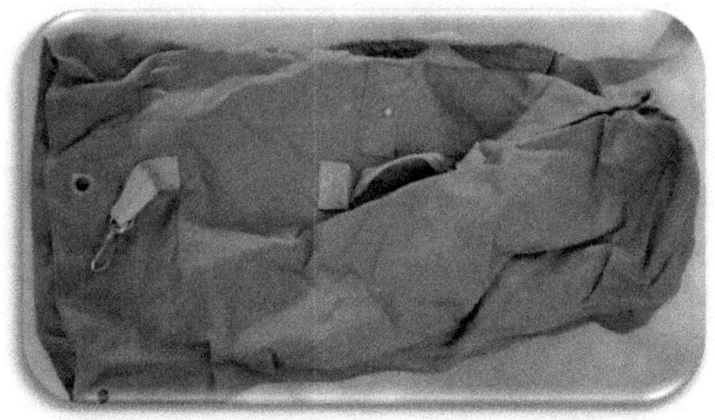

Imagine being given four suitcases of clothes and told to 'make it fit' into two cloth suitcases:

- Two of three sets of Desert Camouflage Uniforms (DCU).
- Six or seven sets of Battle Dress Uniforms (BDU).
- A nighttime camouflage uniform (I have no idea).
- Dust cloths (for the numerous dust storms).
- Goggles, sunglasses, and a Boonie cap.
- One of two pairs of desert boots.
- One of two pairs of black boots (To match the BDUs).
- A two-quart canteen (regular canteens are one quart).
- A flak jacket that weighed 15-20 pounds.
- Another complete set of Mission Oriented Protective Posture (MOPP) protective gear.
- Four days' worth of MREs (12 MREs = one case).

The rucksack was an entirely different story. In addition to one complete MOPP Suit and three days of MREs, we were also required to carry one full set of BDUs, another pair of boots, underwear, a PT uniform including sneakers, and toiletries. Because we were travelling on commercial flights, we also had to pack our helmets and TA-50. TA-50 is a pistol belt with a carry harness, two ammunition pouches, canteens, and likely a butt pack, flashlight, and first aid kit.

Photos 29 & 30. Packed Alice Pack, 1990s era. L – Front; R – Back.

Photos retrieved from https://www.bw-discount.de/outdoor-camping/rucksaecke/1961/us-army-rucksack-alice-pack-large-oliv-gebr.

Photo 31. TA-50 as described on the previous page.

Photo retrieved from https://www.pinterest.com.mx/pin/568157309227404257/.

The 100 Soldiers we sent forward as an Advanced Party only received 24 hours' notice, but had 96 hours to prepare. Our tomorrow, however, was the next day. The Personnel Deployment Schedule was determined based on available space and operational requirements, with unit desires given distant consideration. Because I was responsible for ensuring the shipment of all equipment forward, I should be on the ground to set up the reception before it arrived.

Photo 32. Individual Tactical Gear layout with weapons, flak jacket, ruck sack, TA-50, pistol holster, and map case.

Photo retrieved from https://sipseystreetirregulars.blogspot.com/2012/03/praxis-what-is-ta-50-781782-gear.html.

Now, please don't think I am complaining, because in the subsequent books, the equipment and clothing lists changed dramatically each time, and we received even more equipment! Although it seemed like the 'logical thing to do,' it felt lousy leaving on a moment's notice. Fortunately, Terry had been a Soldier and had a sister assigned to Fort Hood. Her sister was not deployed, and in the ensuing months, Terry would need that 'family' support. Her sister became her Family Support Group (FSG), in addition to the ones formed by the unit and the Army. We were leaving to do what we were trained for, preparing for war, moving out of the firing pan and into the fire.

Part II:
Desert Shield: *"Out of the Frying Pan"*

Safety can always be a matter of life or death.

Safety is of paramount importance, even in war. We should not have been shocked when we received this Leader's Safety Guide about 30 days into our pre-deployment process, but I was. The Army Safety Center was an expertly functioning organization, and one of my first Active-Duty mentors was stationed there before our meeting. I included the cover on the next page and the following Forward because both were profound. The cover has the Army combined arms team of the individual Soldier, an M-1 tank, and an Apache helicopter with Iraq, Kuwait, and Saudi Arabia outlined in the lower right-hand corner. I found the areas outlined as neutral zones between Iraq and Saudi Arabia, and a portion of Kuwait, engaging. Those areas were vital just before the commencement of combat operations.

The Forward outlined the significance of safety and the accident statistics from each war. We lost significant numbers of personnel in each war because of accidents. Yes, everyone hears about every combat casualty and fatality, but not every accident-causing casualty and fatality. Death notifications are heart-wrenching, regardless of the circumstances, but in war, 'accidents' seem less understandable. The military is a dangerous business, which I shared in the introduction.

A low-level accident in peacetime may require an SIR (Serious Incident Report), and the unit and its people may move on. In war, however, the same seemingly simple accident can result in career-ending injuries or, even worse, Death. Death is always a CCIR – Commander's Critical Information Report and is reported immediately for military or civilian deaths. I will recount some of these incidents without disclosing the names of

the individuals, but people need to know the types of things that occurred. Accidents and casualties arise even with the best-laid plans of mice and men and even with extensive risk assessments.

Photo 33. Cover, Leader's Safety Guide—photo provided by the Author.

Photo 34. Forward, Leader's Safety Guide. Photo provided by the Author.

Foreword

In combat, safety is essential to force preservation. Statistics show that—

• In World War II, one out of every five American soldiers killed died as a result of an accident.

• In Korea, more than half the Army personnel who were hospitalized were injured in accidents.

• In Vietnam, accidents killed 5,700 soldiers, disabled more than 106,000 others, and produced nearly 5 million nondisabling injuries.

These are more than just numbers. They're a measurement of a serious loss of combat assets at a time when we could least afford to lose them—in the heat of battle. We must strive to keep such losses from happening on any future battlefield. We can do this by—

• Establishing and enforcing high standards of performance.

• Creating a command climate of "tough caring."

• Using risk management principles to make good decisions.

• Recognizing the effects of stress and fatigue on performance.

Let us not forget that accident prevention is an important weapon in our arsenal; using it will multiply our combat power by preserving our assets.

This pamphlet is a quick reference intended to help unit leaders prevent accidents during Operation Desert Shield, thereby saving lives and preserving their combat assets.

Chapter 6:
"It Began to Sizzle"

I think I know how bacon feels.

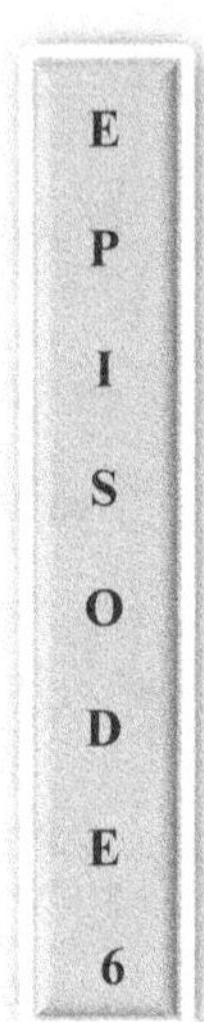

For most of us, this was our first deployment and potential combat tours. This was the first wartime deployment for the entire Army since Vietnam. I wrote about wartime versus major deployment because the Army had plenty of deployments since Vietnam: Panama, Haiti, and Bosnia-Herzegovina, to name a few. Those deployments, however, required only commitment from some of the Army. Some were peacekeeping or contingency missions that may have involved combat operations but were not planned that way. These were eventually labeled as OOTW, pronounced Ow Twa – Operations Other Than War.

Tomorrow Finally Arrived

When 'tomorrow' came, we still had to attend work as usual. As I entered the parking lot near my office, my car began to lose power, so I pulled into the nearest parking space. I walked to the closest office and called a tow truck – remember, 1990, no cellphones, and once he arrived, the driver said all I needed was a new battery. He charged me up, and I went to Western Auto (or someplace like that), got a new battery, and returned to work. I did not work all day because I was leaving that evening, so I went home once I gathered the final deployment information. Although Terry and I ate dinner together, neither of us was hungry because I had to be at the gym at 8 or 9 pm.

The journey began with arriving at a gym packed with about 1,000 other Soldiers from various units and their families, totaling nearly 1,500 people, including support staff. Imagine being at a concert without the band, the music, or the frivolity, just a bunch of sad people. Spouses and children were crying, and Soldiers were attempting not to cry as we moved through the line to pick up weapons, sign the paperwork, and say our final goodbyes. Fear was not a factor in our actions because we were thoroughly trained and ready. Our families, however, had a different story.

I had 'celebrated' my 26th birthday a week earlier, had been promoted to captain 40 days prior, had been married nearly 60 days ago, and this entire event was barely 60 days old! One might refer to this cycle as the 'trauma' incurred by military families. Literally, at a moment's notice, your loved one could be whisked away to a foreign country to perform their military duties. In this case, it meant leaving spouses with children who had just begun school, other spouses in various stages of pregnancy, or some spouses left totally alone.

"When service members deploy, families go through hell."

Although this may look good on paper and brief well to a crowd, turning the plan into reality was a totally separate thing. Envision having to move your entire family elsewhere to maintain an adequate support system. Or your in-laws were moving into your house for the same reason. What about when your child or children need to see the school psychologist, which did not exist back then, about mommy, daddy, cousin, brother, aunt, etc., deploying? Or as a single parent, you must initiate your Family Care Plan (FCP) that was created for occasions like this – deployments, and notify the guardians that the kids needed to live with them for a while.

Even worse, if there is no FCP or at least a valid one, or you cannot bear to deploy and leave your children, you will be chaptered out of the Army within 30 days. Chaptered Out meant discharged without severance pay for refusal to comply with a valid order(s) surrounding deployment. Some Soldiers committed suicide rather than deploy, the conscientious

Objectors who refused to deploy based on religious grounds, or those who just went AWOL – Absent Without Official Leave. And some AWOL did not just leave the unit and the Army high and dry, but also their families.

We were not leaving to attend conferences, symposiums, seminars, or the National Training Center (NTC). We could not return home quickly on a moment's notice or after the event concluded. We were leaving everything behind to conduct the nation's business by brute force. The military is not a diplomatic solution; it is the result when political outcomes fail. We were leaving to do what we were trained for, preparing for war, moving out of the frying pan and into the fire.

After our goodbyes, we boarded buses and headed to the airfield, with our gear loaded onto separate trucks. The Army typically deploys from Army or Air Force airfields rather than from commercial airports. I cannot recall my thoughts on the way to the airfield. I was numb, standing outside my body and watching this scene from the old TV shows 'Combat' or 'Rat Patrol, 'and possibly the movies 'A Few Good Men' or 'Full Metal Jacket.' Although I know that those shows and movies did not have airport scenes and that the military and war/combat were common themes, my experience did not feel like a movie.

The flight began uneventfully as we boarded what I believe was a 747 or larger aircraft. We stored our carry-on bags and found our seats, and because of the time zone difference and the fact that it was about 2200 hours, it was bedtime for many of us. Adequate rest is necessary when you start your day at 0630 with one hour of physical fitness training. The work call was 0900 when your 'eight-hour day' began. Our days typically ended between 17 and 1800ish (5-6 pm) unless there were last-minute tasks. This outlines a typical day without inspections, quarterly or annual training requirements, recall drills, alert exercises, or field training. Yes, the Army keeps long hours, which may be why sleep is a premium luxury when many Soldiers leave the Army, better than a vacation in the Bahamas. The yearning for this luxury was about to increase exponentially, and with some additional anxiety.

Egypt, My Egypt

During my recruiting days, I learned that everyone's DBM – Dominate Buying Motive for joining the Army could be summed up in the acronym TEAMS: Training, Education, Adventure, Money, and Service to Country. DBM is the person's reason for doing something, such as buying a car, a vacation package, or a house. Adventure is a big seller: Join the Army, See the World, etc. Our flight was scheduled for a crew change in Egypt, then on to our destination. Pretty routine stuff, right? We were not required to disembark the plane; we just swapped out the flight crew. Well, the 'adventure' part of our journey began before we even arrived in Saudi Arabia.

As we landed and taxied down the runway, we suddenly heard a 'thud', and the entire plane lurched forward. Then, there were the expected questions and grumblings, "Hey, what the heck happened?" and "Watch where you're going." There was no answer to our questions, only a request to remain seated. The plane began moving what felt like slowly backward, forward, backward again, and from side to side. Finally, we were told that the front landing gear had run off the runway. Hence, the thud and plane jerking forward. As if this were not exciting enough, we were asked to unload the aircraft to reduce the load. This is where the real adventure began.

As we opened the plane door, we were met by what looked like Egyptian military personnel with Uzis, motioning for us to remain on the plane. A Uzi is an Israeli-made mini- or submachine gun that holds a 25 or 32-round clip and can shoot 600-1500 rounds per minute, depending on the model.[5] We had weapons, but our ammunition was in the plane's belly, so we complied without much resistance. This adventure soon turned into a mini nightmare. As the pilot continued trying to move the aircraft back onto the tarmac, the front landing gear wrapped around the ground landing lights. We surmised that, in the dark and without ground guidance, the pilot had not seen the thick cables coiled around the landing gear, like a cobra tightening its grip on its prey. Unfortunately, we were the prey.

The Airport Fandango

After about two hours, we were finally ushered from the airplane onto buses as our bladders reached max capacity. The buses were a step up from the aircraft because each bus had a toilet. Little did we know that this was only another leg of our journey through Egypt's airport. I will explain if you need to become more familiar with the term 'fandango'. A fandango is *a foolish or useless act or thing*. What I will describe next is best defined as a fandango.

As we reached the terminal, we were elated to get off the buses, stretch our legs, and sit in luxury. That didn't happen, and we were not allowed off the bus. Of course, there was grumbling and complaining because we could not understand the big deal about getting off the buses to use the terminal restrooms. At the time, we had no idea that this had nothing to do with us but with alliances. We knew that the United States was building a coalition against Iraq, but had Egypt signed up to attack another Muslim country? That early in the process, I had yet to learn who was on board with the coalition and barely knew what an alliance was. All I knew was that we were not getting off that bus.

After about an hour, we were allowed off the bus, but only to stand next to it and pee into water bottles. Yes, we pee'd into the empty water bottles we had because that was all we could do. Thankfully, we were an all-male unit and only had to worry about offending the people inside the airport, who were likely none at 4 am. After another two hours, we were told to get back on the bus to get a 'headcount' before we could enter the terminal. Our leadership had diligently lobbied on our behalf so that we could have some semblance of decency before entering the chaos that awaited us.

In short, we never went into the terminal. Once we loaded the buses, the buses stormed off towards an airplane. All we could do was holler and scream at the driver, who likely had no idea what we said and never stopped driving until we reached the plane. The Egyptians only wanted us out of their country as badly as we wanted out. Fortunately, another crew that had just flown in heard about the fandango and agreed to fly us to our destination. Apparently, the other captain and crew were so frazzled that flying us anywhere was not an option.

Also, because the plane left the tarmac and did not go into the friendly skies, I am sure there was much paperwork to complete, conversations to be had, head-scratching, and teeth gnashing. All I know is that my butt was in a nice, comfy seat, we had food and beverage service, and we were on our way. The thought crossed my mind:

'Could this be an omen of things to come?' 'Would the entire deployment be like this?'

For the most part, the remainder of the flight was uneventful, without even weather turbulence. We were *on our way…*

…*moving out of the frying pan and into the fire.*

Chapter 7:
"This Ain't No NTC Rotation"

*"**War** is NOT like the movies."*

War is literally not like in the movies. We did not fight our way into the country, evading surface-to-air missiles (SAM) while attempting to land. We did not shoot our way off the plane. We did not call for fire against advancing forces. Once we finally landed in the Kingdom of Saudi Arabia (KSA) at Riyadh International Airport, we safely retrieved our weapons and gear, boarded buses, and rode for 60 minutes to the Port of Damman. Initially, this made no sense to me, but then I remembered that all our vehicles and equipment had been shipped, making it easier to be there to unload them. Another apparent reason was that the Saudis may not have wanted us near population centers should Iraq or some other entity decide to attack us.

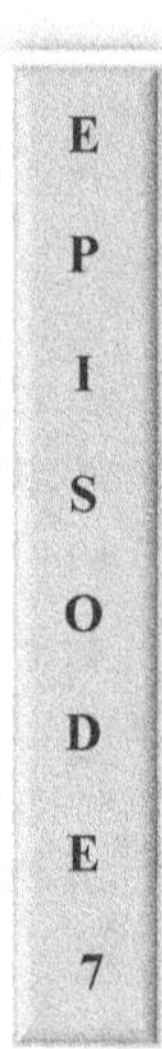

The scenery reminded me a little of the National Training Center (NTC) at Fort Irwin, CA, as we traveled. We would land in Barstow, CA, and take buses to the fort with only one thing

Photo 35. National Training Center Landscape. Photo provided by the Author.

between the two points: a tremendous amount of sand. In California, you can see mountains on the horizon, and according to the time of year, they are either brown or green. In winter, some were even snowcapped. But without the intervening crest, there was no way to judge the distance to any of them. It was nearly the same way to the port: Sand as far as the eye could see, but with significant differences: Almost perfectly flat, lifeless, with no discernible landmarks.

Photo 36. Saudi Arabian Desert. Photo provided by the Author.

The difference between KSA and NTC was that KSA deserts had several Bedouins living there. Bedouins are one of the tribes of the KSA that did not fully embrace modernity and lived in tents in the desert. Many Bedouins, however, took advantage of modern conveniences such as cars, kerosene heaters, and 'portable stoves.' I did not see many Bedouins with both cars and camels, but camels were still a means of travel. Unlike horses, camels did not appear majestic to me; they were large, heavy animals with the giant humped back. The camels also did not walk or gallop with their legs from front to back, but side to side. It was an odd sight to see until someone explained it to you, but I digress.

The Bedouins did not live in large clusters but were scattered across the country's most barren, desolate areas. More about the Bedouins later. The welcoming committee at the port was our Advanced Party, and they looked rough. Everyone appeared to have lost weight, seemed haggard, and appeared battle-hardened, minus the battle. As we unpacked the buses and began unloading our gear, a lieutenant, followed by others, came over and seemed less hospitable, but we soon learned why he was so unpleasant.

"Don't drink the water, even by accident, and always keep your food covered. If you don't, prepare to spend most of your time in the latrine. The flies carry all sorts of diseases and are as big as birds." The instructions continued. *"Keep your boonie cap on at all times, your sleeves down, and wear suntan lotion if you don't want to get burnt to a crisp."* The final comment is what really brought the point home:

"This ain't no NTC rotation."

So, there you have it! Our training environment did not match our reality. NTC has mountains and hills for navigation, as well as valleys that could turn into rivers during the rainy season. I did not recall the flies as much as the mosquitoes; some places provided shade, cover, and concealment, and the terrain was very navigable. Also, maps of NTC were plentiful, another discussion point for later. A training cadre was stationed there who knew the area like the back of their hands, and the enemy was not labeled the enemy but OPFOR – Opposing Forces. Because of those vast differences, this is where the NCO's ingenuity, adaptability, and survivability came into play, helping us adjust and achieve mission success. And then, there was the heat.

The Iraq I Knew...

Like at Fort Hood, TX (now Fort Cavazos), the heat made us sizzle with a tiny difference: We were already somewhat acclimatized. Regarding the other things, however, the Advanced Party lieutenant spoke from experience. As we began to chat, we discovered that everyone had been sick for a few days, either from pestilence, disease, or acclimation. These are other things service members must consider when traveling to foreign lands: familiarizing themselves with and evaluating the new environment. The lieutenant was right – this wasn't an NTC rotation.

The Advanced Party watched us unload our equipment and led us to our accommodations: The largest warehouse I had ever seen. We shared the space with every unit deployed so far and were allotted a section of the area. We set up our cots, which we learned would be 'home' until we received our vehicles and moved out of the port. To better envision this, imagine you were in the top tiers of an enclosed football stadium looking down on two football fields of cots, 500 – 600 deep, neatly aligned, and dress-right-dress. Surrounding the walls were the limited equipment we hand-carried, cases of MREs, pallets of water, and offices where the senior leaders slept. And then, there were the women Soldiers.

Truth In Advertising

When we entered the warehouse, we noticed a curtained-off area using blankets and thought it was for the 'shy' Soldiers who might not want to get dressed and undressed in front of others. That, however, was not the case. That area was for our women warriors. Please remember that this was the first war with a totally (mostly) integrated Army where men and women served side-by-side. Even with the integration of women, there remained a separation between men and women in most areas: latrines, showers, and sleeping areas being the most prevalent. By now, you may have figured out that latrines are restrooms. I will allow your imagination to determine why we were separated; you would likely be correct. Being a brand-new captain, I was on the floor with my crew, so I saw, heard, and experienced things firsthand, like when guards were posted outside the women's shower and latrine.

The bay doors of the warehouse remained open 24 hours a day to provide some semblance of air circulation. The ocean breeze from the Persian Gulf sustained us from cooking inside that tin box. Our next great challenge was finding things to occupy our time until our equipment arrived. This involved conducting physical training (PT) first thing in the morning, playing cards, watching videos sent from home, and trying to remain friendly towards each other.

REMINDER: This was 1990, so the internet, cell phones, iPods and iPads, compact discs (CDs), and DVD devices had yet to be invented. We were also mindful of the religious custom of praying five times a day. I planned out my short respite from my logistical endeavors. I would chill on my cot, either writing letters that wouldn't be sent until much later, reading a book, or listening to cassette tapes. My revelry in doing nothing was short-lived because, after all, I was the Battalion S4.

Barter Joe

The S4 section and supply sergeants had no such challenge as *needing something to do* because something was always required in the supply and logistics world. The water and MREs did not just materialize. Once organized, we set up supply accounts, placed orders, and picked up supplies. It also meant interacting with the local SA (Saudi Arabia) vendors when needed. I was the S4, the Contracting Officer (CO), and the Class A Agent (CAA). The CO entered into contractual agreements, and the CAA paid for the items. I was trained in both duties before departing. Currently, I do not believe the same person can hold those two duties. Fortunately for me, this was not my first rodeo as a CAA. While in the Army Reserves, I served as the Mess Officer (Food Service Officer) and collected meal payments from officers and the Pay Officer, who paid all personnel on extended deployments.

As I like to call it, the 'separation of powers' was for accountability purposes: One person should not have the power to order equipment and supplies, enter into contracts, and pay for them. Because we were at war, many of us were tasked with doing things for practicality's sake. This was never a problem for me because I did not look good in orange, was not a 'favored son,' and did not come from a family with deep pockets. I did the job as it was intended without ever having a problem. My replacement was not so lucky, but that was his problem, not mine, or so I thought.

As we war-gamed what supplies we might need while waiting for our equipment, we quickly realized that most of our supplies were on a ship somewhere. Necessities such as soap, shaving cream, deodorant, and the most essential item – toilet paper - needed to be procured. This wargame session reminded us of the cultural differences between our host nation and us, and that even getting the essentials might be challenging. Enter Barter Joe.

I named myself Barter Joe because I bartered with the SA's and other Army units. That part was like Sergeant Zell, the supply sergeant on the M*A*S*H television series. Thankfully, as more organizations arrived, we were not all stationed at the port or living in that one warehouse. While some units had plenty of toilet paper, they were short on water and MREs. Also, I had a vehicle from somewhere and a driver to pick up items for other units when I went to the airport or King Khalid Military City (KKMC). Of course, they were indebted to me, and when I needed something, I knew who to go to and where. Yes, I kept track of those transactions.

That is really the way most systems work – transactional, and since I had been dubbed the *Lateral Transfer King*, I understood how the Army supply system worked. That was also an excellent benefit for my unit because once I traded for something called Class B Rations. The Mess Sergeant (head cook) told me to get some Class B Rations if I could find them. I had no idea what they were, but neither did the lieutenant I was bartering with, as he traded for some MREs. So, we swapped our individual cases and went our separate ways.

When I returned to the unit and had the Class B Rations unloaded, the Mess Sergeant acted as if I had just unloaded gold. Still baffled, I knew that if my Mess Sergeant were this joyful, the other lieutenant would probably catch heck for the trade. In short, a Class A Ration is a hot meal with real food, and a Class B Ration is a hot meal with reconstituted food.

Photo 37. T-Ration Calculator. Photo provided by the Author.

However, the one thing I learned while serving as the Mess Officer in the Army Reserves was that Army cooks could create a delectable meal out of almost anything. The meals I remember most from the Class B Rations were breakfast, because the cooks made hot biscuits and gravy, scrambled eggs, and what was passed for bacon. While I rose to prominence as Barter Joe, the rest of the unit was not faring well.

The Burden of Abandonment: The Deep End

Although our downtime was only three weeks, it seemed like forever. The card games became stale, reading became dull, and the inevitable occurred: Dear John and Jane letters began to arrive. I recall returning from a supply run after two weeks and noticing a somber mood in our area. Once I arrived at the S4 truck, I asked SFC E,

"What's going on? Why is everyone so sad?"

SFC E replied that, *"An NCO in our sister unit had received a video that he thought was a home movie. It wasn't. It began like many of the other home movies we saw, with the kids holding a poster that read, "We love you, Mommy or Daddy." Each child spoke, and the video ended with a message from the spouse."*

This all sounded like a standard video from home to me, so I asked, *"What's the big deal about a video from home?*

SFC E replied, *"The spouse's message took a weird turn. Her message was an X-rated video featuring her. She finished the video by telling her NCO husband,*

"I want a divorce."

"Sir," said SFC E, *"He played it in front of the unit."*

This was probably the most shocking *Dear John or Jane letter* any of us had heard about at the time. Some of my contemporaries were more graphic in their descriptions of the video, which turned a bad situation into a tragedy. Because we were all starved for information, when someone received a home movie, they would share it with the unit. We acquired a VCR (Video Cassette Recorder) from somewhere because Soldiers were receiving videos from home. Usually, the videos featured spouses and children saying hello to daddy or mommy, sons and daughters, friends, and cousins, and they reminded us of what we were fighting for. That home movie, however, had taken an ominous turn. Everyone watching was stunned, in utter shock and disbelief, but worse yet, the Soldier was humiliated in front of his coworkers and anyone else present.

That ended the blanket distribution of all VHS tapes. When the recordings came in, the individual was notified and allowed to view them in private with a supervisor, and then they could share them with everyone if they wanted to. What happened to the NCO? After the initial shock wore off, he was pissed off to the highest level of pisstivity and uttered several threats against his wife. BTW, just like there are levels of anger: upset, mad, angry, or enraged, being pissed off also has levels. He was not immediately allowed to return home for fear he would carry out his threats. He was also relieved of his weapons for his and everyone else's safety. That is why I referred to this segment as '*The Burden of Abandonment.*'

When service members were about to place themselves in harm's way and were sent a Dear John or Jane letter from spouses or significant others, they felt blindsided. The process seemed like a convenient way to end a relationship, with little recourse for service members: 12,000 miles from home, without any of the conveniences we have today. At that moment, we did not even have AT&T-provided phone banks, so if that happened, you would be stuck like Chuck. Helping service members cope requires much peer counseling, consoling, and constant communication. The unit chaplain was typically involved; if we had mental health professionals assigned to units back then, that would have been beneficial.

Videos were not the only way for spouses or significant others to request a divorce; snail mail was the prevailing method. Also, financial savings were often wiped out, and families moved without notifying service members. All that placed the duty to help *keep the person together* on everyone else, leaving the affected service member feeling abandoned. Sadly, this could happen to anyone regardless of rank, position, or belief about the relationship, affecting the organization's mood daily. This is just one of the many things Soldiers endure when sacrificing for their country. The distraction we needed did not come quickly enough and in fact, another situation presented itself.

BODY BAGS: ONE-SIZE-FITS-ALL

There are some unfortunate truths about war.

The central truth is that people die in war. Another reality is how KIA Soldiers are removed from the battlefield. Still reeling from what SFC E told me and from explaining the organization's climate, I pivoted to a new subject. I was leaning against 8-10 boxes and investigated an open box. I asked SFC E,

"Hey, why do we have so many trash bags?"

"Sir," SFC E replied, *"Those are not trash bags, those are body bags."*

I am amazed at how quickly this day went from bad to worse. We just stood there staring at each other until I removed a bag from the box, opened it, and unfolded it. As if the zipper on the bag weren't enough, I checked the nomenclature tag on the box and saw "Bag, Deceased, Human Remains, 100," or something like that. I asked SFC E, *"What are we supposed to do with these?"* His reply stunned me.

"Pass them out, Sir, one per Soldier."

I knew from the looks on our two junior enlisted Soldiers' faces that, '*This dog don't hunt.*' I knew this decision was well above my pay grade and contacted my boss, the XO, to ask if he, the Old Man, the S3, and the CSM would come to the S4 truck. Fortunately, they respected my request and arrived at our vehicle.

"What's going on S4?" asked the Old Man. I handed him one of the bags. He looked at it and asked,

"'4', you called me down here to look at a trash bag?" he asked.

I grimly responded, *"Sir, that's not a trash bag, it's a body bag, and we are supposed to issue them one per Solder."*

All four senior leaders were speechless and appeared almost nauseous. Finally, the Old Man glumly spoke,

"'4', do you realize the atmosphere around here? If we start issuing body bags, this might send some Soldiers over the deep end." *"No,"* said the Old Man, *"Do not issue the body bags. Don't even mention that we have them."*

"Roger, Sir," I said.

After the Command Group departed, SFC E and I just looked at each other. We both began to speak at the same time.

"We need to make sure our Soldiers do not tell anyone we have these bags."

SFC E said, *"Sir, we will put the bags in the S4 Conex so no one will see them."*

"Probably the best course of action," I said.

THE GHOULISH REALITY

After I placed the body bag back in the box, I began pondering what had happened as I inspected the description tags on each box. Unlike all our other clothing and equipment, there were no sizes on the boxes. That led me to conclude that,

"One-size-fits-all."

It was a ghoulish reality, but true. Although the remains in the bag required 2-4 Soldiers to carry it, the bags did not distinguish between size, shape, race, gender, or rank. The bag accommodated everyone who, unfortunately, needed it. I concluded from this experience that we really needed a distraction from all of this, and we needed it quickly.

Work Therapy

Thank goodness our equipment began to arrive in mass, requiring almost everyone to pitch in with the unloading. That significantly reduced the downtime, card playing, arguments, and rampant imagination that caused Soldiers, NCOs, and officers to stress out. I referred to this as 'work therapy' because it allowed us to refocus our attention on the mission at hand. As the equipment arrived, units slowly deployed to their assigned sections of the desert, referred to as TAAs (Tactical Assembly Areas). The HETs (Heavy Equipment Transport) carried tanks, howitzers, CONEX (Container Express) boxes, and other heavy equipment while we drove the wheeled vehicles to our destinations.

The hardest part of moving out was that we had only a limited number of maps, and unlike NTC, the Saudi Arabian desert had no natural terrain features. There were road networks but no hills and mountains, so, of course, no valleys, trees, or bushes to navigate from. What was prevalent were the Bedouin tents in the desert and the wrecked vehicles alongside the road. Rumor had it that once a car was in an accident of any kind and was wrecked or just broke down, it was believed to be 'possessed' and left on the side of the road. I had a partial map because, like the Battalion Commander, I traveled a great deal; however, we relied on NCO ingenuity to improvise, adapt, and overcome to resolve the map shortfall. We hoped this ingenuity could be used to keep nearly 700 restless artillerymen occupied. After all, if we needed to interact with the local populations, we needed to remember that we were foreigners, not visitors, in a foreign land with vastly different cultures.

THE CULTURAL DIFFERENCES

One experience has always stood out in my mind as an illustration of cultural differences. While picking up some equipment from the airport, my driver parked at the curb, and I ran in to get whatever it was. Obviously, it was not heavy, or we both would have gone. When I returned, I noticed the local men bowed as they passed before the High Mobility Multipurpose Wheeled Vehicle (HMMWV- pronounced Hum-V). I watched this for a moment, trying to understand their actions and why. Finally, after I got in, I asked my driver, *"Why in the world are those men doing that?"*

"Because, the driver said, *they think you are royalty."*

"Yeah, right," I chuckled. *"Who told you that?*

"One of the men, sir." he said. *"I was wondering why they were bowing, so I finally found one who spoke English, and he explained it to me."* The man said,

"Normally, in our military, the officers are from royal or at least wealthy lineage. We are expected to pay tribute to that person, even if we do not know who it is. It is a show of respect."

"What"? I said, but the driver continued, *"Wait, sir, there's more."*

"Headgear and clothing denote your social status or class in society. A white robe with a red checkered headgear was the highest social class in the country. The next highest was the grey robe and headgear, and working-class men wore everyday clothes: jeans, shirts, or whatever they had."

"Come on," I said. *"Surely, the local men know I can't be a Saudi Officer."*

"Sir, you come on," he said. *"Think about what we learned in our cultural and military training classes. Besides, look at us."*

As we sat there, having that conversation, men continued to walk past and bow at the vehicle. I thought Saudi Arabia was an ally; we sold them equipment through Foreign Military Sales (FMS), and their military was somewhat patterned after the US military, including their uniforms. What else I observed sitting there was that the men in the white robes typically had light skin like the driver and me. The ones in the grey robes had slightly darker skin, and what might be considered the working class was the darkest. We also discovered that the working class was not always composed of Saudis.

Based on interactions with the HET drivers, we learned they were from many Middle Eastern countries, including India and Pakistan. They worked daily, were paid monthly, and either sent or took the money back home. This behavior will be a key factor in the next book in the series. At the time, it all made some sense. However, I also had to consider that religion, customs, and climate influenced the dress. Over the years and deployments, I learned that what I called robes are correctly called Thobe, Jubba, and Dishdasha. [6]

Dress was just one of many things we learned, such as the five-times-a-day prayer called salat[7]. Everything stopped for 15 minutes to observe the prayer times. The prayer times began at 0600 and ended at 1800, essentially every three hours. We had already learned not to have contact with any of the local women, and they were covered in black from head to toe in a burqa[8]. We learned about holidays such as Hajj and Eid al-Adha, the annual Islamic pilgrimage, and the Festival of Sacrifice[9].

Everything I just recounted varied between Islamic countries to some degree. As we were stationed in Saudi Arabia with the intent to liberate Kuwait through fighting in Iraq, we needed to be mindful of where we were, what we were doing, and who we were doing it with. I dare say this first deployment set the tone for all future operations and relationships in the region, in my opinion. The beauty of a narrative account is that it is from the person's perspective, not as a government representative.

AND THE BEAT GOES ON...

Little did I know that after this deployment, I would never deploy into or from Saudi Arabia again and that our base of entry and exit into Iraq would be Kuwait. I also did not believe that I would 'visit' Iraq again, uninvited, two more times. I could have never imagined that the reasons for the two additional deployments would be so vastly different from this first one. Much to my chagrin, my drivers' descriptions of what occurred with the bowing made more sense with each deployment.

It felt like I did not know much then, but as I wrote earlier, I had just turned 26, with few deployments and no combat experience. The only thing I did know was this: The waiting felt like it was killing us. It almost felt like we were being toyed with, without the pleasure of playing with toys, and we were no longer children. The mere three weeks we were there felt like three months. Although AT&T had set up phone banks for us by then, three minutes a week was not much.

Yes, three minutes a week to speak with a loved one of your choice. The call was usually made to a spouse for married personnel, and the spouse became responsible for notifying the rest of the family. For single Soldiers, the call was typically to parents, since they were the next of kin, even if the Soldier had children. I did not know many Soldiers, NCOs, or Officers with grown children. That should tell you just how young we all were. Yes, we had snail mail, but it is called that for a reason: When letters arrived, they had been mailed two or three weeks earlier. Old letters, old food, and old routines were getting stale. There were no care packages, video messages, or even news reports. It felt like we were going to wait there forever.

Photo 38. 1st Cavalry Division repositioning in Saudi Arabia.

Photo retrieved from theatlantic.com. https://www.theatlantic.com /photo / 2016/01/operation-desert-storm-25-years-since-the-first-gulf-war/424191/ Greg English, AP

Chapter 8:
"The Waiting Game"

Diplomacy involves lots of waiting.

With all our equipment unloaded and secured, the waiting game continued for us in our base camps. The focus was to keep everyone occupied because it was a waiting game until the diplomatic solutions were totally exhausted. Runners found a way to jog in the desert in the ever-shifting sands while the weight heads created' makeshift weights and pressed iron, or in some cases, bricks, MRE boxes, or 25-gallon pails. I recall an 'improvised' volleyball net without the net, just some 550-cord strung across two camouflage poles. Yes, we did take some recreational equipment because you never know how long the 'waiting game' will last.

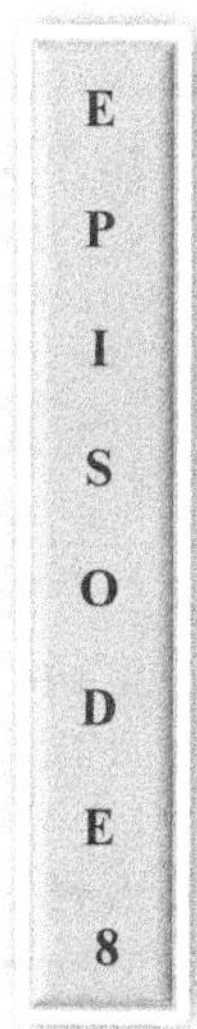

For us less athletic types (I hadn't yet decided to make the Army a career), we just used the plywood floors we'd made and some mats for push-ups and sit-ups. That was done while the UN continued to demand that Saddam Hussein remove the Iraqi Army from Kuwait. We had no idea what was occurring, and our daily thought was that we might either be recalled home or begin fighting. It was an uneasy, eerie feeling I only acknowledged within these pages. Yes, we were young, naïve, and bored, so our thoughts ran rampant with different scenarios. I do not believe that fear was a factor because we were well-trained and equipped, but were just restless for some action. We learned that the day-to-day operations of 'living' in the desert would be a combat within itself.

SURVIVING THE UNEXPECTED

As I mentioned, we were not at the NTC during a four- or six-week rotation, and then you went home. We were stationed in Saudi Arabia for an undetermined period and needed to learn how to live in the desert. The pee tubes were minor inconveniences, but the burn barrels were a different story. As we all used the latrines, things began to 'pile up,' and the half barrels needed to be emptied. Unfortunately, emptying was not an option; the only solution was burning.

What the Burn Barrels Meant

I recall as a child when my dad burned trash in a burn barrel in our backyard. It was a full 55-gallon drum filled with paper and some sticks for kindling. The flame never burned above the top of the barrel, and the smell was minimal. The same cannot be said for burning feces. First, that was a struggle for the Soldiers who had a 'shit-burning detail' and the NCOs who had to supervise them. I recall in the Army Reserves that lime was applied to human waste once or twice a day, and when the waste reached a certain level (three feet, I think), the trench was filled in, and the latrine was moved to a new location downwind. That was not so with the poop barrels.

Second, the latrines had to be closed for cleaning and washing the toilet seats and walls. Also, the barrels had to be removed from underneath the toilet seats. Just let that sink in for a moment – removing barrels full of feces by hand. There was no robot or machine to do that, but the Soldiers did. Notice the gloves on the Soldier in the photo. You can imagine the horrible stench endured at 8 am, when it was already 100 degrees. The barrels were moved safely away from the latrines and any other items in camp, filled with MOGAS, and set on fire.

As the burning began, the smoke billowed throughout the camp, and the smell was horrible. I recall it even as I type this.

Paper could not be used as an accelerant because paper can float when burned, creating even more particulate matter.

Photo 39. Soldier on Crap-Burning Detail Somewhere in Saudi Arabia, 1990.

Photo retrieved from deansrobinson @ https://www.vegasmessageboard.com/ forums/index.php?threads/fact-of-the-day.142889/page-90

Now, consider feces-laced particulate matter floating through the air. The feces alone were bad enough, and they didn't need help spewing toxins everywhere. No, we did not wear gas masks or other protective gear; we just endured the process. That likely went on from the first time we moved in early November 1990 through mid-January 1991.

Photo 40. Soldier Standing at a Piss Tube in Saudi Arabia or Iraq.

Photo retrieved from https://www.ebaumsworld.com/images/you-dont-need-a-urinal-in-iraq/81040693/.

Additionally, there was a requirement to burn trash in 55-gallon drums. That occurred daily for at least an hour or two. The fumes and pollutants could be seen and smelled for at least a mile, but the Soldiers on the detail were the ones who got the worst of it for both duties. Some Soldiers got sick from the smell, nauseous, and even vomited. I came close to puking a couple of times but overcame the urge. Besides, I was too busy with other things. Regardless of our daily routine, combat would have to wait until after Thanksgiving.

Giving Thanks in A Foreign Land

I was almost always home in Kansas City, MO, for Thanksgiving. This would become the second of many missed holidays. Thanksgiving 1989 was spent at Fort Hood, TX, awaiting deployment for an NTC rotation. So, for two of my three years on active duty, I was not home for Thanksgiving. Being in Saudi Arabia for over a month and with Thanksgiving looming, I only *thought* I was busy before. It seemed like every leader in the rank of lieutenant colonel and above was adamant about this,

The Iraq I Knew…

"Being a great Thanksgiving at all costs."

What the heck did that mean? As the VP for Logistics (S4), I soon found out.

Pulling a Turkey Out of a Hat

All the logisticians (of which I was not one) were expected to pull a rabbit out of a hat or, in this case, a few turkeys. A traditional Thanksgiving meal was the order of the day and every day until the event occurred. As Americans, apple or pumpkin pie (neither of which I ate at the time), turkey with all the trimmings, and football are Thanksgiving traditions. Also, we ate ourselves into comas, lining up hours early for the Black Friday sales, and Christmas tree lightings are part of the festivities. This all occurred during the 96 hours surrounding Thanksgiving, from the Wednesday before to the Saturday after; we were in a 'holiday' frenzy, but in a good way. However, none of this would occur for the 400,000+ soldiers deployed to Saudi Arabia.

This year, however, I was worried about securing eight-foot tables with matching chairs, setting up several large GP (General Purpose) tents in the desert to serve as dining facilities, and procuring all the paraphernalia for Turkey Day. Because none of the other traditions surrounding the holiday were available, the food had to be on point to pray and share a meal. One consideration that made planning tremendously easier was removing pork products from the menu. No glazed ham, chitterlings, or other pork products were shipped because they were forbidden in this Muslim country.

We did, however, plan for turkeys with all the fixings and, I am sure, also some baked chicken. All the trimmings included decorations, plates, tablecloths, and almost every festival food you could imagine.

There were two to three types of stuffing: corn, sage, turkey, mashed and sweet potatoes, green beans, rolls, cranberry sauce galore, corn-on-the-cob, macaroni and cheese, salads, etc.

It seemed like my job was consumed with Thanksgiving preparation from November 1st until Thanksgiving Day.

Turkey Mania

Before the food arrived, someone asked, '*Hey, where are we going to store all this stuff?*' The reefer vans (short for refrigerated vans) were already packed, so where would we put at least 50 30-pound turkeys? Fifty was my conservative estimate to feed nearly 600 hungry men, who could quickly eat double or even triple portions since there was nothing else to do. Lo and behold, all the food was delivered in the appropriate number of reefer vans. Problem solved. It was up to the Mess Sergeant to decide where to park and position this extra equipment.

A Hot Meal Is a Hot Meal

This is a good place to review Army chow (meals), since I was writing in detail about food. Based on logistics and the preparation times for serving over 600 meals, we only had hot meals twice a day: for breakfast and dinner, with an MRE for lunch. Many of us who were what I call *Height and Weight Challenged* tried to avoid MREs because of the number of additives, preservatives, and calories, and, from experience, we tended to gain weight. If we had also gained height, the problem would have been solved, but that was impossible. Being on this meal schedule for two, four, six, or even eight weeks during Field Training Exercises (FTX) or Command Post Exercises (CPX) was tolerable, especially when you add Pogey Bait. Pogey Bait is any food that was not issued or prepared by the Army. In other words, snack foods.

Pogey Bait depended on the person and could range from Anchovies to Romain noodles to Vienna sausages, and all the alphabet in between. I became a Romaine-noodles-with-chopped-Vienna-sausage-and-MRE-cheese expert to replace any meal I wasn't in the mood for. I also liked strawberry Twizzlers as a low-calorie snack or for dessert because Twizzlers held up under the heat. Unfortunately, when the weather was cold, you could chip a tooth biting on Twizzlers! Our problem, however, involved time: The amount of time we would be deployed was unknown. With that dilemma, calculating and carrying an unknown cache of pogey bait was impossible.

Expanding My Horizons

There were some foods that I did not eat. In the Army, chipped beef was referred to as Shit-on-a-Shingle, so that was what I saw when I looked at it. Although I had eaten grits before, they just seemed like cooked sandpaper. And then there was chicken cacciatore, which I also did not eat because we had it EVERY evening for one six-week FTX when I was a Fire Support Officer (FSO). I could not blame that on my unit, since FSOs supported maneuver company commanders and were subject to whatever their battalion dining facility served. My old platoon sergeant, SFC P (whom you will become familiar with later), noticed me not eating one day and asked why I was not eating the foods listed above. *"I just don't eat that stuff,"* I told him.

SFC P told me, *"Sir, you need to expand your horizons. Our guys can cook, and besides, it doesn't look right for the Mess Officer not to eat."*

As the S4, I was the organizational Mess Officer by default. I began my culinary foray with chipped beef on a biscuit, smothered in gravy. '*Hey*, I thought, *this tasted pretty good*!' The next day, I ate 'cheese grits' for breakfast. Who knew?

The next time I saw SFC P at breakfast, I told him I had taken his advice, especially with the cheese grits. SFC P just looked at me and said,

"Oh, Sir, I forgot, you're not from the south. Grits come in all types of flavors, like country grits with red-eye gravy." He continued,

"I've been trying to get the cooks to cook some, but they won't listen to me. Of course, as the Mess Officer, you can make a special request that I'm sure they will honor."

I forgot about that and placed my request to the Mess Sergeant, and poof: Country grits with red eye gravy! I had overlooked that cooks have specialties they enjoy making, provided the ingredients are available, and they have permission.

It's Good to Be the King

After speaking with the Mess Sergeant, I authorized him to prepare whatever he thought was appealing to Soldiers, and I would worry about getting the ingredients. Sometimes it's good to be the king, and we began eating like kings! I procured as many A-rations as I possibly could, sometimes even trading T-rations for A-rations. I was also given specific foods to find, such as the biscuit mix and eggs from the T-rations, without the entire ration. They would mix and match the various ingredients from each ration to give us Delicacies in the Desert. This also included desserts such as cookies, cakes, and pies. I forgot to mention that we had full-sized mobile kitchens equipped with stoves, ovens, griddles, and all the kitchen utensils you could think of.

We each had our personal mess kits that we used as we went through the serving line. The photo shows a mess kit with two sides and a metal fork, knife, and tablespoon. After eating, we would wash our kits at the dishwashing station by dipping them in scalding-hot, soapy water, then rinsing them in scalding-hot water. We either air-dried the kit or wiped it down, folded it up, and placed it back in our ruck sack for the next meal. Do not allow anyone to tell you that Army chow is lousy. The cooks and the NCOIC handled the cooking. If it's true that 'An Army travels on its stomach,' then we needed plenty of fuel, especially for what we would face next.

Photo 41. Army Mess Kit.

Scuds, Sandstorms, and Silliness

Sometimes, things happen. The Thanksgiving holiday feast was a huge success. People were 'stuffed' like turkeys, and turkey comas abound, and some had cranberry sauce headaches. Cranberry sauce headaches are caused by consuming massive quantities of cranberry sauce absent atop the dressing. Is this a well-known medical malady? Probably not, but most of the Soldiers who had the headaches only had the 'lone cranberry sauce consumption' in common.

Yes, this sounds silly, but so does mixing antifreeze with orange juice and trying to drink it like a cocktail. Some Soldiers in other units did this and died, while others went blind from mixing this concoction. Unfortunately, this trend is common in the Army today, in deployed units or not[10]. This damaged the 'after party' because the report came in after the Thanksgiving Day festivities. This notification came sometime during our first sandstorm. I might assume everyone knows what a sandstorm is, and I also accept that I would be wrong.

Big Sandy

A sandstorm is like a dust storm except with sand. Think about the coarseness of sand, swirling around in the atmosphere, forcefully contacting every surface it touches. Now, imagine this same abrasive material sweeping against your exposed face and body, seemingly seeping into every pore that will accept it. The pervasiveness of sand is in the granularity of the substance. Now, consider that your body is entirely encapsulated from head to toe, but then you walk into the 'cloth hut' you live in, known as a tent, and all you see is mounds of sand.

Those mounds of sand were the cots, sleeping bags, duffel bags, and every piece of equipment we had because we had no time or experience with this phenomenon. At NTC, only the TOCs' tents and the mess halls were set up. Everything else was conducted outside because deployments were usually only two weeks long. Sand is a leech that only lets go, releases itself, and flees your possessions if you force it to. It blends into its native environment and sneaks back into your belongings with the least provocation. That is why I referred to it as 'Big Sandy.'

> ***"Sand is a leech that only lets go, releases itself, and flees your possessions if you force it to."***

Because there was sand everywhere, and we were in a desert, where did we begin? You cannot 'clean up' during a sandstorm because the sand does not relent. It was not until late in the evening that the torrent stopped, and we could begin to remove the malefactor from our possessions. That is something we endured for the next six months or longer. It may also explain why many Army personnel dislike the beach. Regardless of the ocean breeze and fun in the sun, that does not diminish what we experienced. Something else allegedly occurred during the storm, which can also be classified as 'silly.'

SCUD ALERT! SCUD ALERT!

Around 11 am, the Battalion Tactical Operations Center (TOC) sounded the SCUD Alert. I remember the exact time for two reasons. First, I was walking away from the TOC when the alert sounded, and second, we were in a sandstorm. Recall I was a trained artillery officer and knew the effects of the elements on artillery rounds and rockets, and this was horrible weather to launch a missile. So, although it made no sense and was downright silly, I sounded the alert anyway. I do not believe we did anything because, with the sand flying, you could barely see your hand in front of you, and sand covered every nook and cranny you might have sought cover under. Little did I know that the silliness would not end there.

Before Thanksgiving, I recall hearing about the S2 having a conniption fit over security concerns about the vans. Allegedly, he raved about *"too high a profile"* and *"making us into a larger signature for attack."* If the Iraqi air force got through into Saudi Arabian airspace, we would have far more significant problems. With the US having the best military in the world, I knew the US Air Force would not allow any air incursion. Neither would the Army Air Defense Artillery, our Army Attack Helicopters, or our Naval Battleships. We would see this come to fruition in the coming weeks and months as we were constantly under Scud alerts, with possibly a few FROGs mixed in for good measure.

I just chuckled to myself and thought, *'Who cares? Not me. It's not that serious. My job will be done after Turkey Day.'* Little did I know that my job was only beginning. Eventually, I learned a fundamental lesson about making command decisions, improving your combat multipliers (competitive advantages), and how quickly things can change on the battlefield. I also learned that,

*'You are always being observed,
even when you are just doing your job.'*

I learned the hard way that there was no such thing as 'just doing your job.' Because we are constantly being observed, you can be seen 'just doing your job well, average, not so well, or about to be fired.' My family raised us to work at an average or above-average level, which tended towards consistent excellence. We were not given many accolades for the average things we did because of a simple yet elusive principle:

*"The quality of your character dictates
the excellence of your achievements."*

Some people will only perform at an average level because that is what their character and abilities dictate. Others will always strive to achieve the highest standards because that is how they were made, while most of us learned the expectations for excellence. Whatever the case, I was about to receive another valuable lesson:

*"Don't get too comfortable where you are because
things can and will always change on the battlefield."*

The Iraq I Knew…

Photo 42. Scud B on launcher used in Desert Shield and Storm

Photo 43. Destroyed Scud B used in Desert Shield and Storm.

Chapter 9:
"A Changing of The Guard..."

Sometimes you are the last to know.

Sometimes a change is required whether you notice it or not. I truly enjoyed being the S4 officer and almost considered switching to Quartermaster. I approached the position like I did in the previous jobs I was unqualified for: I jumped right in, immersed myself in learning as much as possible and became an expert. Now, I wrote 'somewhat' because, logically, there was no way I should have been an expert in logistics and supply. After all, that was not my trained specialty, but I acted like it was. With all the praise my team and I received, I did not observe what was happening in the TOC.

Apparently, there were rifts between the S2 officer and everyone else: The S2 Intelligence Section, the S3 officer, Battery Commanders, and finally, the Command Group. With my keen powers of observation, I detected a pattern emerging: The S2 officer did not seem to get along with anyone. I got along fine with him, so I never perceived that he did not get along with others. I should have seen this because this was the guy and the section responsible for the intelligence and security for all 600+ of us. Regarding the enemy, the S2 officer's words were practically gospel. Little did I know that I would be making a new enemy based on decisions beyond my control and would soon be preaching the intel gospel to what I feared would be a skeptical crowd.

Another Major Shift, But Mostly for Me

Things got serious after we survived Thanksgiving, weathered our first sandstorm, and experienced our first SCUD attack. The Battalion XO, Major S, came to my tent that morning and needed to talk with me.

"I'm moving on S4, "he said.

"Moving on to where, sir?" I asked.

"Division Targeting," he said with great remorse.

I began asking why, and he explained that his time was up and that it wasn't working out the way he'd thought. I needed clarification on his statement because we had always worked well together. Before I could wish him well or ask any other questions, he said something that startled me into silence.

"I guess things are changing for you, too," he said.

What? What the heck? I was afraid to ask him what he was talking about. Was I moving with him? Was I moving somewhere else? Was I moving at all? Was I going home? Yeah, right, that was not going to happen. I finally mustered the courage to ask.

"Sir, what does that mean?" I asked.

"Well," he began, *"Two positions are coming open, and your name came up for both."*

He continued, *"I probably shouldn't even be telling you this; your new boss should, but what the heck, what are they going to do? Fire me?"*

I just stood there like the proverbial deer in the headlights.

"A cavalry battalion needs a new Fire Support Officer (FSO), and we need a new Battalion S2 officer," he disclosed.

Once again, summoning the courage to speak, I said, *"Sir, I'm not sure how either of those relate to me, but I'm not interested."*

I had grown very fond of being the S4 officer for several reasons. One reason was the nonstop planning, directing, and executing of missions. It was not tiresome or cumbersome, but fulfilling because I immediately saw the results of our labor. Yes, I whined about the position a few pages back, but I'm trying to make a point here. Second, it allowed me to learn and see how things worked at the organizational/corporate levels before attending the Advanced Course, now called the Captain's Career Course. Third, I was highly competent at my job if I said so myself, and I am saying so. Fourth and quite important, I was a power broker. If you recall my reference to Sergeant Zell from M*A*S*H, I was him with captain's bars.

I had already gone down the road of being selected as a Task Force (TF) FSO and volunteered to be the S4 officer instead. I had served my time in the Fire Support shack and had no intention of making a career in it, regardless of how good I was or my creds with the Fire Support crews. Early in the Army, I learned that if you were good at what you did but did not tell people what you wanted, you would be moved around like a chess piece. Although I thought of myself as a knight or a bishop, there was always an attempt to treat me like a pawn. Once again, Major S solidified my feelings.

"You actually think you have a choice, Captain?" he asked. *"Do you think I am moving to the Division Targeting Cell because I want to? The best you can hope for is that you might have a choice between the two."*

"But why me?" I asked. *"We have other captains."*

"Ya, you're right, but they are not moving a Battery Commander, and you have already proven what you can do. Just remember, no good deed goes unpunished," he said.[11]

So, because I had proven competent, I was punished for it? I only thought this to myself and never voiced it. It was a rotten, stinking deal for someone who had done so much for the organization. But what could I do, quit the Army? I could, but that would be dramatic, so I just waited until someone came and officially told me to move. This also meant that I needed to improve my professional maturity more if I planned to stay in the Army and continue leading. To add insult to injury, Major S continued:

"The Old Man wants you to be the S2 officer but is giving you a choice between the two positions, " he said.

I could no longer hold back and said something sarcastic like,

"Oh, a choice between execution by firing squad or the electric chair. Some choice."

I knew Major S was getting pissed off, which was a monumental task for that to happen, but he maintained his composure and said,

"Look, this is your opportunity to write your own ticket. I know that you'll do fine, and you'll be ahead of your MI peers."

Decisions, Decisions

I listened to the XO, and deep down, I knew he was right: Argue to stay where I was and make things worse for myself, or do what he already told me the Old Man wanted and score some points. BTW, the 'Old Man' was the Battalion Commander – CEO. At this point in an Army career, the CEOs were generally older than almost everyone in the unit; they were literally the 'Old Man' at 39 or 40. That did not change 14 years later when I became a CEO and the 'Old Man.'

Regardless of how I felt or thought, this was a big decision. Providing supplies during wartime was vitally essential, but giving leaders the intelligence needed to make life-changing decisions was totally different. I needed to know the enemy's location, anticipate their actions, and determine the positions of their artillery units. Although we were not the Infantry, armor, or aviation that close with and destroyed the enemy, we still needed to be able to do the same thing, albeit from a distance. This still required timely, accurate, and actionable intelligence.

No one could really make this decision for me. I already knew what the commander wanted and why, and had the old XO's full faith and confidence. I wanted to know what the new XO thought and how I would get along with the S3, Battery Commanders, and the rest of the staff. I fully understood how things worked in the Army and knew the rank structure and positional Authority. Still, I did not intend to have numerous bosses. Although I was a 'new' captain, I was still the *'same old Burl,'* who would not be bullied or manhandled on something this important. After this assignment, I knew I would be transitioning to the MI (Military Intelligence) Corps. Still, the key was to make it out of this assignment alive.

That may sound intense, and it was because we might be told to move out and draw fire at any time. The enemy was not the OPFOR at the National Training Center, where, if we were shot, our MILES (Multiple Integrated Laser Engagement System) gear could be rekeyed. MILES equipment is the military version of the laser tag before laser tag was invented. However, in war, if we were shot, we were either WIA - Wounded in Action at various levels or KIA – Killed in Action. As I typed this, I realized that this was likely the most crucial decision I made in my 32-year Army career. Although I would visit Iraq uninvited two more times, my positions were more transparent, I had some semblance of training, and I understood the battlespace better based on education and experience.

And I would be a bona fide Army intelligence officer versus 'The Pretender.' Well, I made up for what I have always lacked in formal education with intellectual and operational experience, so I decided that if asked, I would accept the position of Battalion S2 officer. The question now was, *'Would I ever be asked?'*

And The Question Is…

It is incredible how fleeting military secrets are.

Allegedly, no one knew anything about these pending 'personnel decisions,' but everyone seemed to know about them except me. The following 24 hours were grueling, spent trying to keep a secret that wasn't a secret. However, I could discuss it only after the official announcement. Oddly enough, who should show up at my office (Deuce-and-a-half truck with a makeshift shelter on the bed)? The Battalion S2 officer!

He said, *"Yes, we need some supplies. Lots of markers in all colors, as many rolls of acetate as you could spare, and bottles of alcohol."*

I began piling it on, since SFC E had provided him with the 'normal' amount.

"Here you go, take some extra markers, plastic, alcohol, and anything else you need," I said.

"Really?" he replied. Like a kid in a candy store, the S2 officer looked around and said, *"I think that's it for now. Thanks, man!"* I replied, *"No problem, man. Here to serve."* Turning around after waving him goodbye, my crew was just staring at me.

SFC E began with, *"What's up, sir?" "You never give out supplies like that."*

Well, I admit that I was a miser when it came to the government's equipment and supplies. Although I did not have the responsibility of being a Battery Commander, because of my position, I had a great deal of accountability with no intention of jail time in my future.

Little-known fact: an officer found negligent for the loss of government property can be held pecuniarily liable for the full amount. Losing something and being careless are not the same, and I had no intention of being caught short with either!

All I replied was,

"Nothing's up, just trying to be more friendly and cooperative."

I am sure they did not believe me for one second, but were too respectful to say so. Well, I was about to begin another waiting game.

My Own Waiting Game

I do not recall if it was late Friday or Saturday night, but waiting on the notification of my move was an all-day affair. I went up to the TOC to see what was happening, and SFC P and SSG K greeted me with big smiles. Both NCOs used to work for me when I was a Firing Battery Platoon Leader, SFC P as the Platoon Sergeant, and SSG K as the Special Weapons NCOIC (Non-Commissioned Officer in Charge). Both were excellent NCOs, and I had no qualms about working with them again. *"So, sir, when are you coming up here?"* asked SFC P. I looked at him quizzically because something was amiss.

Why would an officer pick up supplies for his replacement? That made no sense, so I could only surmise that the S2 officer did not know he was moving! Based on this quick thinking, I stated,

"Moving up here? Why would I be moving up here? No one has told me I was moving."

My answer was true and false. I had been told, but it was unofficial. They just looked at me, and I asked,

"Did you get all the supplies the S2 picked up yesterday?"

"Yes, sir," replied SSG K. *"More than enough."*

"That's great," I said. I continued, *"You might want to ensure you have everything you need while you can get it without a problem."*

Both NCOs looked at each other and said, *"HOOAH, sir, we'll send the list down in a few minutes."*

"Okay," I said. *"I'll see you later."*

I would be remiss if I did not explain the term 'Hooah!' Hooah, pronounced Hoo-Ah, is the Army term for an enthusiastic, Yes! 'Hell Yes!,' 'You got it!' 'WILCO! (Will Comply). Do you get the picture?

SFC P and SSG K nodded, and I knew they had caught the coded message I had sent: they knew *I knew* I was moving to join them, but could not say anything. Just like civilian life has innuendoes, sidebars, and indirect agreements, so does the Army. Although it was great that they knew I was moving, it did not ease my angst about not being 'officially' notified.

Big Dave

I knew that my new boss would be Major D, whom we all affectionately called 'Big Dave' because he was big. Big Dave was a high school and college wrestler and looked like he could rip a person's head off. Big Dave also had another interesting feature: an extreme Boston accent. Major D was a 'gentle giant,' friendly and cordial, and avoided confrontation.

Please don't read into what I didn't write: avoiding confrontation does not mean running from it. One definition for avoiding is *preventing*. Big Dave did not condone arguing, fussing, cussing, or fighting between officers, but as I later discovered in my Army career, firing or removing someone from a position was easier said than done.

It was early evening, but after chow, I found Big Dave. He was moving into his new, posh, mobile-flex tent. A mobile-flew tent was also called a 'pop-up' tent because once you took it out of the package, you just threw it out, and it 'popped up.' Both majors had them, but they were in short supply because they were new to the Army inventory. As I 'knocked' on the tent door (I know, it sounds silly), he said,

"Come." My question was a simple one,

"Sir, have you told the S2 he's no longer the S2?"

"Keep your voice down," he said, *"He's right next door."*

He could see my disappointment and frustration since he had already visited me hours ago at my tent and told me he was my new boss. I wondered if he had said the S2, and he answered, *"I'm getting around to it."*

Because to that point in my career, I had never fired anyone, so I wondered what the big deal was. The big deal had several factors to consider:

1. It should have been his predecessor who fired him.

2. It should have been done sooner rather than later, as early as before deployment.

3. It should have been considered when the maneuver Brigade S2 officer mentioned the numerous contrasting intelligence briefings that the Old Man had briefed.

4. This would impact the officer's career. That is always the most challenging part because we are humans and do not necessarily want to end someone's career.

    I had yet to learn how long this had gone on, but I had heard about the numerous mistakes the S2 officer made back home. Although frustrated, I knew I had to be compassionate about the situation.

"Sir," I said, *"The longer you wait, the worse it will be for everyone, especially him. He deserves to know since, apparently, everyone else does."*

As far as we knew, Big Dave looked sad, likely because the S2 officer was not a bad person. Sometimes, we all deal with things, physically, mentally, and emotionally, that might cause us significant distractions.

"I'll tell him," said Big Dave. *"I'll tell him tonight."*

That was all I could ask for, no matter how much I did NOT want the position.

A Bruised Ego

My predecessor did not go quietly into that good night. Although Captain B did not pitch a fit, he did not want anything to do with me. There was no left-seat, right-seat ride or smooth transition of power, and initially, it appeared he would not leave. Although I was asking him questions, I was not receiving answers or even responses. He ignored me. I decided that we needed to 'take this outside.'

"Dude," I said, *"You know I don't want your job, right?"*

He only looked at me inquisitively, so I continued.

"Why would I want your job, where I might be up day and night, trying to assess a very uncertain situation, and I have no training?" Although what I said next might have been arrogant, it was how I felt.

"As the S4, I'm the kingpin, the supply dealmaker and power broker who never has to go to the front lines but simply shuttles back and forth from here rearward to the support battalions," I said.

"Why in the world would I want to be the S2?" I stated. Captain B finally spoke.

"I know," he said. *"I guess you are right. I always knew this day would come, and the Command Group was unhappy with my performance."*

That response satisfied my need to move this transition forward. Sometimes, you must know when to 'settle' and declare victory. Captain B took me through his filing systems, intelligence-gathering processes, and reports and presentations he had completed. Captain B did not offer insightful recommendations about the job and asked for time with his crew. That was an easy request to fulfill. Although the situation was arriving at an amicable resolution, my thought process was different. Given what had happened, I needed to make an impact fast, and I knew exactly what it would be.

Chapter 10:
"Getting the Quick Win"

Sometimes the quick win is not so quick.

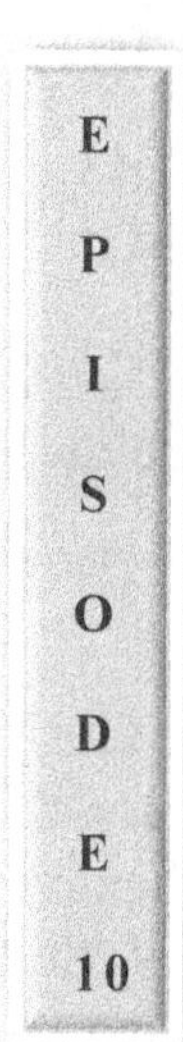

My first order of business as the new S2 officer was to "*Pass out the damn maps!*" Since we arrived at our tactical assembly area (TAA), the S2 track was surrounded outside by maps. For the most part, only the Command Group, the Tactical Operations Center (TOC), and the S4 had complete maps. The Battery Commanders were livid, and with good reason, because the stacks of maps came up to my knees! I know that is low, but high enough to make a mess of things! After I reported for my new position, we did a terrain walk straight to the maps, and I wanted an explanation for why the maps had not been issued.

"Captain B said that's what the colonel wanted; not to issue any maps until the battle started," said SFC P.

I looked at SFC P, then at SSG Ski, then back at SFC P. I shook my head and said,

"That's the dumbest thing I've ever heard. I don't believe the Old Man said that."

"Well, sir," said SSG Ski, *"That's what CPT B told us."*

"So, sir," said SFC P, *"You think we can finally get rid of all this shit and issue it to the Batteries?"*

"We'll see," I replied.

PASS OUT THE DAMN MAPS!

Sometimes, to get a quick win, you must be bold. I went straight to the Old Man and asked him about it, and he replied, *"Hell no, why would I say something like that? I was wondering myself why all the maps were around the TOC."*

That was my green light to begin distribution. I went back and told my team,

"Let's get ready to pass out the damn maps."

They were elated. Then I told the Battery Commanders,

"When we ask you, send someone to pick up your maps."

They about passed out from shock. This one action established instant goodwill throughout the organization. In later years, this technique was dubbed 'The Quick Win,' and I used it whenever needed. The magic of 'The Quick Win' is that you find something meaningful to most people in the organization, it is easy to address, it is within your purview, and you can act on it. Why some actions were not previously taken, I have never known. Maybe ego, fear, or confusion, but inaction mainly creates confusion, and trust me, we were trying to reduce confusion, but, as I was told, *"No good deed goes unpunished."*

HOLY SHEET! Where are the Damn Maps?

The following action was to create a system to determine which maps we needed, because apparently, Saudi Arabia and Iraq were not kept in ample supply within the US Army topographic inventory. Once we began separating the maps for distribution, we made a startling discovery: we had 'map sheets,' not 'map sets.' The 1:50,000 map sets are usually comprised of four map sheets that outline an area. I thought,

'Holy sheet! Where are the DAMN maps?

I was curious how long this 'Quick Win' would last once we began passing out the maps. That is why preparing our own map-tracking system was so vitally important. We needed a means to tell the Battery Commanders precisely what they were missing and requested the same information to order more maps.

To make matters worse, topography was included in the S2 section when ordering the maps. I thought,

'You gotta be shittin me? I raised all this hell about what had not happened, and now I'm back in the supply & ordering business?'

I felt like I was now up 'sheet creek without a paddle.' Yes, I'm milking this metaphor! We may have had enough maps to provide the Command Group and each Battery Commander with a somewhat complete set.

I recall some of us drawing the sheets we did not have on butcher paper, which we had plenty of. So, we were basically creating our own maps on the fly. And, of course, the S3 and S2 sections had complete map sets. The last nail in my proverbial coffin was when the Global Positioning Devices or GPS' I ordered when I was the S4 arrived. We had no GPS before deployment because that was a relatively new device. And we still did not have any when the order came in, and once I saw them, I thought,

'Oh death, where is thy sting?'

Sweet Loran…

In the middle of my map mayhem, SFC E called me at the TOC and asked me to visit the S4 truck. Once I arrived, he said,

"Sir, you need to see this."

"What is it?" I asked. *"The GPS we ordered,"* he said.

I stood there, my mouth gaping open, wondering what was happening. Long story short, we were sent Mobile Handheld LORAN devices, not GPS. LORAN is short for **Lo**ng **Ra**nge **N**avigation and is generally used by the Navy and Air Force, but mainly by the Navy. I thought,

'They are going to think I've gone bat shit.'

Honestly, I thought maybe I had gone bat shit.

"Sergeant E, how did this happen?" I asked.
"Sir, I already called and asked the same thing. They figured something was better than nothing," he replied.

"Well, it can't get any worse," I said. All the S4 personnel looked at each other until SFC E said, *"Sir, yes, it can."*

LORAN does not use a grid system on maps because it is for naval navigation, not land navigation, so it uses LAT/LONG coordinates. LAT LONGs are Latitude and Longitude, calculated in degrees, not grid coordinates. My career was flashing before my eyes. I could not believe what was happening, but delaying the inevitable would not improve the dilemma. I returned to the TOC, took a LORAN with me, and explained to the S3 what had occurred. He looked at the LORAN then at me, and I received the response I expected:

"S2, what the fuck are we supposed to do with these?"

All I could do was tell him we would figure out how to use it before issuing it. I will not bore you with all the details, but we discovered that maps have grid coordinates, as well as latitude and longitude along the edges. This was all part of the UTM (Universal Transverse Mercator) coordinate system [12]. If this wasn't making my head hurt again like in 1990, I might explain it in greater detail, but the best I can do is give you the reference so you can look it up yourself.

It was a manageable stretch because, as artillerymen, we dealt in both coordinates and degrees. Especially for all the other captains, since they were advanced course graduates, had studied at an elevated level, and performed as such. Hence, they were the Battery Commanders. The system was beneficial when we had satellite coverage, especially since we needed our full complement of maps. I used Sweet Loran as a spinoff from M*A*S*H and LTC Henry Blake when he referred to his wife as

"Sweet Lorraine." The LORAN did not solve our immediate problem: A lack of complete map sets or the more significant problem of using three different map sets.

Three Blind Mice

Unfortunately, we were not only short of our standard 1:50,000 maps. We used three different map systems based on the operation we were about to execute. Our usual maps were 1:50,000; however, we were also issued some 1:100,000, which covered a much larger area, about twice the size of the 1:50,000 map set. Lastly, 1:250,000 satellite imagery was placed on a map three times the size of the 1:50,000 map set. To add insult to injury, we also needed the full complement of those maps. The incomplete map sets were like three blind mice: We ran around like blind mice, not knowing where we were going. The pictures below were the beginnings of what resulted in a much larger system. It was the best we could do with very little to work with.

We did not derive our map requirements from any scientific method or Army Regulation. We simply looked at what we needed, who needed it, and the initial minimum requirement. Remember, if we were doing this, so were the rest of the units in the division. Our only advantage was that, although I was the S2 officer, I was still Joe Barter. We decided to reach out across the rest of the DIVARTY and the 2nd Brigade to determine who had what and who needed what. Then, horse-trading began.

Author's Note. No horses were traded during the exchange process or during the writing of this book.

The three types of maps are outlined in this sketch from the Author's notebook. The 1:50,000 and 1:100,000 map series were numbered in the 5,000s. The 1:250,000 map series used letters beginning with N and numbered in the late 30s.

Sketch 1. The three types of Maps Required – 1:50,000; 1-100,000; 1-250,000.

MAPS

1:250,000   NG 38-3 & NH 38-15
1:50,000   5146 I-IV & 5147 I-IV

MSG K has maps. Not the ones we need.

1:250,000
NG - 38-2, 38-3, 38-4, 39-1
NH - 38-1 to 38-16 39-13

1:50,000

5045	I-IV	5346	I & IV
5145	"	5347	I - IV
5146	"	5447	"
5147	"	5444	"
5148	" II & IV	5445	"
5246	" I & IV	5446	"
5247	"	5447	"
5248	" II & III		

1:100,000   5046 5045
Satellite   5146 5145

Sketch provided by the Author.

Sketch 2. Unit Map Requirements. Sketch provided by the Author.

Sketch 3. An expanded version of the 1:250,000 map series requirements.

Sketch provided by the Author.

The title *'From Here to There'* (Sketches 3 & 4) was the map sheet we needed to move to our follow-on positions. Those map sheets contained the road networks we were required to travel on. As you can see from my scribblings, the map requirements were constant based on movement and the operations orders.

Sketch 4. Composite notes of Map Systems.

Sketch provided by the Author.

Sketch 5 is one of our final products. It shows the five 1:50,000map sheets embedded within the three 1:250,000 map sheets. This shows the enormity of what we were working with and the ingenuity required to create this tracking system. Trust me, my two great senior NCOs did the heavy lifting on this. The second final product is depicted in a sketch after much hard work, gnashing of teeth on my team's part, and lots of searching through my old files. Those illustrations were provided to show that, despite significant shortcomings, we overcame the odds and prevailed.

Sketch 5. 1:50,000 map sheets embedded into 1:250,000 map sheets.

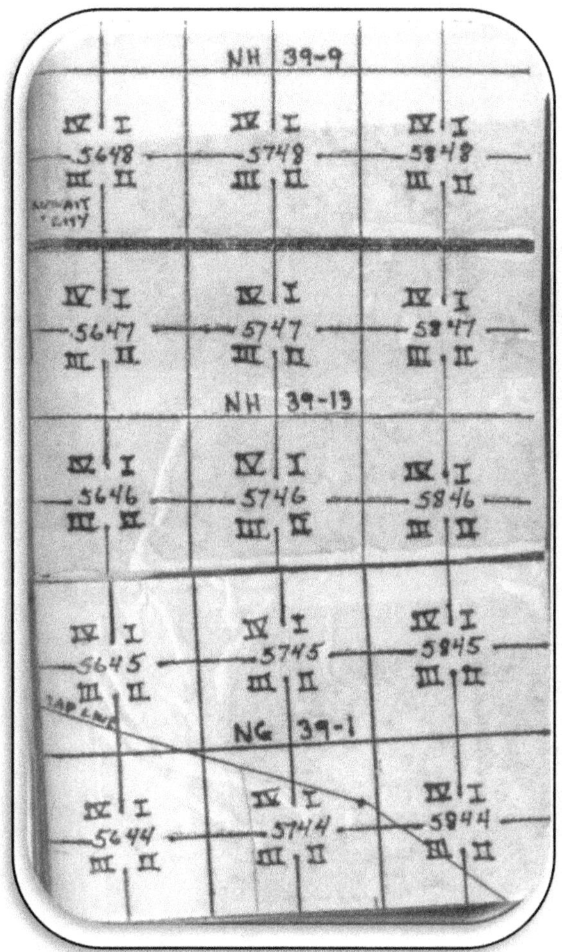

Sketch provided by the Author.

A lack of maps and navigational systems was only the start, but we overcame each successive obstacle—even the obstacle of transition. Once we got past the hurt, anger, and anguish of the previous S2, the tone in the TOC and with the Old Man shifted to a mentoring mode, with me as the mentee. This was likely because things were heating up.

Sketch 6. 1:250,000 map sets.

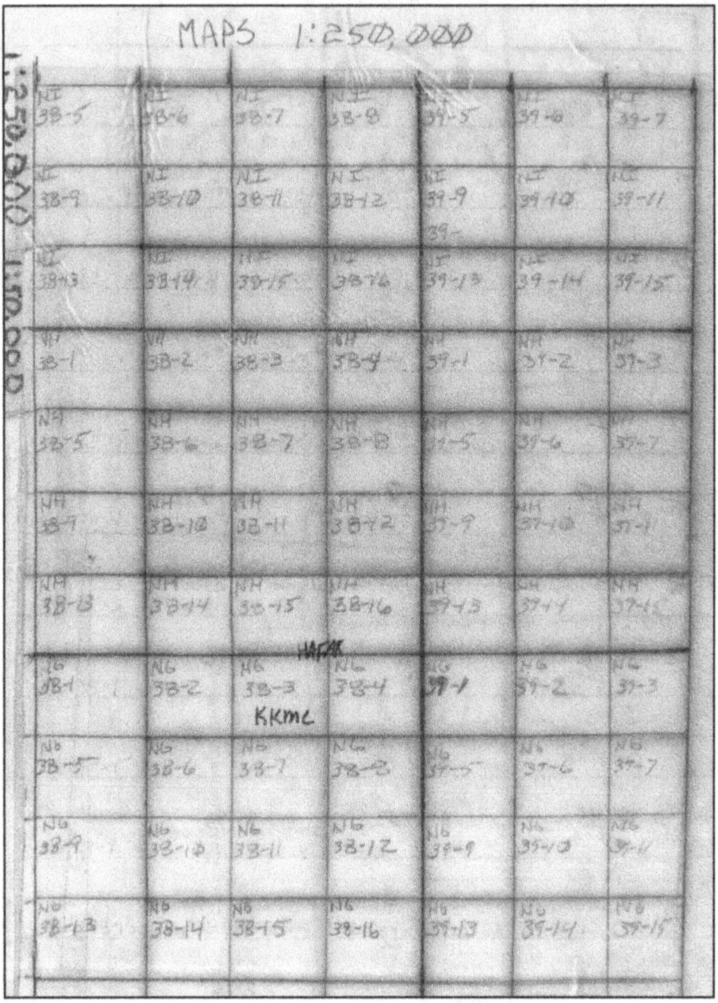

Sketch provided by the Author.

Author's Note. If you do not understand anything I explained about our maps system, that's alright. It took us some time to develop and understand it ourselves.

Part III:
Desert Storm: *"Into A Firey Storm"*

The time really had come...

Remember, we had been in the country since mid-October 1990, and it was now mid-January 1991. As each day passed, we could feel it getting hotter and hotter. The funny thing about Iraq is that there is winter. We wore our field jackets and sometimes even our 'snivel gear,' also known as long johns. The new year had come and gone. We celebrated with something called 'Near Beer' – a nonalcoholic version of beer with every characteristic except alcohol. I thought, *Really? Near beer? How about a 'Near Pork Chop' or 'Near McRib'?'* Please. We had not had a pork product since October 1990, and I was jonesing badly, but I digress.

I do not recall Christmas being the flurry of activity that Thanksgiving was, mainly because we already had the precise process and because food is typically not the emphasis at Christmas time. I am confident that we had meals fit for royalty. Still, by that time, I was no longer the S4 officer but the S2 officer – Vice President for Intelligence and Security. What I do recall is that it was great to just sit back, relax, and eat the meal, vice being the person to procure it.

The relaxation occurred only at the dinner table because, as we entered January 1991, the talks between Iraq and the UN continued to deteriorate. We were hoping against hope that the war would be called off on account of rain, disinterest, or something. While listening to Armed Forces Radio Network (AFRN), we heard that President George H. W. Bush was visiting Camp David one weekend, so we thought, *'Hey, there must have been a breakthrough!'* That was faulty thinking on our part, but I learned that regardless of the situation, leaders MUST get adequate rest to be effective. Yes, the handwriting was on the wall: We were about to enter a Firey Storm.

Chapter 11:
"Becoming the S2"

Talk about the weight of the world...

I can honestly say that this may have been the only job I had in the Army that it felt like I was going in 'Cold Turkey.' At least with the S4 job, we had a Leader's Right-Seat Ride, referred to in civilian life as a 'warm handoff' or leader onboarding. The previous S4 was my buddy, 1LT Craig, who was prior service, meaning he had previously enlisted in the Army. He had reached the rank of Sergeant First Class (SFC, E7) and decided to become an officer. I learned much later in my career that this was normal, especially since a 2LT earns more than each enlisted rank. Because LT Craig was transferring to the Quartermaster branch, he ran the S4 shop on a tight ship, did things right, and I was his ticket out of the organization. At the time, without a replacement, officers were held captive until a replacement showed up.

At the time, this was a very selfish tactic by the CEOs, creating stressful situations and tumultuous transitions for officers. Throughout my Army career, I learned that many senior leaders used this technique to keep the best and brightest, as well as a warm body. The late 1980s and early 1990s were the lean years in the Army, so with officer accessions down and resignations up, the fight for bodies was at a premium. Premium requirements sometimes provide premium results. Still, in my case, everyone thought it was a good deal for the organization. My predecessor, however, felt different.

Making An S2 Through Mentoring

The Old Man took me under his wing to help me learn how to become an S2. The Old Man began by telling me, *"'2', you're going to ride with me to all my meetings so you can see and hear how things are done."* I can honestly say that God showed me favor in this instance because the Old Man, a lieutenant colonel, was not my direct supervisor, so he had no requirement to help train me. I also knew that we could be simply days away from combat and that the stakes were high. The Battery Commanders and staff primaries were supportive throughout my very short but memorable training phase.

Getting My Feet Wet

On my first outing with the Old Man, my first mentoring moment came when he said, *"Lock and load, S2. We're about to enter a possibly not-so-secure area."* If it were not for my complexion, I'm confident I would have looked pale, even white as a ghost. As I watched the driver place a 20-round magazine of 5.56-caliber rounds into his M16A2 rifle and the Old Man lock and cock a magazine into his Colt .45-caliber pistol, it all seemed surreal. I was getting my feet wet, and locking and loading made me a little nervous. Being an expert marksman with the Colt .45 pistol did not replace the firepower of the M16A2 with a 20- or 30-round ammunition magazine.

My delusions of grandeur in being the S4 kingpin were a thing of the past, but it did make me appreciate the position much more. As an S4, I had traveled as much or more than the Old Man. Still, I was traveling rearward toward the support battalions and the division headquarters. Moving forward on the battlefield made all this very real because the artillery units were in front of the support units but behind the infantry and armor units. The idea of engaging enemy Combat Reconnaissance Patrols (CRP) and insurgents was the initial S2 education I received. My education increased daily, especially after I spent time with the DIVARTY (Division Artillery) S2.

Getting The Bum's Rush: Off to The DIVARTY S2

Although the Old Man had greased the skids for me to train with the DIVARTY S2 officer, the transition could have been smoother. One day, the XO (Executive Officer) suddenly told me, "*Pack your rucksack and take your sleeping bag; you're going to DIVARTY.*" It felt like I was getting the bum's rush. When we arrived at the DIVARTY TOC for the first time, the DIVARTY S2 officer, Captain Tim, ushered me into his 'Intelligence Lair.' I learned that military intelligence folks like to keep the air of mystery and secrecy alive because they keep secrets! I immediately noticed the difference between his setup and mine.

He had more space, people, his own MSRT – **M**obile **S**ubscriber **R**adio **T**erminal, and more 'gadgets.' It looked like he had a bank of radios, multiple map boards with all kinds of overlays and graphics, and an overlay 'bin' stacked three rows deep and high. He also had something called a SCIF.

In 1990, I was not versed in the intelligence lingo, but knew I could not go into the SCIF (pronounced "skiff") – **S**ensitive **C**ompartmented **I**nformation **F**acility because I had not been 'Read On.' A SCIF is an extraordinarily secure room or area where US Government officials and contractors review highly classified information if they have the proper clearances and Authorizations. Even though I had top-secret clearance, I did not need to access that level of information. I had spent plenty of time in the S2 office back
home, but now I realized it was not a SCIF because we did not maintain that material level. Of course, this was war, and I was now in the S2, which significantly changed the landscape. Also, the other thing keeping me out of the SCIF at that moment was the armed Soldier at the entrance, who had his weapon locked and loaded.

The Iraq I Knew…

CPT Tim was not a branch detail officer like me and was voluntarily transferring to the Military Intelligence Corps. This is a massive problem in most branches because it seems offensive to the senior leaders of those branches, but not to CPT Tim. He was a knowledgeable guy and remained an asset to the field artillery. He explained that being S2's was an excellent opportunity for both of us that many intel officers might never get: Being an S2 in combat. Oddly enough, I would serve as the S2 or G2 in all three combat deployments to Iraq.

We only had one afternoon, evening, and morning to ramp me up on what I needed to do and know. Some of the particulars CPT Tim trained me on were:

- Maintaining the enemy versus friendly Situation Map.
- How to read INTREPs – Intelligence Reports from various intelligence sources.
- What were the sources of intelligence?
- How to prepare an EXSUM (Executive Summary) of what I had read.
- How to prepare my 'Elevator Speech' for the Old Man if we were asked for a quick turn intel briefing.
- How to prepare the Intelligence Briefing Book for the Command Group.
- How to provide a daily morning Intel Briefing.
- How to brief the enemy situation to a friendly audience.
- Obtain 100% knowledge of enemy artillery capabilities.

Yes, this was very ambitious for a short time. Still, leaders must rise to the occasion when it calls for it. These were the tactical requirements I needed to know about the job. I would learn a plethora of other requirements through **OJT** (On—the—Job Training).

I soaked in as much as possible, took copious notes, and asked for copies of what I thought was important. Being the stellar officer he was, CPT Tim provided me with an S2 Handbook, which I added to as my knowledge grew. As this short training session ended, I thanked CPT Tim and his team profusely for the education, and they told me that we would be talking regularly. Feeling much better, I soon learned this was only the beginning of my S2 training.

FROM GETTING WET TO GETTING SOAKED

As the Old Man arrived for the morning briefing and spoke with CPT Tim, there was a different air about him. As we returned to our unit, I sensed something was about to happen, and I was right. The Old Man told me he would keep me *"under wraps,"* and I would only provide intel updates to the Command Group. He followed the *"under wraps"* comment with,

"Because I don't want the Battery Commanders to eat you alive."

That began my 10 days of Two-A-Days. Many competitive organizations use Two-A-Days to increase training intensity and improve proficiency in a shorter period, and time was not on our side. I was being invested in as a leader, and I had no intention of failing. Training with the DIVARTY S2 had certain advantages, including getting a better map of Iraq.

It is incredible what a starving man will think is a feast. When CPT Tim provided me with the maps in Photos 44 & 45, I felt like George Jefferson: *'Movin' on up!'* Seeing the rivers labeled (natural barriers), Kuwait's total size, and even more Iraqi cities was fantastic. If our final objective were to reach Baghdad, it would be a 300-mile (480-kilometer) trek diagonally across the border from the Saudi border. At the time, we were much deeper inside Saudi Arabia, so you could easily add another 100 miles (160 kilometers, or km), bringing the total to about 540 km.

Photo 44. Iraq map with greater details.

Photo provided by the Author.

This will be much more significant later in the story. Having an even better map made me feel more confident, and I received this as a 'training graduation present.' All the maps were in color; however, because this is a black-and-white book, the colors were converted to black and white.

Photo 45. Detailed map of Iraq with major cities and other countries.

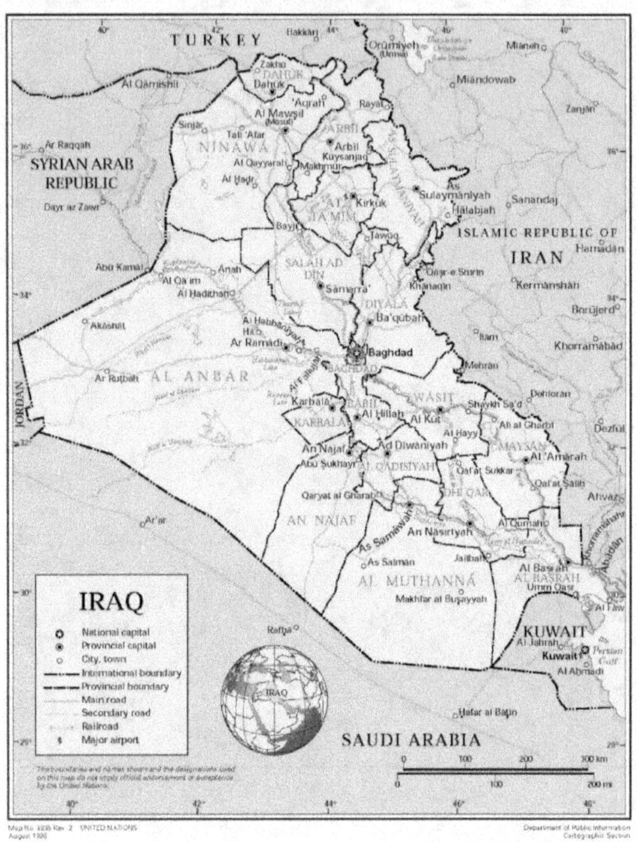

Photo provided by the Author.

My 'graduation gift' excited me because it allowed me to study the country more deeply. Also, because I was not providing morning intel briefings, I needed another way to keep the Battery Commanders and anyone else who wanted to know informed. The opportunity presented itself when the Headquarters and Headquarters Battery (HHB) Commander asked if he could read the raw intel reports. I told him, *"Sure, just give me two days to get my system into place."* He looked at me, puzzled, but said,

"Okay." This allowed me to apply what I had learned from CPT Tim and to use it whenever possible for the remainder of my intel career.

The Vaunted Briefing Book

If we already provided a briefing book for the Command Group, why not to the Battery Commanders? Their book would not be as concise as the Command Groups because I assumed that all of them would want to read the raw intelligence reports. I wanted to provide an EXSUM of the reports, with a brief analysis of what the enemy artillery might do. After all, I was a trained field artillery officer, so I knew how to speak that language. Now, I could add something else they did not have: A detailed map of Iraq to reference when reading the reports.

After I was ready, I told the HHB Commander he could read the reports. When he arrived, we had set aside a special place for him; I provided a brief overview of how this would work and asked him what he would like his daily scheduled time to be. Again, a blank look came across his face because it was unexpected. Finally, he spoke and said,

"You know, your predecessor NEVER, and I mean NEVER, allowed us to read the intel reports. It was as if reading them meant breaking some sacred vow or trying to take his job. What gives?"

"Well," I said, *"Because I am the 'keeper of the security clearances,' I know what level everyone can see and read. Since you are interested in what is occurring, the more you know, the better it is for us, as you are better informed. Lastly, what does it hurt?"*

He just shook his head and began reading. After about 30 minutes, he told us that he was done. We asked if he had any questions, thanked him for coming by, and asked if he wanted to come by again the next day. This went on for about three days, and on the fourth day, the HHB Commander mentioned some intel nuggets during the morning briefing. The other Battery Commanders looked at him and said,

"How do you know that?" The HHB Commander replied,

"Because I read it."

"Read it where?" they asked in unison.

"From the S2 Intel Read Book, that's where," he replied.

"Yeah, right," someone said. *"That doesn't exist for us."*

"Well, said the HHB Commander, *"There's a new sheriff in town, Boys. Ask, and ye shall receive."*

One by one, for the remainder of the day, the Battery Commanders asked when they could see this 'vaunted' S2 Intel Read Book. I said they just needed to make an appointment so we could have it ready, and that it wouldn't conflict with anyone else. We would set that time aside for them daily. Over the next few days, we had a booming intel business. We even made a second intel book because there were sometimes scheduling conflicts. I thought, '*This is great. At this rate, I will never have to brief them.*' Well, that thought was short-lived, as all good things must come to an end.

MY D-DAY: The 10th of December 1990…

We were on a fast-moving train traveling at breakneck speed, and I felt like a flailing passenger. My personal and professional D-Day had arrived. It was not the 6th of June, and we were not storming the beaches of Normandy. Still, it sure felt like I was being stormed as I was scheduled to give my first full intelligence briefing to the Battery Commanders and other captains. I was nervous because my predecessor briefed like an expert, even though it was all his opinion versus collected information synthesized into vetted intelligence.

I provided the briefing as I had given it to the Command Group many times before. The Battery Commanders challenged me on almost every aspect of my briefing, helping me improve, because their lives also depended on my success. Once I concluded, those few minutes of silence seemed like the longest of my life. Once the briefing was officially over, various people took me aside and offered briefings tips. One comment that stood out was,

"Not a bad briefing for someone who has not attended the Advanced Course, but you will get better in time."

The Officer Advanced Course (now known as the Captain's Career Course) taught captains how to be captains. That included classes on administration, operations, briefings, and, most importantly, command. I was not trained in any of those areas at the captain's level, but training and learning are different. Many people are 'trained' in various subjects but have yet to 'learn' anything. Another resonating comment was to have a well-developed outline of what I would brief. I used this technique in my next venture: Briefing Alpha Battery.

A Test Beyond Test: Scared Shitless

When the Alpha Battery Commander approached me about briefing his battery, I was shocked and told him so. His reply was,

"You know I wouldn't let you near my guys if I didn't trust you."

Okay, everything was back to normal. CPT B+ made the remarks I expected. I am referring to him as B+ because there were 2-3 captains whose last name began with B, but if any were B+, it was him.

He was tough because he commanded the cohort battery, composed of the permanent party NCOs, and all the Soldiers went through basic and advanced individual training together. They were also assigned to their first unit together. I wonder if they had been with us for a month when we were activated for deployment. This was a Firing Battery full of high-strung privates concerned with what was going on. As we set the time and date, I arrived, set up my equipment, and the company's First Sergeant led the Soldiers in. It was only the cohort Soldiers.

I began my briefing by outlining the scenario as I understood it and reviewing the enemy situation. I followed this by showing the enemy's situation on the map in a graphic depiction of everything I had just said. I made sure to pause at the end of each section and ask if there were any questions. All I received was silence. I continued with an update on recent enemy events and an estimate of possible future enemy events. Before I knew it, about 45 minutes had passed. Once again, I asked if there were any questions. Silence. The First Sergeant called the group to attention and told them to file out from the rear.

As I began to take my maps down, the First Sergeant thanked me for coming. *"Well,"* I said, continuing to take down my equipment. *"I just wish the Soldiers had more questions."*
"Sir," said the First Sergeant. As I turned around, I was face-to-face with 20 privates. As the First Sergeant began shooing them away, I said, *"No, I will answer questions."* Apparently, they were listening to what I briefed and began asking insightful questions of Soldiers of their rank and experience. I was feeling much better about my briefing skills and knowledge until I was asked the question that changed my life:

"Sir, are we gonna die?"

Being quick on my feet and with a poker face, I said,

"Not if I can help it."

"Good answer, sir," the First Sergeant whispered as he began shooing the Soldiers away, but not before they thanked me, shook my hand, and told me they felt much better.

I was glad they felt much better because I was now scared shitless. I am trembling even as I type this. The enormity of what we had done was nothing compared to what that Soldier asked me. People often ask me why I was so uptight, and that is your answer. Being asked to predict the fate of others was a humbling experience, and nothing has humbled me so much since that day. I was never asked that question again over the next 20 years of my military career.

When I returned to the TOC, my guys asked me how it went, and I said 'great' and began barking orders. Both of my NCOs asked me if I was okay, and I said,

"No, we need to up our game."

I feel bad now that I never told them what they asked, and, to my knowledge, no one else knew except the First Sergeant and those 20 Soldiers. I went into overdrive because I was going to make damn skippy so that I could keep my promise. I must have been overdoing it because my NCOs told me I needed to sleep. Fortunately, we had the kind of rapport that allowed me to listen to their wise counsel. I needed it.

Now, it seemed like time was moving extremely fast. That Soldier removed any nuances about what we were there to do. This all had just become deadly serious to me. I went from slinging turkeys and toilet paper a month before to having acetate up to my ass with markers, maps, and assorted mayhem to figure out where the enemy might attack. That was if we had not yet attacked them first. That seemed unlikely, but it could happen. Worse yet, they could attack us sooner than we expected at a vulnerable point. This just became worse yet.

A MAD DASH TO THE BORDER

When a unit calls in distress, we all answer. I will not disclose the organization, but the unit reported that they were severely outnumbered and outgunned and requested reinforcements. Oddly enough, we were the closest unit that could respond and respond as we did. At that moment, all our training kicked in. As the S3 issued the Warning Order (WARNO) to move out, the S2 section plotted the supposed enemy position on the map and wargame where they might attack from, and we all began to pack. Between packing, the Old Man wanted a complete intelligence and operations briefing for the Battery Commanders and staff. Although the call was for immediate assistance, we dared not move in the daylight so the enemy could see us coming and shoot us like fish in a barrel.

Once the S3 received an order from DIVARTY, we wondered, *'Was this it?' 'Was the waiting game over?'* Well, it was for us as we finished packing, identified routes of march and attack, and determined if other units were moving around us. Thankfully, at least an armor battalion was also moving, so we would maintain our supporting role as artillery, answering calls for fire from a standoff position. This required me to coordinate with the counter-artillery radars to verify if they were also moving. My job shifted from identifying the enemy in a frontal attack to assessing whether the enemy might attack us on our flanks (sides).

"The Anticipation Far Exceeded the Actual Event"

As nightfall came, we lined up, revved our engines, and took off on a great race across the desert. The more we moved, the more I saw the actual operation. I thought an armor battalion was moving, but it looked like our entire brigade. In 1991, a brigade had three combat battalions and one artillery, signal, engineer, and logistics battalion in support. How could I see all of this? NVGs – Night Vision Goggles. I had procured our full complement before deployment. We were rolling, traveling all night, and arriving at our designated positions just before dawn. Unfortunately, we were not 100 percent sure about it because traveling at night can be tricky, especially in a desert.

As the sun rose, we reconfigured to use the available firepower. Fortunately, it would be moot. Preliminary reports from the scouts were that we were literally the only ones there. There were no enemy units, friendly units, or movement. There were not even Bedouins or field mice, just us. The early reporting was accurate once the sun came up: Nothing as far as the eye could see. I do not recall if we ever figured out what happened, but we were a heck of a lot closer to the Iraq border.

We spent the time policing our straggling units, resetting for the next mission, and forming a recovery party to retrieve all the equipment we had left behind at a moment's notice. We also discovered that we were experiencing calm before the storm.

Photo 46. The S2 Crew for 3rd/82nd FA BN.

L-R: SFC P, CPT Me, SSG Ski, SPC T, PFC H.

Photo provided by the Author.

Chapter 12:
"Before the Storm"

There is not always calm before the storm...

This was the most challenging portion of the book to write because it began the most intense period of the deployment. Over the years, I have heard comments about, 'How easy Desert Storm was because it was so short.' My retort to this was and is:

1. It was only *short* if you were **not** there.
2. Regardless of how *short* it was, Soldiers **died** in that *short* period.
3. Operations began well before the commitment of ground forces.

As with any military operation, prepping the battlefield begins weeks before the main effort attacks/advances.

E P I S O D E 12

Prepping The Battlefield

WHOOSH, WHOOSH, WHOOSH were the sounds the Tomahawk missiles made as they left the decks of the battle cruisers and aircraft carriers they were launched from. Of course, I only knew this from the television reports I saw years later, after the war. When the Tomahawks were launched into Baghdad, we were still securely in Saudi Arabia at the border with Iraq. Those attacks began on January 15, 1991, when Desert Storm was officially declared. Of course, once the US started combat operations, so did Iraq.

Iraq, however, pointed its aggression towards Israel and fired SCUDs towards Tel Aviv. Iraq's strategy was to draw Israel into the war, which might mean Palestine would enter the war on Iraq's side. With the numerous SCUDs lobbed at Israel, they showed great restraint and never took the bait. That meant Iraq's aggression had to go somewhere, and they turned it towards us.

Dancing with the Scuds

It may seem like I have a morbid sense of humor, but as I look back on the events, I must laugh to keep from crying. Long before we fired a shot, we were under SCUD alerts almost hourly. Because we never knew where the SCUDs were aimed, we always went into MOPP IV. We were also instructed to begin taking our PB-Pyridostigmine pills. The PB pills were anti-nerve agent pills issued to us to prevent death from a soman nerve agent chemical attack. We were issued 21-tablet blister packs, and once we began taking them, we took one 30-mg tablet every 8 hours.

We only took the tablets for two or three days at the beginning of the war for two reasons. First, I noticed that I was feeling no pain, like I was drunk or something, and my urine smelled horrible. Once I confirmed my suspicions with the section, I brought this up with the Old Man, and we requested, through DIVARTY, a better way to track SCUD attacks and stop taking the tablets. That led to the second reason: The PATRIOT Missile Batteries had AN/MPQ-53 radars that could track the direction of launched missiles. That allowed us to stop taking the pills and suit up in MOPP IV. We remained in MOPP II – jacket and pants and wore the uniforms for most of the war.

As the charcoal from the MOPP suits rubbed off on our regular uniforms, those uniforms were normally ruined. Remember, we began wearing MOPP suits on January 15, 1991, and until we left in March or April 1991. Even with changing our uniforms regularly, most of us decided to sacrifice a couple of uniforms to what I called the MSM - MOPP Suit Monster, not to be confused with the Meritorious Service Medal. About this time, I mentioned the proverbial *bullet with my name on it*. My two stellar NCOs quickly brought me to reality when they said,

"Sir, it's not the bullet with your name on it that you have to worry about," said SSG Ski.

"Hell, no," said SFC P, *"It's the ones labeled, '**To Whom It May Concern**' you have to look out for because there are plenty of those."*

I never forgot this sage advice and shared it on my subsequent two deployments. As we danced with the SCUDs, we continued preparing for our missions. Iraqi SCUDs, however, were not the only thing we had to worry about.

Photo 47. SCUD Missile Ranges. Photo provided by the Author.

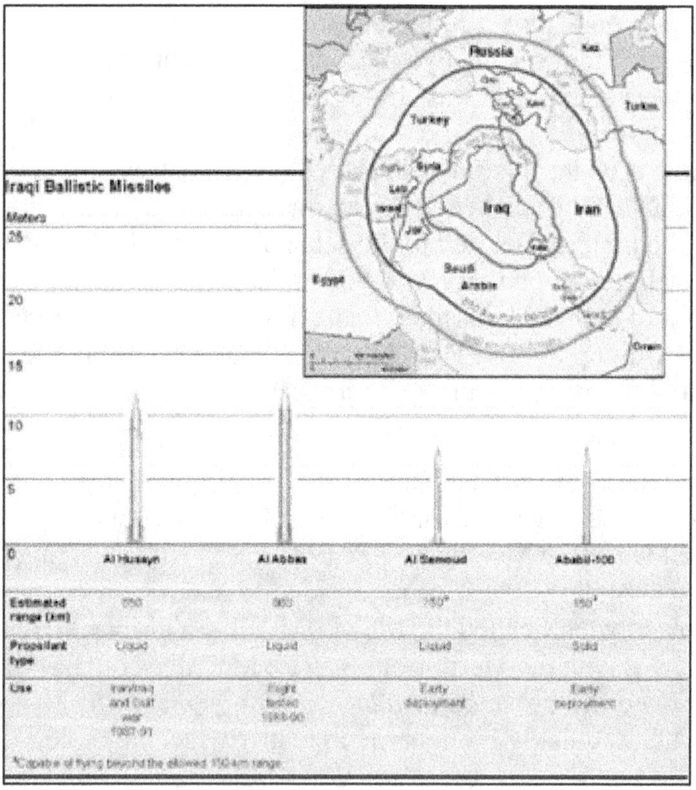

A-Holes and Elbows: CHEMICAL ALERT!

Imagine being in a war zone and having a halfway decent day. We had grown accustomed to the SCUD alerts and knew what to do, since the ever-efficient S2 section learned how to track the angle of trajectory and flight path. All in a day's work for trained artillerymen, right? We had a great breakfast, completed the morning briefing, and were standing around shooting-the-shit when suddenly,

RANT, RANT, RANT!!! RANT, RANT, RANT.!!! RANT…

That was the unmistakable blaring of the M42 chemical agent alarm attached to the M43A1 Detector Unit, which indicated nerve agents were in the air. Talk about assholes and elbows! Everyone stopped breathing, put on their gas mask, made sure that it was fitted correctly, and repeatedly began yelling,

GAS, GAS, GAS! GAS, GAS, GAS!

My NCOIC, SFC P, ran out of the track like Jamaican sprinter Usain Bolt, and then I realized, *'Oh shit, the night crew!'* I ran out right behind him, and we were all trying to wake everyone who was outside or in tents, continuously yelling, "GAS, GAS, GAS!" I shook one cot, and the person did not move. I shook it repeatedly, and finally the person rolled over: It was the Battalion Chemical Officer! As I was steadily sounding the alarm, he was shouting,

"WHAT? WHAT?

I finally grabbed him by the upper arms and began shaking him and shouting,

"LOOK AT ME!!!! LOOK AT ME!!!

His following response was just about what anyone might say,

"OH FUCK!!!

…as he scrambled to stop breathing and find his gas mask. It was under his cot, and as I stuffed it into his chest, he hurriedly put it on. We continued sounding the alarm and ensuring everyone wore their masks.

And the Pucker Factor Began...

Just so the reader understands why things were done a certain way, Stop Breathing or holding your breath was step one in a suspected chemical attack because whatever the chemical – VX, mustard, or sarin gas, you did not want to inhale it. If you did inhale, the mask was even more crucial, and now someone had to stay with you to observe if you were showing signs of chemical agent poisoning. We usually kept a pocket card in our upper left-hand pocket outlining the symptoms of each chemical agent.

Photo 48. Personnel in MOPP IV.

Everything I described occurred in seconds: Don the mask, proper fit, and sound the alarm. More than a minute could be the difference between life and death. Now, for the next test.

The Chemical Officer and NCOIC are not just titles in the Army. These personnel were school-trained in every facet there is to know about chemical weapons, their deployment, the effects, and all the equipment. It was a standard operating procedure (SOP) to leave the alarms blaring until it could be determined if the alert was real. Yes, the alarms could be triggered by various things, so the chemical officer and NCOIC conducted the appropriate test to determine the type of agent in the air. As they went about their business, the pucker factor was mighty high. All sorts of thoughts ran through my mind until finally, they yelled the two sweetest words in the chemical weapons vocabulary when you are in a gas mask:

"ALL CLEAR! ALL CLEAR! ALL CLEAR!"

The chemical officer first took off his mask to show his confidence in his equipment. The actual procedure is for the lowest-ranking person to break the seal on their mask, take a breath, reseal it, and sit in a separate place with someone observing them for 3-5 minutes. As archaic as that may sound, and even cruel, it was 1991, not 2024, when the current technology was used to detect what seems like everything. The chemical NCOIC followed suit, and we all slowly removed our masks. We never discovered what triggered the alarm, but we were just thankful it was a false alarm. Our following standard procedure was a pain in the butt, but we became used to it.

PACKEM UP, MOVEEM OUT!

We did not resume what we were doing, but began packing to move. Our brigade commander was a Vietnam veteran, and so was the Assistant Division Commander for Support. Initially, we relocated two to three times a day. Because of the chemical alert, we had to move anyway. Most of us did not mind, but we were still a little shaken up. My Dad was in the 10th Cavalry in World War II, and the first time he yelled, *"PACKEM UP, MOVEM OUT,"* while we were fishing, I asked him what that meant. He said, *"In the cavalry, that means 'it's time to go.'"* As a young kid who got bored easily, it was music to my ears when Dad said that. Not so much in this case, but what could I do?

We began preparing for our subsequent missions at our new location. The days blurred together during that very short time. Before the ground offensive in late February 1991, our portion of the war began over a week earlier with continued battlefield preparation. That was meant to give the Iraqi units a taste of their medicine.

Chapter 13:
"Our G-Day Came Early"

There's nothing like being first.

The feints required engaging in combat operations in a pre–G–Day (Ground Forces Day) manner. In essence, this was our G-Day. Although I always referred to the pre—G-Day operations as The Battle of Wadi Al Batin, the official name was The Battle of Ruqi Pocket. [13] Our portion of the campaign plan focused on a series of artillery tactics with names like Red Storm (Our motto was Red Dragons) and Knight Strike (The Old Man's last name was Knight). Those operations were always in support of the larger maneuver feint campaigns that moved fast and furiously, with the TOC's ability to keep up almost impossible. We did the best we could, attempted to stay in radio range to provide operations and intelligence support to these complex operations designed to draw the Iraqi Army towards us.

Artillery Raids and Maneuver Feints

I am about to describe what I call 'textbook' stuff. Never in a million years, well, at least a hundred years, did I expect ever to exercise any of those tactics. Because imagery indicated that the Iraqi Army was well dug in, had fortified underground positions, and had a system of interlocking trenches, those targets required softening before our infantry and armor advances. The Tomahawks could only do so much firing from the Persian Gulf, where the artillery came from.

"THIS IS A" RAID…

"(This Is a) **Raid**…" is a song by the group Lakeside released in 1983 on their album *Untouchables*. Yes, 1983 albums and Lakeside are likely unfamiliar to most readers. To me, however, this is very familiar since in 1983, I was a sophomore in college, had an afro (back when I had hair), and believed I was going to be a DJ (Disc Jockey). According to ' When' the song was released, I could have been a college junior, but I digress. Remember, there were not many years between 1983 and 1991, so the song's lyrics came to mind when I was informed that we would be conducting artillery raids.

Our mission was to conduct a series of artillery raids on those dug-in positions by delivering massive amounts of artillery rounds. As we had danced with SCUDs for the previous three weeks, we were about to 'rain' artillery rounds on the Iraqi Army. By their nature, raids are not necessarily designed to be direct, well-known attacks against an enemy. Raids are swift, penetrating attacks meant to surprise, suppress, confuse, and/or crush the enemy or their positions.

For our raids, our goal was to enter Iraq undetected, pound the specific enemy sites along expected routes of advance, and return to our Tactical Assembly Areas (TAA) in Saudi Arabia. 'Undetected' could only mean one thing for an artillery unit: at night or under the cover of darkness. My job was to ensure that the 'undetected' part remained that way and to detect and report ANY enemy movements in our areas of operations.

That operation required the utmost skill, efficiency, and stealth. We had the skill and efficiency down cold, but stealth? Now, go back to the picture of the M109A2 howitzer and tell me how stealth would occur. The plans were sand-tabled (no pun intended), rock-drilled, and walked through extensively during the last two weeks of January 1991. Every Soldier was given precise instructions on how to stay 'stealthy', or quiet and undetected. That also meant only the bare necessities were taken for the mission: A full complement of artillery rounds, powders, and fuses, and with the most basic equipment on the howitzers. No camouflage nets or ammunition carriers were included. The crews wore MOPP II and carried their rucksacks with the standard fare.

Imagine 8, 16, or 24 howitzers tiptoeing across the desert from Saudi Arabia to the Iraqi border. If you have an imagination like mine, it seems like something from a cartoon. Showering steel onto Iraqi Army targets, however, was not cartoonish. I can only imagine that the Batteries firing at night must have looked spectacular. To accomplish my portion of the task, our section monitored the Battalion Operations, Division Artillery (DIVARTY), and Brigade Operations radio nets.

Photo 49. 155mm Self-Propelled Howitzer firing at night.

The battalion conducted several iterations of raids, and waiting for the Batteries to return each time was like waiting for a baby to be born. You want the baby to be born healthy and happy, but mostly, you want it to arrive! After each mission, we would high-five each other, conduct a debriefing, and then the dayshift went to bed. Although we did not conduct the raids nightly, the planning and practices filled up the remainder of our time until D-Day. Because we supported the 2nd (Blackjack)

Brigade and the 1st Brigade had artillery, the raids were a shared responsibility across the division. Ours was a small portion of a much larger plan.

FEINT OR FAINT?

Some might say that our plan could make you faint if you looked at it in totality. We, the 1st Cavalry Division, were held in Corps Reserve, which meant we were the Rapid Reaction Force (RRF) for the Corps and were required to move anywhere across the battlefield within 2-4 hours. I will discuss Corps operations later. The plan was to make the Iraqis believe that the VII Corps was attacking through the Wadi Al Batin, while the VII Corps actually attacked from somewhere else. This deception operation is known as a feint. Those battle deception operations may have been the riskiest part of the war. If we were successful, the enemy might quickly mass its Army in our area, and a numerically superior force could attack us. As nerve-rattling as it may sound, that was all part of the job.

That is where the fainting may come from, in any Army other than the US Army and the 1st Cavalry Division. We were lean, mean, fighting machines and dared anyone, friendly or enemy, to tell us differently. The Cavalry was always used in this fashion, and the term 'Here comes the cavalry!' came from it. The deception planning began immediately after the air war, around January 18, 1991. Once the deception operations started in early February, they lasted about 10 days. They stopped just short of the time when the offensive was scheduled to begin. Our artillery raids were successful for the most part.

The maneuver brigades simultaneously began their subterfuge operations by posturing near the Wadi Al Batin. That was the attack corridor we wanted the Iraqi Army to believe we were attacking from. That meant digging shallow fighting positions, creating makeshift structures, and giving the illusion that we were 'camping' in that area before the big attack. The goal was to draw as many Iraqi armor units to that area as possible. That would allow several US divisions to flank several Iraqi divisions, while our other US divisions simultaneously head to Baghdad. As we began the reconnaissance missions as part of the feint, the tenor of our operations changed.

All our movements, sights, and sounds had to mimic a force far greater than we were. This required us to be far apart, with tank-sized fighting positions between each tank and Bradley Fighting Vehicle. Our artillery could not be spread as far apart because it is designed as a precision weapon fired in mass. I remember walking our perimeter several times to check security using the challenge-and-password system. I did not catch anyone asleep on duty, and every sentry challenged me. This success was mostly because I notified the Batteries during the morning staff meeting about what we were doing, so no one thought an enemy was approaching.

When Our High Fives Ended

We were blessed during the artillery raids that no one was seriously hurt, wounded, or killed. Even during the beginning of the feint, we were still fortunate to return unscathed. Just as the enemy deploys a Forward Security Element (FSE), we use a tactic referred to as Reconnaissance in Force. Scouts' standard recon mission is to observe and report, not engage the enemy. In a reconnaissance in force, an entire infantry battalion deploys to execute the scout mission, with one exception: it is prepared and authorized to engage the enemy. Prepared they were, but the enemy needed to be in a fighting mood.

To this day, I do not know if the following enemy operation was a trap. Still, as one mission began, some Iraqi soldiers indicated surrender: Hands up, moving slowly towards our friendly forces. I remember the high fives started when the report of EPWs (Enemy Prisoners of War) came in. But the celebration ended when the calls for MEDEVAC (Medical

Evacuation), the call for artillery fire, and general chaos began. As the mechanized infantry unit began to collect and process the EPWs, enemy antitank weapons started firing, and several Soldiers were killed and wounded. We anticipated antitank weapons and to possibly engage other enemy combat vehicles, but did not expect to encounter EPWs. Being stationary for that long allowed the enemy to cause havoc.

You Can't Feint Death

We had practiced air and ground MEDEVACs before we began operations for events like this, but the preparation did not make us feel better. The infantry scouts were now observing enemy troops and positions, calls for artillery fires were radioed in, and we could hear the MEDVAC helicopters flying forward. Remember, these operations were occurring at night, and once the dust settled, we had 10 personnel either killed or wounded. The first combat force-on-force operations had just happened, and we needed to wrap our minds around it.

Those were our first casualties during the war and may have been the first fatalities of the war; they created a somber atmosphere, and the high-fives never resumed. After we withdrew from Iraq and returned to Saudi Arabia, we met at the TOC the next morning for an AAR (After–Action Review). One thing I recall is the message from the Brigade Commander that,

"We got our noses bloodied, and they got in the first punch, but we'll be ready next time."

That boxing analogy always stayed with me. As with anything involving the unknown or the first time an event occurs, once the action happens, good or bad, our angst dissipates and allows us to settle down into what we need to do. For the S2 section, this meant that we needed to be sharper on what to look for so that the Batteries did not meet the same fate. We also learned from experience that we needed to increase our security.

Ensuring We Could Defend Ourselves

Because I had wonderful NCOs who wanted to learn and grow, SFC P designed a 'duty roster' for the security checks so we could rotate the duty between the three of us. Those checks were critical because we had no idea where the enemy might be. To our knowledge, the Iraqi Army was modeled after the Russian Army, using T-72 tanks, AK-47 rifles, and RPG – Rocket Propelled Grenade launchers. This meant they may have followed their doctrine of sending combat reconnaissance patrols (CRP) to gather information on the opposing forces. Although we had night vision goggles (NVG), imagery, ground surveillance radars (GSR), and a few other toys, that did not mean the enemy could not move stealthily on foot, observe us from afar, or attempt to probe our camps, so we needed to be prepared.

Making The Rounds

To sell the feint, we also built dug-in observation posts and fighting positions using our materials, including sandbags and a small amount of lumber. The sandbags braced the observation posts on both sides, and the plywood served as an overhead cover, with sandbags stacked on top. Each battery had at least two observation posts, one on each flank of the battery assembly areas, to watch for enemy scouts. We needed 7-10 positions to check spread across two to three kilometers in a circle with the TOC in the middle. We did not need to check the positions during the day because they were easily visible. SFC P drew Sketch 7 in my personal field book so that we would all have accurate orientation points for the checks at dusk, with me making the rounds first.

We were checking to ensure that the guards on duty were awake, knew the challenge and password, knew their general orders, and whatever additional orders the Battery Commanders and first sergeants gave them. We were also not fools, and we called each battery to let them know that we would be checking security at dusk. That was done so we did not surprise anyone as we walked up, and they, 'shot first and asked questions later.'

Sketch 7. Battalion Tactical Assembly Area sketch from Author notes.

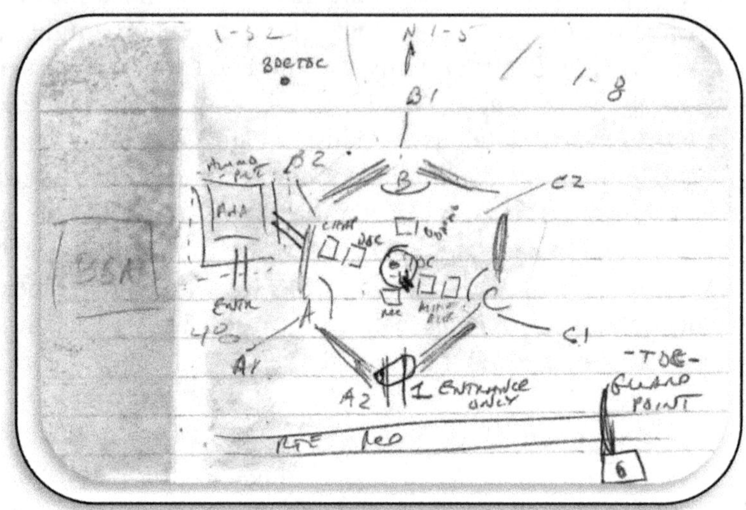

The first check went as I expected, and as I approached a position, I heard,

"Halt, who goes there?" said the guard.
"Captain Randolph, Battalion S2," I said.

"Advanced to be recognized," said the guard. I took three steps forward until he told me to halt.

"Challenge word or phrase," said the guard.
"Challenge Response, " I said.
"You may pass, " said the guard.

That was the typical exchange when checking observation posts and fighting positions, and is called the Challenge and Password. I cannot remember any of the exact challenges and passwords, so I used Challenge Word or Phrase and Challenge Response. These are predetermined by day and change every 24 hours. That allowed us to distinguish between friend and enemy without the enemy compromising our system.

I began chatting with the guard and told him to let his partner know who I was.

I asked the guards if they had seen anything on the horizon or out of the ordinary. I then asked about one of the general orders and what additional instructions they were given. The first outpost passed with flying colors, and I continued to the next position, and an hour later, I returned to the TOC, done for the day. I ensured that I completed this first security run before our shift change, and SFC P asked me how it went.

"Peachy," I replied. *The guards were alert and well-informed and didn't shoot me, so it's all good, except I'm tired as hell!"*

"I'll do it tomorrow," said SFC P, *"So we can change it up a bit."*

Tomorrow came, and SFC P made the rounds for the second security check. When he returned, he said,

"Sir, what the hell are you talking about, 'peachy'? That was a damn hump!"

I replied, *"I assumed after working with me this long, you knew how sarcastic I am."* SSG Ski and I both laughed.

From then on, it seemed like the days ticked by slowly. The Batteries went out as required to provide artillery support to those infantry and cavalry units maintaining the feint by continuing recon missions. We checked, double-checked, and triple-checked all our equipment to ensure everything was fully operational or could be replaced before D-Day. We conducted rock drills and sand tables to ensure we knew exactly what to do. We also became intimately familiar with the Q36 and Q37 radars so that if the counterbattery fire was needed, we could 'Cue Radars' without hesitation to pinpoint the enemy artillery. We believed we were prepared and ready, but at this point, we were too close to stop operations and too far forward to turn back.

Chapter 14:

"Into the Eye of The Storm"

It was here before we realized it.

The G-Day or D-Day for the Coalition to attack into Iraq was Sunday, February 24, 1991. Four Theater Commands and Two Army Corps were locked, cocked, and ready to rock and roll with the enemy. An Army Corps may comprise three or more Army divisions of 20,000+ Soldiers. The 'more' units were the Armored Cavalry Regiments, Special Forces Groups, separate brigades, and additional divisions. The four theaters were US Army Central Command, Joint Forces Command North, Marine Central Command, and Joint Forces Command East. The XVIII Airborne Corps from Fort Bragg, NC (now Fort Liberty), and the VII Corps (deactivated) from Europe were the Army Corps. Each Corps had Coalition Partner Divisions, which boosted their strength to 4-5 divisions and over 100,000 personnel.

The Coalition and Marine Corps were supplemented with coalition partners and US Army brigades. Our combat coalition partners were the United Kingdom (UK), Syria, Egypt, Saudi Arabia, Kuwait, and the United Arab Emirates (UAE). VII Corps had three armored divisions: 1st Armored, 3rd Armored, and 1st UK Armored Divisions; 1st Infantry Division (Big Red One); 2d Armored Cavalry Regiment; and our unit, 1st Cavalry Division.[14]

While I was aware of the entire campaign plan, someone much more capable, who was paid significantly more than me, was responsible for it. My most fantastic familiarity was with and focused on what our division was tasked with: The Feint to End

The Iraq I Knew…

All Feints. Before that, we needed to move into position under constant SCUD attacks. That did not matter as we moved into the eye of the storm.

Photo 50. Operational map for Operation Desert Storm, Friendly Forces.

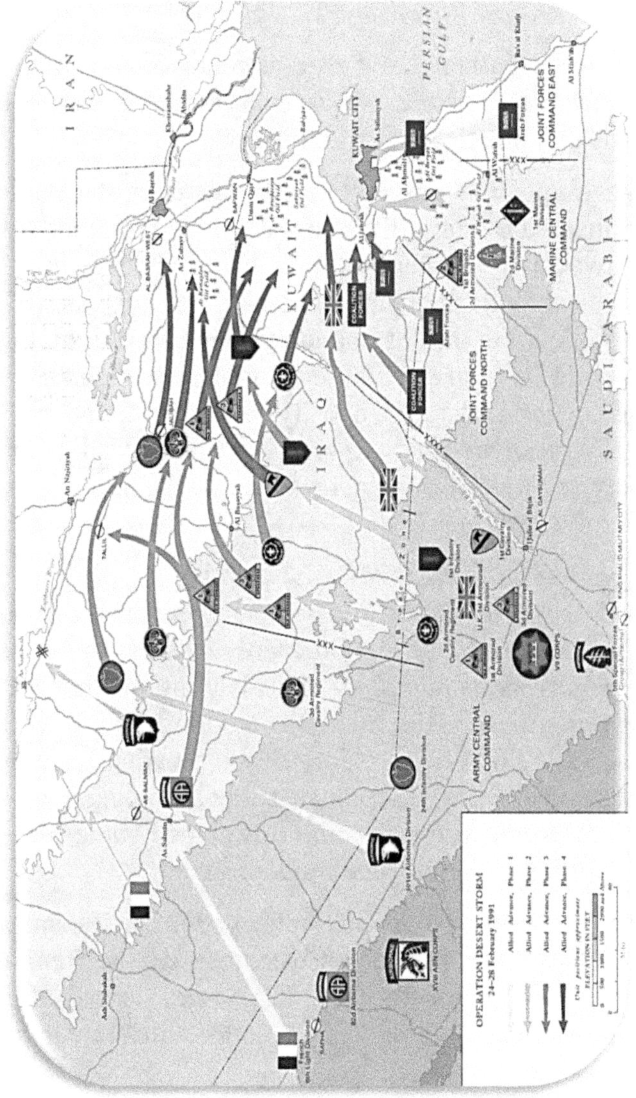

Know Thy Enemy, Know Thyself

Although I provided the 'big picture' view of our side of the war, my primary job was to know the enemy. The Chinese philosopher Sun Tzu, the Author of The Art of War, wrote,

"Know thy enemy, know thyself."[15]

In a short time, I gathered and read as much Iraqi military and cultural doctrine as possible to learn everything I could about the Iraqi Army's composition and fighting style.

The Iraqi Divisions within our AO were the 20th, 27th, 31st, and unnamed infantry divisions. The 12th Armored Division and the Tawakalna Mechanized Infantry Division were to the north. As you look at the map, this isn't a big deal for a Corps, right? But look at the theater boundary to our east/right. On that border were the 30th and an unnamed infantry division and, in my worst-case scenario, the 16th and 21st infantry divisions. What does all this mean in English? The 1st Cavalry Division was wedged between four Iraqi Divisions: One to the immediate west and three to the east.

If we had to fight, the odds would be 4:1, with us being the ones. If I just used our division numbers in a one-to-one comparison, we could face 80,000 enemy soldiers or 120,000 if the other two divisions joined in. This also implied that the feint may be working to draw the enemy forces to the Wadi Al Batin! A wadi is a valley or valley region. Based on what I saw, water must have been flowing through that area, creating a valley. I have no pictures because it was too difficult to guide a vehicle, listen to a radio, read a map, and hold a camera!!

The Iraqi-named divisions Nebuchadnezzar, Hammurabi, Madina, Al Faw, and Tawakalna were part of the Republican Guard Forces Command (RGFC). They were described as the 'elite' units, politically screened, and pledged absolute loyalty to Saddam Hussein.

Photo 51. Operational map showing Enemy Forces Circled.

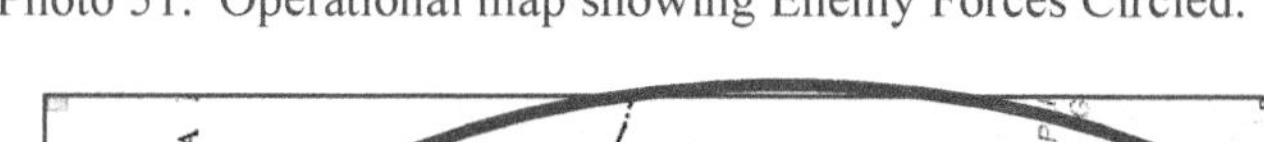

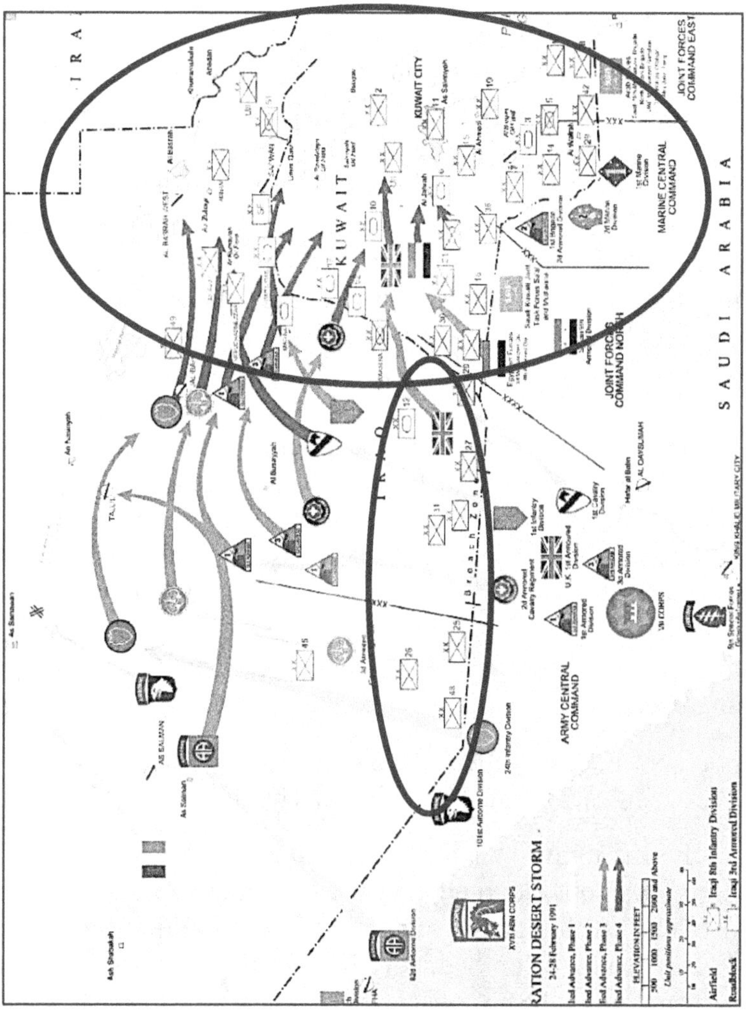

Those forces had the best of everything Iraq offered, including training, equipment, and preferential treatment. Our intelligence reported that because of their ability to move quickly and strike with precision, the RGFC led the attack into Kuwait. We would soon see how elite they were.

There was also a unit named the Fedayeen Saddam, which we initially believed was Saddam Hussein's personal security detachment (PSD). Well, at its height, it was more of a paramilitary force, numbering 30,000 to 40,000. We did not engage them much during Desert Storm, but I would learn a great deal about them through my next Iraq deployment. Iraqi personnel were not the only thing we had to worry about, or I would have known. Shortly, we would discover some very unorthodox tactics.

100 Hours and No Turning Back...

The next four days were the quickest and almost the most intense of my three combat tours in Iraq. When people read or see four days and 100 hours, it doesn't seem to match, but with the give-and-take of when the ceasefire began, the time can easily be rounded up to 100 hours or more. With the tank-on-tank battles, constant artillery prep missions and barrages, and the scrimmages between all-sized units, we knew there was no turning back.

ACT I, DAY ONE - FEB 24, 1991:
Crossing The "Line in The Sand"

It was time for the US Army and US Marines to make good on President George H.W. Bush's promise about *"A Line in the Sand."* Although the war officially began after January 15, 1991, the deadline for Saddam Hussein to withdraw the Iraqi Army from Kuwait, the 'official' ground war did not start until February 24, 1991. We knew that the LD – Lines of Departure or 'Line of the Sand' was the border between Saudi Arabia and Iraq. Think of the LD as the starting line for a race. Instead of beginning the race by firing a gun (we all had guns of various shapes and sizes), we timed our movements. We had all synchronized our watches and were at our SP – Start Points with engines revving. We were not going to simply wait and be attacked. We took the fight to the enemy.

As with any good attack plan, you always *'prep the battlefield.'* This meant peppering the enemy with numerous artillery rounds to soften them. That occurred as the Firing Batteries reached the berm around noon. We could no longer hide our intentions: We were going in. Our battalion did not attack alone; the entire DIVARTY participated in suppressing enemy artillery, forcing any enemy scouts watching the berm into defilade positions and 'selling' the feint. Defilade means going into hiding so that the enemy cannot see you. That applies to troops in the open, vehicles, and even tanks.

After reviewing the maps on the previous pages, you can see where each division entered the fray. As the 1st Cavalry Division, we were held in reserve to a certain point. Some might say,

'Wow, you guys weren't in the fight,' or 'What was wrong with you guys, that you weren't in the fight?'

To answer those questions and thoughts, not only were we in the fight, but we may even have started it! It was the most challenging mission I had ever participated in at that point in my career or life. Because we were the 1st Cavalry Division, one of our core capabilities was swift movement in action. The term 'held in reserve' was a misnomer. The term 'flex fighting force' or something like that sounded more fitting, in my opinion.

Moving any place on the battlefield that the Theater Commander directed via the Corps Commander was our mission. You may have heard of the theater commander, General H. Norman Schwarzkopf, also known as 'Stormin Norman' With 2-4 hours' notice, we reinforced any of the other 20,000 Soldier divisions within the theater. We were placed strategically on the battlefield to shift in any direction required. As an artillery battalion, we were poised to support our brigade or the division with artillery fires. We could respond to calls for fire from any unit within the 18-kilometer range of our howitzers. Thankfully, that did not happen, and we only had to worry about everything else in the combat zone, such as encountering our first unconventional method.

Who You Gonna Call? Berm Busters!

We encountered our first round of unconventional Iraqi tactics as we raced across the desert to reach the border. Because US imagery had detected a berm between Iraq and Saudi Arabia, which allowed us to develop what we called a 'berm busters' strategy. Those 'berm busters' were Army Corps of Engineers units assigned to each division that used armored combat earthmovers (ACE), essentially armored bulldozers. Although we had punched through the berm at specific points during the feints, those lanes were not enough to support the entire division.

Berms were a tactic used in World War I to slow or stop the Allied advance, and apparently, Saddam Hussein thought the same would deter us. Because this was 1991, soldiers were not required to fight through the sand berms with mere hand shovels; we had the ultimate shovels. We were about 10 kilometers out, and as the pace slowed to a crawl, SFC P said over the intercom,

You gotta see this shit."

Photo 52. Armored Combat Engineers (ACE) vehicle

Photo retrieved from U.S. Army Photos.

Photo 53. M1A1 tank behind a berm in Iraq.

Photo retrieved from the National Archives.

Another Changing of The Guard

I climbed up into the Commander's Hatch with SFC P and viewed a sight to behold. Vehicles as far as the eye could see with artillery firing, but more importantly, a giant berm between the two countries, miles long. The berm varied in height along the border and could be driven over in some places. With our trusty, dusty M577 Command Track Vehicle, there was no way, so we were in the 'breach' lane. Since we had stopped, I thought it was time to change the guard again. I let SFC P know he could step down and man the radio, and I would stand in the Commander's Hatch.

"Sir, why would we do that?" he asked.

"Because those are the risks I get paid to take," I said. *"All the armor and infantry officers are commanding their tanks and Bradleys, so I should be taking the same risk."*

Photo 54. Another view of the berm in Iraq.

From my point of view, the breaching process might be the most dangerous part of the entire operation because vehicles could only cross the berm through the holes punched. That put us in single-file lines, with our flanks exposed by the slow pace. In theory, there were no Iraqi tanks in Saudi Arabia, but hey, they invaded Kuwait, didn't they? What would stop them from firing at us as we crossed into Iraq? Because we were in a metal versus armored vehicle, an anti-tank round or rocket-propelled grenade (RPG) would go through our side like a hot knife through butter. Or the vehicle commanders could also be shot by small arms fire.

SFC P just stared at me and said,

"Sir, it's not your job to get shot-to-hell. Your job is to stay alive to get us all through this shit!"

And I said, *"Lord, willing and the sand don't rise, I can do both!"* I know that the cliché is 'The creek doesn't rise', but that didn't make much sense in a desert. Finally, he said, *"Okay, sir,"* and moved down from the Hatch. He knew everything that I did, probably more, but my conscience would not allow me to let him take those risks.

As SFC P climbed down from the Hatch and I got situated, I cannot say that I was not frightened. The thought had crossed my mind that any number of enemy weapons – RPG, incoming air burst artillery, tank round, or a hail of gunfire could take me out. As we slowly moved forward, I got taken out by a different type of weapon: *A royal **ass chewing***. Long before we reached our crossing lane, I received a message from SFC P:

Photo 55. Captain Randolph peeking out of the Commander's Hatch on the M577.

Photo provided by the Author.

*"Sir, the Colonel wants to know, and I quote, '**What the hell is Captain Randolph doing?**' When I told him, he said,"*

*"**How noble. Tell Captain Randolph to get his ass back on this radio! He does us no good shot up or worse.**"*

I thought, 'Hmm, so much for personal courage.'

SFC P and I switched out, and the Old Man called me on the radio.

" '2'," he said, *"The only voice I want to hear when I call is yours. Is that clear? "Crystal clear, sir,"* I said.

I failed to consider that a tank platoon leader fights his tank while commanding the four tanks of the platoon, which consists of 12 to 16 Soldiers. As the S2, I was not a platoon leader but led a C-level staff section that provided intelligence for over 600 Soldiers, including 24 howitzers, to support a 4-5,000-Soldier brigade. My place was behind that map board, listening to the radio and fighting my own battle: 'The Battle for Accurate Information.' I soon found myself fighting more battles than that.

AW, SHIT WHAT?

On one of our many stops, I heard SFC P utter over the intercom, *"Aw shit,"* and he directed us out of the vehicle. We set up a perimeter while he checked out our track. The inspection was short-lived as he said, *"Sir, we might be a little screwed."* A little screwed, I thought! You think? We are in enemy territory, and our vehicle is not moving! Fortunately, everyone else had come to a stop, so our stop was not so obvious. It just so happened that a wrecker truck (tow-truck) happened by, and SFC P knew the sergeant. The wrecker driver jumped out, looked under the hood, and exclaimed,

"Sarge, I think you guys might be fucked."

SFC P asked, *"What the hell does that mean, specialist?"*

The young Soldier chose the following words very carefully.

"Sergeant, I think you blew a gasket." His boss then said,
"Oh yeah, sarge, if that's it, you guys are fucked. The best we can do is hook you up and tow you."

My mind began to race on how many ways I would get my ass chewed and be blamed for something we had no control over. Worse yet, I wondered what my kids would ask me in 20 years.

"Daddy, what did you do in the war?" my answer would be,

The Iraq I Knew…

"I rode in the back of my tracked vehicle while it was being towed across Iraq."

Oh, the shame of it all! And our pucker factors increased by 10 because we were sitting ducks. Now, for the worst part: Reporting this to the S3, who would report it to the Old Man. We still had radio communications so I could do my job, but it was from the back of a towed vehicle. Just writing it sounds like a Saturday Night Live (SNL) skit. Things became much more tolerable for me as we were hooked up and moving.

My Name Is Gumby, DAMN IT!

Sitting securely at the back of the track, it felt like we could feel every bump as if there were bumps in the sand. We inched slowly towards the border as the reports came in from other units. As I mentioned, I remained on our battalion and DIVARTY radio networks. I had the brigade radio net on the Aux, an auxiliary device that only receives without the means to transmit. The battalion and brigade nets were where the action was, but DIVARTY controlled the Q36 and Q37 counterbattery radars. If Iraqi artillery fired toward friendly units within the scope of the radars, it would alert the radar operators, who would inform DIVARTY with the pertinent information. DIVARTY would notify the impacted unit. This sounds complicated, but it takes less than a minute because time is not a luxury in combat.

It is incredible how fast a towed vehicle can move. I didn't feel so bad because we were doing the same things as before, except someone else was driving! Hey, we joked, 'We're being chauffeured across Iraq.' The jokes ended when we stopped again, one of many stops, and SFC P said, *"Hey, sir, the S3 just pulled up."* That seemed odd, so I climbed up into the commander's hatch with SFC P when the S3 said,

"Hey '2', grab your shit, you're going with me."

I thought: *Oh no! Court-martial and firing squad for dereliction of duty!'* I grabbed my rucksack, maps, and everything else I needed from inside the track. As SFC P began to untie my bags from on top of the vehicle, the S3 hollered,

"Hey, you don't need all that shit. Just bring your go-bag, your maps, and your S2 shit, whatever that is."

A go-bag is what the Army refers to as our 'carry-on', where we keep our most personal and precious items, such as letters from home, photos, a camera, a cassette player, etc.

As I entered the S3 vehicle behind his driver, I asked,

"Sir, what's going on?"

"S2', my boy, you're about to earn your damn pay, that's what!"

Bend Over, Gumby

I was still puzzled by the S3's comments, and it must have shown on my face. He sensed my confusion and continued.

"Boy 2, the Old Man must really like you. He made sure your ass would be in the fight."

I must have looked dumbfounded, so he resumed.

"'2', did you actually believe you would sit out the war in the back of a broke dick vehicle? Hell no! The Old Man wants you where he can talk to his S2, so you're stuck with me. Or I'm stuck with you, or whatever."

All I could think of was, 'Here we go again; I'm getting the bum's rush.' Then, he added insult to injury by saying,

"Boy '2', you must feel like Gumby."

I vaguely knew that Gumby was an Eddie Murphy character from SNL. Truth be told, I had never seen a complete episode of SNL. Apparently, my comedy palette is more refined today. Eventually, I replied, *"Yes, sir,"* but I thought,

'Bend over, Gumby.'

Writer Oscar Wilde wrote, *"No good deed goes unpunished."*

The only thing I could think of was, *"I need to stop being so damn good! It's not getting me anywhere!'* But the day was still young.

Cruising The Battlefield in Style, **NOT!**

I felt like I was back at square one. I began this war in an excellent, cushy, rearward-oriented job. The S4 job was not easy, but at least I knew exactly what I was doing and had little chance of being shot. Then, I took over the S2 section somewhat against my will, but it was better than being in a thin-skinned deuce-in-a-half or an HMMWV because the 577 was at least metal. Now, back in an HMMWV bouncing around the battlefield. The S3 ensured that all operations went smoothly and troubleshot any issues. The Old Man was already forward with the Brigade Commander and radioed back what he saw.

"Hey, '3', do you have the '2' yet?" said the Old Man.

"Yes, Sir. He's right here listening," said the S3.

"Good. You both listen up. We're not seeing much up here, but that doesn't mean nothing is here. '2', you ensure to keep up with us and cue those radars at the first sign of enemy artillery," said the Old Man.

"Roger, sir," I said.

"Sir," I said to the S3, *"Can you put your aux on the brigade operations channel?"* I had a feeling of what was coming next.

"What the fuck S2?" said the S3. *"Do you think this is your intel vehicle?"*

"No, sir," I replied. *"But that's the only way we can hear the battle, and I can know to cue the radars. You are already on the battalion and DIVARTY radio frequencies, and I just need to hear the battle, not transmit."*

The S3 sighed, shook his head, and turned the aux to the brigade operations radio frequency. As we crisscrossed the battlefield to avoid being acquired by an RPG, the Batteries began reporting their ammunition statuses to the S3, who, in turn, gave the ammo request to the Service Battery Commander. The ammo HEMMTs were the same ones we discussed earlier, but they were now full of ammo and returning to the Ammunition Supply Depots (ASP) to draw more. The Batteries were continuously firing, and the ammo HEMMTs were 'hauling ass' to resupply them.

A Different Perspective

Sitting in the back of an HMMWV gave me an entirely different perspective of the battlefield. Before, I was *told* about the battlefield, but now I <u>see it</u> for myself. I was in awe as I watched the tanks speeding across the sand to their destinations. Even as a Fire Support Team Leader (FIST), I did not command the vehicle; I rode in the back, looking at a map, listening to the radio, and processing calls for fire.

Occasionally, I commanded the FIST-V—Fire Support Team Vehicle through the often muddy or dusty training fields of Fort Hood, TX, and maybe once at the National Training Center (NTC), but nothing like this. I also wondered what was going on with my vehicle and my guys. I'm sure they did not want to sit out the war like this. What mattered most as we resumed our race across the desert was engaging the first Iraqi units the tank commanders encountered or responding to any calls for artillery fire. The photo below shows what it was like to fly across an open desert without a care in the world, NOT! If you look closely, you can see vehicles in the distance. When I expanded the photo, it looked like US vehicles based on the shapes and alignment. I was right because I am here to write about it.

Photo 56. M1A1 Abrams tanks racing across the Iraqi desert.

As I listened to the radio, I knew that we had not engaged any Iraqi units yet, and as the day wore on, the tanks and BFVs poured through the crossing at the berm and into Iraq. As the night sky emerged, we were ordered to keep moving into Iraq to keep up with our brigade. As the radio chatter was heating up, the S3 said,

"This is it. We're crossing into Iraq."

I think I said a few 'Mother Marys' and 'Saints preserve us,' and I'm not even Catholic! The old cliché, however, holds:

There are no atheists in foxholes.

Is that because atheists declare that they are not required to deploy as soon as the balloon goes up? The term "conscientious objector" came to mind, but that is someone who refuses to deploy on religious grounds. Anywho, we were there, and I was praying and following my father's advice from a letter he sent to me on November 28, 1990:

"So, you do the Best you can and don't Forgit to Pray."

After I remembered that, the rest didn't matter. We followed the Batteries across the berm and kept traveling until we reached our destination. We had our full complement of NVGs (Night Vision Goggles) and the few LORAN systems the Battery Commanders and Command Group had, so we knew where we were going. Once the Batteries were emplaced, calls for fire came in, and the Batteries began firing. Night fire is always a sight, especially if you are an artilleryman. There is no fear, just the awe of seeing your craft in action. That allowed me to contact my crew and learn that they were still hooked up to the tow truck but safe.

And that was just **Day One** of the ground offensive.

Chapter 15:
"Time – It's All Relative"

Time is relative when you're fighting the good fight.

With the first day of battle behind us, there was a certain amount of calm in the air, at least for me. Still stuck in the S3 vehicle, hoping that my vehicle could be repaired, I gained a better appreciation of what we were doing. I knew the brigade was poised to attack if ordered but did not know the immediate game plan. My crew was still being towed; we were all refueled, refitted, and ready to fight. However, it was night, and that would likely not have occurred. We would need to wait until dawn to determine our next moves.

ACT II, DAY TWO – FEB 25, 1991:
Where the Hell Are We?

EPISODE 15

No matter how much noise occurred, I know that I fell asleep at some point. We discovered during this first Middle Eastern tour that there is little movement at night. Because of this and being stationary, we stopped several kilometers behind the firing lines. When I woke from one of my snoozes, the sun was coming up, and I thought to myself,

'Where the hell are we?'

As I mentioned, our job was to execute a feint up the Wadi Al Batin to draw most Iraqi forces into that area. The XVIII Airborne and VII Armored Corps entered Iraq from the middle to the far west and headed towards Baghdad. As I shook off the fog, I realized that we were somewhere in the wadi, and the best place for a thin-skinned HMMWV.

Being in a wadi was a strange, eerie feeling because all I could see was sand around and above us. I thought to myself,

'Lord, please let us get the heck out of here!'

If you have ever watched The Ten Commandments, when Moses parted the Red Sea and walls of water stood an unknown number of feet tall on each side, that is what came to my mind. I wondered how the heck all that sand stayed in place, but I guess over the years it became compacted, almost petrified, and didn't move.

I likely ate an MRE before our 0800 SP. As we began to move, I felt mixed emotions after we emerged from the wadi. I saw the majestic fighting force known as the 2nd Blackjack Brigade. M1A1 Abrams tanks, Bradley Fighting Vehicles, and our 24 howitzers, all flying across the desert. My amazement would soon turn to surprise, then horror, as I saw what awaited us.

IT WAS TRUE: There Were Fire Trenches Everywhere!

We suddenly stopped as we moved forward 5, 10, 15, and 20 kilometers. I tried to navigate and find landmarks on this barren, waterless beach, so my focus was not always forward. I knew something was up when the S3 said,

"Holy shit! '2', do you see this?"

In front of the brigade was a maze of trenches, with what appeared to be Iraqis inside. This must have been their last line of defense before engaging us. We saw them light the trenches. First one trench, then another, then another, and then I said,

"What the fuck are they doing?"

The S3 and his driver looked at me because I was not known for cursing. I shouted, *"Sir, look at what they're doing!!"* As he and the driver looked, all three of us began screaming,

"Get out of there!

"No, you dumb fucks! Stop!!

"NOOOOO!!!!"

The Iraq I Knew...

For unknown reasons, an Iraqi in the trench on the right lit the oil while the squad of men were inside. Usually, they stood in the corridor between trenches, lit the oil, and ran like heck towards their side and out of the trenches. They may even have had a vehicle in the corridor and jumped in it, but not this crew.

Photo 57. Kuwait Oil fires.

Once the Iraqi Soldiers in the trench realized they would be burned alive, they began to jump to try to climb out, but the trenches were dug too deeply. We just looked in horror, and while we did not see them burn, I imagined what had occurred. That sight haunted my dreams for a while after we redeployed and returned right before I retired, almost 25 years later.

This Was Even More Real

We sat in silence for a period. Finally, the S3 broke the silence with,

"Those poor, dumb bastards..."

I just sat there and shook my head. From their frantic efforts to get out of the trench, we knew that was not a sacrifice, just a dumb move. They were lighting the trenches so fast that there was a significant human error. As the fires began to burn, we knew we would be sitting there for a while because they were oil fires, and the oil needed to burn off completely before we could move forward.

Now, fast forward to 1996, when I was notified that I may have been exposed to toxins in Iraq. Who knows what was in that smoke besides oil, and how far the particulate matter floated? We were not masked because we believed we were far enough back, but what if we were not? That is just one example of why the PACT Act was approved in 2022 and is so important.

The S3 decided that because we would be there for hours, we should set up the TOC when suddenly we heard the unmistakable sound of artillery being fired, and we weren't doing the firing! From across the trenches, the Iraqis were firing artillery at us, never hitting us but close enough! This allowed me the opportunity to grab the DIVARTY radio mic and holler,

"CUE RADARS!"

I gave them our location, and the radars did the rest. We were allocated a platoon of MLRS, and once they received the mission, it was all over for the Iraqi artillery, except for the crying. Be that as it may, the S3 told us to stop and move the TOC back about five kilometers. He said it was,

"Just to be on the safe side, in case they get lucky!"

Photo 58. AN/Q36 Radar.

As the S3 side of the TOC began to set up, I saw a 577 coming toward us like it was coming home because it was: It was the S2 Track! With SFC P in the commander's hatch, I shouted, *"Hey, I thought you guys were still broken down?"* SFC P replied, *"Sir, it's a long story, but a good one. I'll tell you what happened after we set up."* Even the S3 seemed happy, probably because this meant he was no longer my taxi. One item I need to point out is that military vehicles do not have air conditioning. Even worse, tracked vehicles have no windows, so it feels like you are baking. As we waited, we received a 'Change of Mission' order, and I was back in my old vehicle.

Photo 59. The Battalion S2 track and crew, January 1991, somewhere in Iraq. Photo provided by the Author.

Moving Back but Not Retreating

Our mission change was to move back to Saudi Arabia to await further instructions. Looking at the carnage on the battlefield, it appeared that the feint had worked, and as I mentioned before, the cavalry goes where we are needed. Out of nowhere, the Old Man showed up, staggered into the TOC, and hollered, '**2**', because the S3 was already in place. The Old Man looked worn out as he attempted to give us a situation update. When the Old Man almost fell over, we sat him down and got him water to catch his breath. There were portions of what he told us that he asked us not to disclose, and I will not do so here, even over 30 years later.

He could only disclose that we were pulling back into Saudi Arabia, changing our mission, and were likely to engage one of the Iraqi divisions to either the north or the west. We recommended he sleep until the brigade began to move out.

The Iraq I Knew…

Because we were in Iraq, and there were always fragments and bypassed forces on the battlefield, we were required to fire a smoke screen to obscure our repositioning back into Saudi Arabia. Bypassed forces are platoons or smaller that the armor and infantry units might not engage because they were considered too small. That also meant that while the Batteries fired and the tanks and BFVs moved out, we needed to stay in place until they passed us by. Fortunately, at least one tank platoon usually secures the brigade's rear to engage any enemy that might appear. As the sun set and we continued packing, we knew it would be another long night.

Another Long Night

Unfortunately, a war in a direct, immature theater of action is not a 9-5 job. After we finally moved out of Iraq, it was about 2100 or 2200 hours. We needed to refuel, refit, and move even further back—about another 40-50 kilometers—to a staging area. SSG K was in the Commander's Hatch so SFC P could get some sleep. When you are tired, you can sleep anywhere. On the floor or in a seat, sleeping is sleeping. I was glad to be back with my crew and in my 'assigned' seat and snoozed a little myself.

This next road march took another 2-3 hours, based on where you were in the convoy. We arrived at our position around midnight or 0100 on February 26, 1991. Setup, security, and the day shift went to bed for real. We simply placed our cots outside the tracked vehicle because setting up tents was impractical. I did not know if I was on the dayshift, nightshift, or 24-7, but my eyelids told me to shut down. After checking for new INTREPs with new enemy battle damage assessments (EBDA), and to see if the Old Man needed me, I hit the rack myself for the new mission.

ACT III, DAY THREE – FEB 26, 1991: SEND IN THE FIRST TEAM!

Out of habit, I popped awake at 0600ish, cleaned up, and reported to the TOC. I left my 'S6' Record Book with my team when I moved forward with the S3 and used my 'pocket' S6 book. That was necessary because we received numerous reports, requests, and updates during the battle that were not about the enemy. Nearly every hour, depending on how fierce the fight was, I would switch from the O & I – Operations and Intelligence net to the Logistics and Supply net to provide updates. Our 'battalion supply trains' did not accompany us into the battle because the HEMMT tankers and supply trucks were too vulnerable to enemy fire from RPGs and AT-4s. When someone did not call them, they called us for updates.

We maintained a standard Army log (DA 1594), the Daily Staff Journal, or the Duty Officer's Log to provide you with a sense of what we reported and how we tracked it. The logs covered each day from 0001 to 2359. We included all the radio reports we received and sent. However, the battle only sometimes allowed time for paperwork, so we used my S6 Record Book to record the initial reports and then transferred the information to the Army log. The main reason for this was that we could be called to provide an enemy update at any moment, and it was easier to grab the book than the log. An example from my book is:

From February 25, 1991:

1725 – Such-and-Such unit reports BMPs and tanks smoking at grid xxxxxx.

1730 – Such-and-Such unit reports T-55 dummy position at grid xxxxxx near PL XXXX. (PL is Phase Line)

1740 – Such-and-Such unit reports Bunker complex at grid xxxxxx.
Such-and-Such unit reports friendlies at grid xxxxxx, M577 and…
Such-and-Such unit reports, ammo cache at grid xxxxxx.

1804 – 54 vehicles with Republican Guard markings.
Muzzle flashes, vicinity grid xxxxxx.

1805 – Vic grid xxxxxx, dismounts.

Those were just a few of the entries in the book from the prior day. Today might prove even more interesting as we received the following classified order:

> *"Send in the First Team."*
> *"Destroy the Republican Guard."*
> *"Let's go home."*
> **Schwarzkopf**

We really enjoyed the last part, *"Let's go home."* However, we needed to complete parts one and two before we could get to part three.

Go West, Young Men...

We were ordered to move west into the 1st Infantry Division (1st ID) AO. The 1st Infantry Division was known as 'The Big Red One' for its exploits in World War II, so we had to be on our game to follow them. Oddly enough, we had the morning O&I briefing for the first time in days. The Old Man wanted to see everyone, share his insights, and ensure the Battery Commanders knew what we were facing. We were scheduled to begin moving out at 0900, and after the briefing, we started tearing down at 0800. After three months of moving twice a day, we were experts at tearing down and setting back up because we each had our assigned tasks.

As the brigade began to assemble, it appeared a spear was forming, with the operations centers positioned toward the middle to ensure we had the tanks' cover. It takes a few hours for a brigade with over 4-5,000 Soldiers to get into position, so our departure time was 1200. On a previous map, the Breech Zone for VII Corps was outlined. The seven to nine hours we traveled were uneventful, and we took full advantage of napping because we knew it would be another long night. Once we arrived at the breech sites, we needed to refuel using a ROM – Refuel on the Move. After refueling was completed, SFC P and SSG K changed shifts and shared some interesting information.

SSG K said we would be led to a 'passage lane' to move towards Iraq. To avoid mines, booby traps, and other obstacles, and to ensure that no fratricide occurred, this was necessary. A fratricide is, in simple terms, friendly fire – when friendly units confuse another friendly unit for the enemy. It reminded me of a 'passage of lines' maneuver, explained in greater detail later in the book. Our journey was slow because we were essentially in a single file. This was probably the best formation for us, considering it was dark, we had two days of fighting behind us, and the battlefield was likely torn up. I recall beginning our travel, but the next sound I heard was SSG K's, *"We're here."*

ACT IV, DAY FOUR – FEB 27, 1991:
Taking It to The Enemy

We did a lot of traveling and sleeping because we were on the road so much. We had gone at least 20 kilometers to reach our destination just past the 1st ID breach point. Everyone who needed to be awake was awake as we assumed attack formation. Although I knew what was supposed to occur, I could not see it because I was not in the commander's hatch, and it was still night, likely around 0300 or 0400. We refueled again because we needed to be ready for anything when we started around dawn. I recall the TOC vehicles parked side by side so we could talk, confer, and exchange information as needed.

I needed a little time to get my bearings, find out where the friendly units were, and estimate where the enemy units might be. According to my notes, previous reporting indicated that the Tawakalna Mechanized Division - a Republican Guard unit- was in our vicinity. JSTARS – Joint Surveillance and Target Attack

Radar System states that the 17th, 10th, and 6th Iraqi Armored Divisions were heading north. They were likely to take up defensive positions around Al Basrah, but that was just surmising.

At dawn, we began moving to our next objective, only to find the 2nd Armored Cavalry Regiment (ACR) engaged with the Tawakalna Mechanized Division, confirming the intel was correct. As they fought, we waited to avoid friendly-fire incidents, as previously mentioned. According to the report, the ACR was taking care of business, and soon, we were allowed to keep moving north. The only problems that came to mind were bypassing enemy forces and running out of fuel. When we refueled, we also picked up MREs and water if needed, so we had plenty of food, but fuel was constantly being expended. We were running on fumes by the time we reached the division objective title OBJ Horse (after the horse on the 1st Cavalry Division patch). Fortunately, another part of the cavalry showed up, and we refueled and took a short breath.

Time To Get It Done!

Fueled, fed, and informed, we continued our march to engage and destroy whatever we were told. Although I could not see what was happening, based on what I heard on the radio, not much was happening. SFC P was back on duty, and I asked,

"Hey, what's going on? SFC P replied,

"Not a damn thing, Sir. Just a lot of Iraqi vehicles shot-to-shit."

As we continued traveling, reports were coming in about the enemy situation. The Tawakalna Mech and Iraqi 12th AD were reported as combat ineffective; the Hammurabi and Madina Divisions were heading north, and the Al Faw Division was somewhere in the mix. In my mind, I wondered where the Nebuchadnezzar and Adnan Divisions might be intact and lethal because they were part of the Republican Guard. With nothing else to do but listen and travel, I began to record enemy Battle Damage Assessments (EBDA).

Table 2. Enemy Battle Damage Assessment. Author notes.

Unit	Location	Vehicles	Time
26 ID	NTxxxx	4 tanks, 2U/I, 4 ATRY pieces	1340
25 ID	PTxxxx	4 tanks, 2U/I	"
16 ID	PTxxxx	4 vehicles	"

Once we stopped, I believed we were at our objective, but that was no longer necessary. The S3 confirmed what I was tracking: The Iraqi Army was getting beaten down on every front and moving north, likely towards Baghdad. We all thought, 'Baghdad, yeah! Let's put an end to this.' Unfortunately, our thoughts were not the powers that be's thoughts, so we began setting up again. Once we were set up and doing business, the first inkling of a ceasefire was reported.

Ceasefire? Did someone say ceasefire? Really? We were elated, but it was unofficial. Because we would be there for a minute, we put up the tent, and I went to bed. Little did I know that I would wake up to the loudest alarm clock in my life.

Photo 60. Multiple Launch Rocket System, M270

PART IV
After the Storm...I Think FEB 28, 1991

Someone must always clean up after the storm.

I could not believe a tentative ceasefire had been declared, but I went to bed anyway. I am certain it sounds odd, me sleeping all the time but, combat operations are not on a regular schedule. We needed to be agile to advance against the enemy when we had the initiative. You may be sitting for two hours, traveling for three hours, stationery for an hour, then engaged in battle tracking for the next four hours, so you have an irregular sleep cycle. Knowing when to shut down was a critical skill that would serve me well as I navigated an uncertain future.

Because the ceasefire was tentative, hostilities could resume at any time, so we needed to rest while we could. Yes, we still maintained a perimeter, had guards at our entry and exit points, and crew-served weapons placed in overwatch at our vulnerable positions, covering road networks. That was the tricky part about being consolidated: All the necessary duties that junior enlisted were required to perform. We had a private and a specialist, and the only break we received as a section was that they were both not on detail duty at the same time. Detailed duties are the guard duties, kitchen duties, burn details, etc., that were shared within the headquarters battery.

Although we were all dragging, everyone else was too excited to care about sleep, rest, or relaxation. Had the reporting indicated a permanent ceasefire, I would likely have been dancing in the sand myself. I went to bed thinking I would get at least 40 winks, but by this point, I should have known better.

Chapter 16:
"It's Not Over, Till It's Over"

It's not over until the resilient soprano sings.

SWOOSH! SWOOSH, SWOOSH, SWOOSH were the unmistakable sounds of missiles firing from an MLRS (Last photo, 60, Episode 15). When I went to bed a few hours earlier, a cease fire was mentioned. We were elated, but I was tired and needed some well-deserved rest, so I went to my tent for a bit of R&R (Rest and Relaxation). The sound startled me awake, and it was not long before my lieutenant knocked on the tent flap, and I told him to enter, and he said,

E
P
I
S
O
D
E

16

"Sir, you're wanted in the TOC."

What a shocker! A ceasefire was mentioned four or five hours earlier, but now we are firing rockets. Who could sleep through that? As I put on my battle-rattle and observed the time as 0400, I stumbled into the S2 portion of the TOC and said, *"SITREP"* (Situation Report). SFC P began with,

"Sir, what the hell! We don't really know what's going on, but we received some fire missions from DIVARTY, and we're obligated to comply," he said.

I groggily said, *"Okay. I thought we were in a ceasefire?"*

"Yes sir, you thought right," said SFC P. *"Nothing was rescinded since you went to bed, but it seems like we're still at war."*

SSG K then chimed in, *"Sir, **you** know there's a ceasefire, **SFC P** knows there's a ceasefire, and **I** know there's a ceasefire, but do the **<u>Iraqi's</u>** know it's a ceasefire?"*

The Iraq I Knew…

SSG K had presented an interesting quandary: Did all the Iraqi Army know there was a ceasefire? One thing I learned over the ensuing years was the uniqueness of our Army.

Was This for Real?

It was still 0-dark-thirty, and I was caffeine-deficient. No matter how horrible the canteen coffee was, it was still better than nothing. Canteen coffee is the coffee you fixed in your canteen cup from the instant coffee packets in the MREs. Now, TOC coffee could be a considerable step up, depending on who fixed it, and mess hall coffee was generally the best. Please don't ask me any of the usual questions like, *'What brand of coffee was it?'* *'Did you guys have Starbucks?'* *'Did you have flavored K-cups?'* The answers are **"*I don't know, No, and No*."** This was 1991, and the last two had not yet been invented.

I got on the radio and started the 'You, this is me…' game to try and figure out what was going on. The S3 was doing the same thing, and we wanted to have answers before the Old Man woke up. This also included using the 'Bat-phones' to make the appropriate calls. The three senior officers had phones in their vehicles, and because most of us had no idea how they worked, we just called them the 'Bat-phones.' Sometimes, we non-caped crusaders were even allowed to use them.

It was the crack of dawn when we discovered that the ceasefire was scheduled for 0800 Eastern Standard Time (EST). For us, that would be high noon – 12 pm because of the time difference. Until then, who knows what was going to happen? We were still asking questions when we heard the S3 Major shout,

"You gotta be shittin' me?!?"

For the uninitiated, that means, 'You gotta be kidding' or 'Is this for real?'

We military folk have a colorful way of expressing America's slang. About that time, the Old Man and CSM walked in and asked, *"What's all the hollering about S3?*

"Sir," he said, *"They want us to do a passage of lines with the retreating Iraqi's."*

I thought, 'Is the S3 popping doxycycline or something?' We were all puzzled because a passage of lines is when one unit passes through another unit's position to move into or out of enemy contact. Why in the world would we be doing that with the enemy?

The Old Man was even more befuddled.

"'3', my head already hurts. Start from the beginning," he said.

By this time, the Battery Commanders were also arriving.

"Alright everybody," began the S3. *"Get over here so I don't have to repeat this."* As we gathered around, this sounded like a science fiction tale.

"Because we have advanced so far into Iraq, and there are so many Iraqi troops behind us," he said, and paused because he seemed angry. *"And there is a ceasefire pending,"* he began again. *"They want us to allow all Iraqi troops to return to Baghdad using the quickest route possible, and that is driving right through us!"*

It was so quiet; you could have heard a gnat sneeze. We looked back and forth at each other, shaking our heads in disbelief. You must remember that we were combat arms officers, steeped in friendly and enemy tactics, so this was unheard of to our knowledge. This was just the appetizer, however, to the main course of information.

But It Got Better…

As we all stood there, our mouths gaping open, the S3 continued.

"On the howitzers, the gun tubes are supposed to be straight up in the air, and for the tanks, the gun tubes are over the back deck. They (the Iraqis) wanted us to take down our machine guns, but someone probably said, 'HELL NO!' We just turn the machine guns around, so they don't point at the enemy as they drive by."

My first thought was, 'So, why don't we just give them a piggyback ride home?' but I thought better of it. The Old Man asked, *"So when is this supposed to happen?"*

"Within the next 6-12 hours, Sir," said the S3. *"We need to notify everybody now, get those tubes in the air, and clear the roadway. We don't want any equipment even close to the road."* The Battery Commanders began to voice their concerns:

"How long do we need to have those tubes in the air?"

"What time is this supposed to happen?"

"How many Iraqi units are coming through?"

"Why the hell are we letting them go home?"

"Pipe down," said the S3. *"We didn't make these decisions; the higher mucky mucks did. We just follow orders."*

The next hour or two was spent moving, shifting, and clearing equipment from near the road. And what was the S2 section doing? We were trying to figure out what enemy units to expect based on where we were on the battlefield. As the morning drew on, we were told an Iraqi tank unit was coming through at 1300 hours. The Old Man instructed everyone to remain awake and alert, even if they had been on the night shift. What we didn't need was a mishap because someone went to take a piss, saw an Iraqi tank, and began firing.

As we anxiously waited for 1300 to arrive, life went on. Lunch was served early so everyone could be at their post at 1300 hours. Every howitzer crew was manned with the crew chief standing in the turret hatch, and a Soldier by the machine guns. Just because we had to let them drive through us did not mean we needed to look weak. So, 1300 hours came and went, as did 1330, 1400, 1430, and 1500 hours. As the time ticked down, antsy-ness turned to curiosity, then to agitation and anger. Even I began to think that the Iraqi's were going to be a no-show and that maybe this was a hoax to keep us off guard.

Sometime between 1530 and 1600 hours, we saw large dust clouds in the distance. This might be it, so we made sure everyone was awake and alert. As the clouds moved closer, we could hear a slight rumble. As the dust clouds moved closer and rumbling shook the ground, we could see the Russian T-72 tanks with something flapping in the breeze. We all put on our goggles and dust rags and made sure our weapons were ready, just in case. We were also ordered not to take pictures because we were in combat, not a photoshoot, and we didn't want cameras mistaken for weapons, or all hell to break loose.

As the Iraqi tanks roared through our position, the flapping we saw earlier was Iraqi flags tied to antennas. Those tanks were moving so fast that you would have thought they were being chased. About 20 tanks or a regiment sped through at maximum speed. The wait was longer than the event itself, and the S3 called DIVARTY HQ to ask whether any other Iraqi units were expected. Once we received the 'negative', we were allowed to stand down and resume normal operations. The nightshift personnel tried to catch a couple of hours' sleep, the cooks began preparing dinner, and we all started preparing for our next mission. The next few days, however, would be anything but normal.

The Undefeated

After the ceasefire was official, there was policing of the battlefield of enemy ammunition, equipment, enemy prisoners of war (EPW), and enemy Killed in Action (EKIA), as appropriate. During the next few days, there were sweep-in-zone missions, helicopter recons, and the scariest occurrence of all: Iraqi soldiers who refused defeat. Friendly units were reporting shots fired that resulted in outright battles for one of two reasons: First, some Iraqi units did not get the memo about the ceasefire. With the extensive bombing campaign that occurred as part of the 'air war', once the 'ground war' began, many Iraqi units were likely cut off from communications. I referred to those units as ***The Unacknowledged.***

Second, some units received the ceasefire order but *refused* to accept it. The reader must recall that we were no longer in Saudi Arabia but in Iraq. Recall how you may have felt some 10 years later when the U.S. was attacked on 9-11, and you were fighting mad after the initial shock. Now, place yourself in the position of an Iraqi soldier in combat, in *your* country, and you are being told to stand down, ceasefire, and ultimately, quit fighting. Quit fighting is a better posture than 'giving up.' 'Giving up' would mean that we were taking prisoners, but that was not the case. The diplomatic solution was to allow the Iraqi Army to return home. Our job was the liberation of Kuwait, not the occupation of Iraq.

Even with that distinction, to stop fighting in your own country and return to a designated area would be a bitter pill to swallow for any soldier in any Army. Some Iraqi soldiers and units did not care about the semantics or wordplay and were not going to swallow defeat. Hence, they became ***The Undefeated***, whom we would fight until we left Iraq and another day in the future.

All those events coincided, which makes it seem like it was another '*most dangerous portion*' of the very short ground offensive. I know that I have written 'most dangerous' several times, but when I wrote it, that's how it felt at the time. Can you imagine allowing those Iraqi units to conduct a passage of lines through our ranks back to Baghdad, knowing that some enemies were not on board with the ceasefire decision? We were still wrapping our minds around everything that was occurring while preparing to redeploy home, but it made us wonder.

Was This a Cease Fire?

Ceasefire didn't mean the fighting stopped. With everything that was happening, it was hard to believe that this was a ceasefire. Words and phrases mean everything. In World War II, the Allies required the *Unconditional Surrender* of the Axis powers. That meant there was no negotiation and no ceasefire. The Axis forces were taken prisoner, and that was that. There may have been undefeated and unacknowledged units and personnel, but I am sure they did not fare well. Because this was March 1, 1991, and the situation was so volatile, we were also assigned a mission.

Sweeping Without Getting Swept Away

I can attest that the sweep-in-zone missions were dangerous because I was allowed to go on two. Truth in advertising, for me, those missions were less of sweep-in-zone and more like battlefield surveys, which my second one was by helicopter. Walking on the road and looking at the damage that had been inflicted was a sight. Once we were inside an Iraqi tank position, I believe all our curiosities changed because the amount of unexploded ordnance was staggering. Everywhere we looked and possibly stepped, there were rounds of various sizes and calibers. There were rounds still in the bustle racks of some tanks and artillery pieces, although the rest of the vehicle was destroyed. (A bustle rack is what holds the rounds in place.)

The more we surveyed, the less we wanted to be there for fear of stepping on and detonating an unexploded ordinance. Another reason we departed was that we apparently drifted into another unit's zone, and their First Sergeant let us know about it with his team. I recall this because the First Sergeant was carrying a nickel-plated Colt .45 pistol. POWs – Privately Owned Weapons were forbidden to be brought into the country, so I had no idea where that weapon came from. The First Sergeant told us that they had just taken some Iraqi soldiers' prisoners, and the battlefield was full of dug-in fighting positions and underground bunkers.

The bunkers housed everything from massive supplies to offices with furniture for Iraqi officers. We just had to see this for ourselves, so we asked the First Sergeant and his unit to provide security while we explored. This request quickly became a test.

"Sir, what is the first thing you are supposed to do before entering any enemy structure?" said the First Sergeant.

"Check for booby traps before entry and along the way. These are mostly tripwires that could be attached to just about anything: a mine, a grenade, or an automatic weapon. Anything," I said.

Then came the final question: *"Do you guys still want to go in?"*

Well, at that point, we couldn't back down without looking like wimps, so I said, *"Heck yes!"* Fortunately, we had designated who would do what if the time came. The time had come, and we probed for mines at the entrance and found no tripwires. Using our flashlights to illuminate the way entirely, we were amazed at the construction and passed one office that had all the luxuries of an office. A wooden desk larger than the one we used and a leather chair. We had seen enough and made our way out the way we came in. Once we were excited, we noticed an entrance at the other end.

That let us know how long the tunnel was because we could not see to the other end. That meant that at any time, an Iraqi soldier or soldiers could have emerged from one end of those bunkers, surprised us, and could have taken us out. The First Sergeant, however, had sent a team to the other end as soon as we came out to ensure that did not happen. As if that was not harrowing enough, my following battlefield survey had me thinking about my life insurance policy.

Photo 61. This might be my ride for the aerial survey, but it looks more like an Apache helicopter. Photo provided by the Author.

Flying The Unfriendly Skies

I went on an aerial survey via helicopter. The only thing I honestly recall about that mission was that **The Undefeated** were firing at U.S. helicopters. So, why were we doing this? Likely to be able to visualize the carnage that had occurred in a short period, identify helicopter landing pads, and see if there were Iraqi units and soldiers still scattered across the terrain. There were reports of Iraqi soldiers surrendering to helicopters, which I thought was exaggerated until I saw Iraqi soldiers with arms in the air, waving them and waiting for us to take them captive. What we discovered later was that the reason so many Iraqi soldiers were eager to surrender was that they had not eaten in who knows when, hence, **The Unacknowledged**.

Photo 62. Iraqi Soldiers surrendering to a Kuwait helicopter.

With the enemy supply lines cut to shreds by the air campaign, many units had likely exhausted their food supplies days or weeks earlier. Whether in the air or on the ground, there was always the possibility of being swept away in the confusion of war. What I recall most vividly was returning from that aerial excursion to find that we had seven living Iraqi prisoners with one eKIA because of our unit sweep. As the S2, everything about the enemy fell on me, including EPWs – Enemy Prisoners of War and equipment. What I read in the manuals was interesting, but hardly enough to know how to take people as prisoners.

The DIVARTY S2 told me to,

"Search them (search) just stay away from them (separate), keep them away from each other (segregated), keep everyone else away from them, and make certain they have plenty of water and food. And by the way," he added, *"Unless you or someone in your unit speaks Farsi, Arabic, or both, or the prisoners speak English, don't try to interrogate them.*

Search, separate, and segregate were the standard procedures when dealing with prisoners. Interrogating the Iraqi prisoners was the least of my concerns, as everyone wanted to know how we managed to create an enemy KIA during a ceasefire.

And The Rest of The Story…

Charlie Battery was the capturing unit that had already searched the EPWs, confiscated their weapons, identifications, and any other items on their persons. They had tied them up, segregated them, given them water, placed them in a tent away from the rest of the organization, and posted guards inside and outside. That was the easy part. The hard part was explaining why one EPW died of smoke inhalation.

"Sir," said the First Sergeant, *"We told them in Arabic to come out, but apparently he was the only one who refused to comply."*

"Maybe he did not understand you," I said.

"Sir, if seven others understood, then he probably did too," said the First Sergeant.

"Then why toss in the smoke grenade?" I asked.

The First Sergeant replied, *"I threw in the smoke grenade to coax them out a little quicker. Apparently, he wasn't quick enough. We went in after the smoke cleared and found him."*

This small sample of what happened in our unit likely occurred in any of the hundreds of units operating across Iraq. Many Iraqi soldiers were unaware of the ceasefire; some were defiant about the truce, while others were just plain scared. Then there were the language and cultural barriers, whatever propaganda the Iraqi army was told about the U.S. military, and how they would be treated if they were captured. Add in the tremendous stress of the entire process: preparing for war, waiting for and hoping for a diplomatic solution, constantly being on guard, and then combat itself. This caused tension even before the war began.

This, however, was not the best of circumstances, as we continued to hear about firefights, EPWs being taken, and the cataloguing of enemy equipment. As we began the task of recording the information on the small arms weapons collected –

AR-15s and pistols, this quickly came to an end for two reasons. First, there were too many weapons for my small five-man section to store and safeguard. Second, we were told that weapons were going to be destroyed, with only a few taken back to the U.S. as artifacts and placed in the military museums. Just when we thought the worst was over, that's when the explosions began, and the worst was just beginning.

Photo 63. Captain Randolph holds an M-16A2 and an AK-47 after returning from the sweep-in-zone mission in Iraq. Notice the American flag flying in the background. Photo provided by the author

Chapter 17:
"*MEDIC!!! MEDIC!!! MEDIC!!!*"

Regardless of training, you are never prepared for some things.

T he day began as any other day in the Iraq ceasefire era. We were preparing to go home, and everything seemed to be in place. The days after the ceasefire were a blur because the pace of operations remained blistering, and the events felt very real. It was finally a lazy afternoon, and everyone seemed to be doing their own thing.

Alpha Battery was playing a rousing game of volleyball. The competition was fierce, as no one wanted to lose. We watched for a while, then went back inside. After a time, we heard two things: One that should not have occurred and another that no one wanted to happen. First, we were all startled by an explosion for no reason, since we were in a ceasefire and had cleared our zone. Then suddenly, we heard the one-word screams that were worse than 'incoming':

MEDIC!!! MEDIC!!! MEDIC!!!

It sounded like 1,000 voices were screaming "MEDIC!!!," but only the 20 or 30 Soldiers at the volleyball game. As I called the BSA (Battalion Supply Area) and asked for Doc C, SFC P raced out of the TOC and asked for him, too. I did not have time to explain; we just needed him here, but he was not at the BSA!!! As I quickly turned to run out, Doc C strolled into the TOC.

I directed him toward Alpha Battery as we scrambled to determine what had occurred. SFC P returned and said that a private stepped on a landmine or something. All we could report to higher was the soldier's name – Private (PVT V); what we believed happened – stepped on a mine, and that we had a trauma team on site, but needed an ambulance. Once the ambulance arrived, we saw Doc and his team do their thing, place the Soldier on a gurney, load him into the ambulance, then roar off. We knew if anyone could save him, it was Doc C.

The Worrisome Wait

In my opinion, the next few hours were horrible. All we could do was sit and wait for the BSA's report on PVT V's condition. Doc C, our Battalion Surgeon, showed up just before we deployed. He was an Army Reservist, affectionately known back then as a Weekend Warrior. In civilian life, he was an Emergency Room surgeon. When we asked if he was ordered to active duty, his answer shocked and impressed us all:

"No, I volunteered. I'm in the emergency room 5-6 nights a week, seeing what we do to each other. I knew where I could help the most, so I volunteered."

Laid-back and easygoing, Doc C had a great sense of humor and took everything in stride. Our chief medic may have felt a little something when Doc showed up, but before we deployed, all the medics sang his praises. We still believed that if anyone could save PVT V, Doc C could.

The Awful Anguish

Five or six hours passed with no word on PVT V, when suddenly Doc C appeared in the TOC. We were all happy to see him and asked how PVT V was doing. Doc said,

"PVT V died an hour ago."

The word "shock" was too mild to describe how we felt. We were stunned, floored, and could not believe our ears. Doc C told us he wanted to come back and tell us in person.

Before everyone arrived, I had time to ask Doc,

"What happened?"

"Burl," said Doc, *"I knew he was dead before we left."* Doc continued,

"He didn't step on a mine but stepped on unexploded ordnance. Unfortunately, the blast blew straight up his body into and underneath his flak jacket."

"What?" I said. *"How did that happen?"* Doc answered,

Because the flak jackets are just that, jackets. They do not cover down to the waist or pelvic area, and the blast and shrapnel blew underneath the coat. The shrapnel then went into the softest place it could: His body. When we opened the jacket, I knew it was a mess, and we'd be lucky if we kept him alive until we made it to the MASH unit.

As I gazed at Doc in disbelief, he began speaking again.

"We never gave up, though, and operated and did all we could, but there was too much internal damage. One of the primary pieces of equipment that was supposed to keep us safe was what caused the most injuries."

As the Command Group and Battery Commanders arrived, the look on Doc's face told it all. The wind had deflated from everyone's sails, and the victory we were enjoying disappeared.

I never told anyone what Doc told me first because he asked me not to. As I barely listened to Doc give his report, and he eventually began telling them what he had just told me, I felt numb. We were genuinely learning about the harshness of war and all it entailed. The heaviness of combat was now squarely on our shoulders, and the weight was crushing. PVT V was the only KIA in our 600+ man artillery battalion. To me, this one death made the war feel like a defeat, but we had to learn something from this experience.

Honoring Our Dead

The Army has something called 'The Missing Man' ceremony. The other services may also have it, but I am uncertain. I had never heard of this nor attended a military funeral, and did not know what to expect. As a lieutenant, I never performed funeral details because of a leg injury. Alpha Battery was the only unit in formation as the rest of us formed a U-shaped posture. The Battalion S1 officer officiated the service, ensuring military protocol was observed.

There was a small table in front of Alpha Battery, with a helmet, a pair of boots, and an empty chair. I do not recall the remarks from the Alpha Battery Commander, the Battalion Commander, or anyone else who spoke. I remember when the Old Man said,

"Call the Roll."

The Battalion S1 officer stepped forward and began calling out for PVT V. Soldiers in the formation answered as he called.

"PVT V." "Here, sir. "PVT V." "Here, sir." "PVT V." "Here, sir."

The Battalion S1 called PVT V's name six times, but on the seventh and subsequent times, everything changed,

"PVT V." PVT V." "PVT V."

There were no answers to the calls for PVT V. This illustrated the Missing Man.

The Alpha Battery Commander commanded,

"BATTERY, ATTENTION. PRESENT, ARMS."

Everyone in and out of the formation came to attention, presented arms, and then Taps began. Taps are the music played via a single trumpet when a service member dies, and they signify the end of service. Echoed taps are even more heart-wrenching. That is when two trumpets play Taps, but one echoes the other. I do not recall if we cried while Taps played, but I did not. I saved my crying up 33 years later as I was writing this portion of the story. The Alpha Battery Commander commanded,

"ORDER ARMS."

I had just witnessed my first 'Missing Man' ceremony, but unfortunately, it would not be my last. PVT V's body was not present because it was being prepared for transport back to the United States. The body would arrive at Dover Air Force Base, Delaware, and then be transported to his hometown in Texas. The body would be greeted at Dover by an Army ceremonial detail, a General Officer, and likely the next of kin. Our memorial ceremony was only the first part of a more extensive, more distressing experience.

Adding Insult to Injury

As with any incident that causes injury in the Army, the Army Safety Center was tasked with tracking the event and, when necessary, conducting investigations. The death of a Soldier in combat was even more urgent. After Doc's report that it was an unexploded ordnance, we could not help but wonder if it was one of ours or one of theirs. Many wondered what we could have done to prevent this tragic situation. Risk management is taken very seriously in the Army, even in combat. Our goal is to accept the least risk possible but accomplish the mission. The investigation results were shocking.

PVT V had stepped on a DPICM bomblet, a submunition of the round. DPICM is a Dual-Purpose Improved Conventional Munition. The rounds consist of over 70 grenade devices referred to as bomblets. Theoretically, the shell should explode, releasing the grenades, and when those grenades hit the target, they would explode. The result was that whatever they hit turned into Swiss cheese from the sheer number of grenades. Although the round deployed the bomblets perfectly, in many cases, there was nothing for them to hit but soft sand, so they never exploded.

Photo 64. Unexploded bomb, origin unknown. Photo provided by the Author.

Photo 65. DPICM grenades.

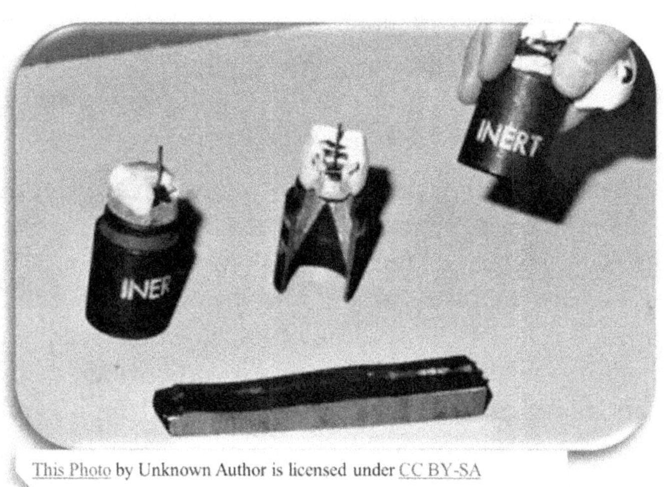

Another reason the bomblets did not explode was because of a 10-20 percent dud rate, regardless of what the grenade hit. If you add the standard dud rate when hitting the sandy surfaces, the dud rate increases to 50 or 60 percent, almost triple. Also, such a great area was covered with the bomblets; it was surmised that they came from either Army MLRS or a US Air Force blanket bombing run. The injury part is that a US artillery round bomblet killed a US artillery Soldier. As our minds began to race, the investigators reminded us that this was not just a problem for our unit but for Iraq and possibly Kuwait as well. We were now facing a new threat.

The Enemy from Within

With this new information, we needed to get the word out to the entire battalion. Some of the measures we took beyond *'Don't touch unexploded ordnance'* were:

- Watch where you walk.
- Stay on known paths if possible.
- Check your immediate area for possible unexploded munitions.
- If you see a small device protruding from the sand, <u>STOP.</u>
- Do a quick scan of your area to ensure nothing else is visible and mark the area with a strip of engineer tape.
- Do not kick or step on anything unidentified because it might explode.

This information needed to be disseminated throughout the theater because those bomblets were likely everywhere. Even with the best dissemination in the world, not everyone gets the message, and some do not heed the message. Most injuries were caused by Soldiers accidentally stepping on something they did not see because it was covered with sand. Others, not knowing what it was, kicked it, and it exploded. Still others decided to tempt fate by picking up the bomblet. As you look at the grenade, it does remind you of a firework on the 4th of July. This bomblet, however, did not need anyone to ignite the fuse, as it were.

The Iraq I Knew...

One story we heard was that a logistics sergeant on a bus headed to a departing helicopter pulled a device out of her bag. A Soldier, seeing the device, had everyone evacuate the bus except for the sergeant. She was told not to move and to wait for EOD, but when she attempted to place the device back in her bag, it exploded. They say she was fortunate only to lose a hand because her flak jacket and whatever was in her bag absorbed the blast.

Those are the stories the public never heard: The intimate details of moving hundreds of kilometers in hours versus days, going without sleep, hot meals, and showers for days, and the firefights with the enemy even after the announced ceasefire. And the sacrifices many Soldiers gave in the last full measure – their life fighting for their country. Those stories are the nonfiction realities many of us dealt with and carried off the battlefield. We were destined to bring those stories home with us, etched in the hidden recesses of our minds. But not before other events added to what would become more suppressed memories.

Chapter 18:
"Uncontrolled Controlled Detonations "And Other Mischief

Even the best-laid plans of mice and men can go south quickly.

It was a couple of days into the beginning of March 1991 when things *seemed* like they were beginning to stabilize as we prepared to redeploy back home to Fort Hood (now, Fort Cavazos), Texas. Although our hearts were heavy from losing a member of our unit, the happiness and excitement of returning home were present. That was until we suddenly heard,

BOOM-BOOM, BOOM-BOOM, BOOM-BOOM!!!

We all ran for our fighting positions, vehicles, or any cover we could get to when we saw the plumes of smoke in the not-too-far distance. None of the chemical alarms went off, and after the ground finally stopped shaking, another set of,

BOOM-BOOM, BOOM-BOOM, BOOM-BOOM!!!

The S3 motioned me to his vehicle and muttered something about *'figuring this crap out.'* We grabbed our rucksacks, put on our battle rattle, i.e., helmet, flak jacket, weapon, gas mask carrier, etc., and hit the road. As we approached from the rear, which looked like a staging area, we saw it was a US Army unit. They stopped fiddling with whatever they were doing when they saw us coming.

"Hey, guys," said the S3. *"What the hell's going on?"*

"Controlled detonations, sir," replied the person in charge.

"Who did you guys tell that you would be blowing shit up?" said the S3.

Looking puzzled, the Soldier asked, *"Tell, sir?"*

"Yeah, tell," said the Major. *"We're about three clicks* (kilometers) *south of here, and those explosions about shook my teeth out."*

A bit more authoritative person came out, who was likely the NCOIC, and said,

"Sir, we were just told to come out here and begin controlled detonations of enemy ammunition. That's all we know."

"Well," said the Major, *"I need you guys to stop until we can sort this out. What's your unit, and who's the commander?"*

As they began to sort out the administration, I looked around at the massive amounts of ammunition. I assumed it had been collected across this battlefield section and stockpiled here for destruction. Little did I know that we were near an Iraqi army ammunition depot.

After the S3 completed his phone call, he said,

"Well, from now on, they will put out an alert of when and where the detonations will occur since they are supposed to be 'controlled detonations.' The next ones are at 1400 hours today."

With that settled, we returned to our unit. We notified everyone of what was happening and what would occur. Once 1400 hours came, we sat outside and watched the explosions. This schedule of 1000-hours and 1400-hours controlled detonations happened for another day or two, when suddenly, we were notified that,

"You have to move your unit."

"What? Move? Are you kidding me?" I heard the S3 officer shout.

"Why?" he asked.

Well, this time, the Explosive Ordinance Detachment (EOD) NCOIC came to us to explain.

"After the last couple of detonations, some of our guys got sick. There may be something in those munitions that we don't know about or recognize," said the NCOIC. *"We recommend moving at least 10 kilometers from the blast site because we will move here once you depart."*

I thought to myself, '*What could be making them sick?*' The only thing it might be is chemical weapons. But (the infamous 'but'), none of our chemical detection alarms activated. Back then, the thought of biological weapons was not something that circulated much. On the side, I asked the NCOIC if they were setting out radiacmeters and he said *"Yes."* They would also be in MOPP 4 when conducting the detonations, but we would not need to be because we would be far enough away. Then he said,

"But it wouldn't hurt to have your radiacmeters on also."

When we got into the Hummer, I let the S3 know this so he could notify the Old Man. The S3 told the Old Man when we returned, and the Old Man wanted this done quietly so as not to cause a panic. He let the XO and the CSM know what was happening and had the '3' alert the Battery Commanders in a low-key manner through a Warning Order. Things were officially set in motion once the S3 had coordinated the movement orders with our higher headquarters. We did not know what this meant at the time, but deep down, we had our suspicions. Meanwhile, we had earned a little rest, relaxation, and a shower. We were beginning to smell, but even showering was not incident-free.

A Nervous R&R

We were stabilized long enough to begin getting a little R&R – Rest and Relaxation, and the process of resuming natural personal hygiene. When we were told we could take showers, we jumped for joy until we were told we had to sign up for them. The Main Support Battalion (MSB) had established a shower point in a large building within the nearby city for all the units in that area, so it was not our private shower. The HHB XO was my battle buddy, and I went with him, recalling that we arrived at the shower point an hour early and were allowed to walk through town. Boy, was that an experience.

As we scanned each side of the street, we were amazed that Iraqi men walked the streets with rifles slung over their shoulders. From a distance, they looked like a rough, tough, ominous squad of rebels with intent on doing us harm. As we approached the five men on our side of the street, the men looked like they were 100 years old, and so did the rifles. Although I never saw this in the cartoon, the rifles looked like something from the Flintstones era. Some were wrapped in tattered cloth at the top, while others did not have a butt on the weapon. Even though the rifles looked archaic, we did not intend to test them and returned to the shower point.

Shortly after arriving back, we heard a tremendous explosion and felt the ground shake as if it were an earthquake. We scrambled for cover and checked to ensure we were all still in one piece. This was odd because we were in a ceasefire and just days away from sending out the advance party for redeployment. After the explosion, the shower area was cleared except for the operators, and we asked if the showers were still open. They said, of course, and we disrobed and jumped right in. The hot water felt excellent, and we hogged it as long as we could. The standard limit was 10 minutes, but we were taking advantage of an empty building. The luxury soon ended as we were asked to move along.

We could see the line begin to reform, and that our 15 minutes of fame were 20 minutes of liquid heaven. We were amazed at how our skin tone changed color after the grime was removed. Yes, we were dirty, grimy, and even stinky from days of only throwing water on our faces and key body parts. Wearing MOPP suits for several weeks caused our skin to become almost as black as the charcoal inside the suits.

Earning My Disinformation Officer Pay

When we returned to the TOC smelling and looking good, almost like rock stars, I heard someone say,

'Hey S2', you missed all the fun. We just got hit with a SCUD. Almost knocked me on my butt."

I responded, *"If a SCUD hit the TOC, you'd all be dead."*

Once I got inside the track, SFC P reported that the intel indicated the Iraqis had, in fact, fired a SCUD missile. In classic SFC P manner, he said,

"Hell, sir, I don't know where the hell they were shooting, but a Patriot missile hit it and knocked the warhead off."

"Oh my God!" I said. *"What if that thing had exploded?"*

We surmised that, based on the tremor the warhead caused when it struck the ground, it may have been at least the SCUD-B 1,000-pound warhead, the largest SCUD warhead, but had the shortest range of only 190 miles. This indicated that the missile was meant to remain in Iraq. That event made me realize a new storm was on the horizon.

Chapter 19:
"A Storm Front Was a Brewin"

The storm is never really over until you get back home.

We were finally headed home! We could not believe it! We had won (or so we thought) the war by beating down the Iraqi Army in conventional Force-on-Force and heavy combat operations. We used Abrams tanks, Bradley fighting vehicles, self-propelled artillery, attack aviation, and battles for air, naval, and land superiority. The US military and coalition forces had deployed all the necessary assets to close with and destroy the enemy. We are planning to go home now! I was about to be rewarded for my administrative acumen in two positions. I was completely unaware of the great blessing coming my way.

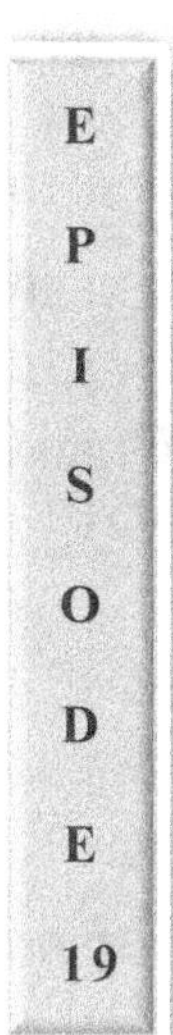

2 + 4 = 6: BEING THE S6

As the plans for the advanced party were discussed, my sources told me my name was mentioned. As you know, I began the deployment as the Battalion S4 – Vice President for Logistics and Supply during Desert Shield. I moved to the Battalion S2 position – Vice President for Intelligence and Security, about two months before Desert Storm began. Little did I know how all of that would work in my favor. Redeployment required the same skills at the battalion level that deployment did: An almost intimate knowledge of the Army supply and transportation system.

I would not claim to be 'all that,' but I got us to Saudi Arabia, right? As we were developing the Advanced Party redeployment plan, we discussed who might be best qualified to help with the redeployment. The conversation took an unexpected turn:

The XO recommended that I return as the Advanced Party S4!

The Old Man showed partiality to the current S4 and asked why he shouldn't redeploy in his current position.

"Sir, the guy was out the door before all this deployment stuff started, and all he has talked about since the ceasefire is getting back home to his 'new' job," said the XO.

Unexpectedly, the S3 said, *"Sir, this guy's probably gonna bolt as soon as he hits the ground in the States. He doesn't have our best interests at heart. At least with the '2' (S2), we know he will be around."*

I was stunned and sat silently, wondering what would occur next. The Old Man asked the CSM (Command Sergeant Major) what he thought.

"Hell, sir," said the CSM, *"I'm surprised he hasn't tried to pop smoke already."*

The XO said again, *"Besides, Sir, he's the contracting officer and must close out all those accounts and settle the books before we release him. I'm sure none of us want to pay off any 'misplaced funds' after he's gone."*

I knew the Old Man didn't like the recommendations of his senior staff and trusted agents, but he placed the unit's needs above his desires.

"Okay, '2'," said the Old Man. *It looks like you're the '4' for the Advanced Party and redeployment, but you're still the S2, making you the S6.*

Everyone chuckled, but I knew one person who would not be laughing: The current S4. After all, this was his job, and he had every right and reason to do it, but that was the million-dollar question—*would he* do his job and redeploy the battalion home?

Today, in 2024, the S6 is an Army position: the Information Technology (IT) officer and section. We just referred to them as commo, short for communications, since we did not need IT. My newfound position also made me the XO of the advanced party because I was the second-highest-ranking person, which meant the XO needed to impart his 'XO' knowledge to me. All of this was placed on hold after what happened next.

The First Storm Front: Making It Work

Although the meeting was a closed session, the word got around about the redeployment decisions. It was mainly the Battery Commanders who made the comments when they saw me:

"Glad to have you back."

"We need you back in the position."

"I feel a whole lot better now."

I felt somewhat guilty, but it was the right decision. My eight months as the S4 officer were extensive compared to the current S4 officer's eight weeks.

I had prepared the battalion for two deployments, executed one deployment, and stabilized the organization logistically before I moved to the S2 position. We also completed several initiatives that provided me with extensive knowledge, experience, and credibility. The moment of truth finally arrived as I ran into the S4.

"I hear you're taking over the S4," said the S4.

"Nope," I said. *"I'm just doing the paperwork on the other end."*

"Well, I'm glad to turn everything over to you," he said.

"That's impossible, "I said," because I won't be here."

The S4 looked puzzled.

I continued, *"I'm not taking over the S4 shop; I'm redeploying with the advanced party to set things up back in the States."*

All the color left the S4's face as his shoulders began to slump, and he dropped whatever was in his hand. He only had one response: *"What?"* in a monotone voice.

"I'm redeploying on the advanced party as the S2 and the S4," I said. *"To get things ready for the battalion to redeploy."*

"That can't be right," said the S4, slightly raising his voice.

"I'm going to talk to the Old Man about this," as he stomped off.

I do not recall speaking with the S4 again after that, even when he returned to the US. I stopped by the old section to let them know I was not returning to the section but just filling in for the advanced party. They were noticeably disappointed but said they understood.

"We got this, sir," said SFC E, *"But it sure would have been nice if you were returning."*

I thought the S4 ignored me as I passed him while walking back to the TOC. 'That's fine,' I thought. He can sulk here in the country while I'm back in the States.' It may sound cold and selfish, but all's fair in love and war. We were making it work, and the XO had no words of wisdom for me.

Before redeploying, I ensured the S2 section was ready and that all intelligence and security matters were handled. And then there was the classified material. It was not like I was a walking safe or could carry a safe around. The classified material was hand-carried during deployment and was required upon returning home. It was a minor inconvenience on my part compared to returning home three to four weeks earlier than planned.

I would never be left alone; I still had my weapon, ammunition, and a reason to use it if necessary. I might need the gun and ammo, since the S4 discovered he wasn't redeploying early. We should have all been happy. Little did we know that the most significant task now was to leave Iraq alive. There was also the matter of the broken vehicle story. In short, SFC P said the Specialist worked on the track whenever we stopped. The crew set up security as the mechanic worked until the track was fixed, about eight hours later.

How A Bronze Medal Was Really Earned

SFC P said there were a few hairy times during the advance, but the mechanic never gave up. I thought he should be rewarded for his bravery under fire. As we recommended awards for everyone, I recommended the mechanic for the Bronze Star.

"That'll never happen," said the XO. *"He's just a specialist, and we have a cap on how many we can award."*

"Then he can have mine, sir," I said.

"S6," said the XO, *"You may not have a Bronze Star to give away. I don't think anyone on the staff will receive Bronze Stars because we are staff and didn't face the same dangers."*

"Speak for yourself, sir," I said. *"I feel like I was in plenty of danger daily."*

"Okay, '2', I mean '6', or whatever you are," said the XO. *"Have the recommendation done before you leave. I'll submit it, and we'll see what happens."*

I could only hope for that since my reward was redeploying early. There are various ways to earn a Bronze Star, but what that mechanic did impressed me. As the days went by quickly, departure day arrived, and we learned that departing Iraq might take a lot of work.

The Second Stormfront

Leaving Iraq was just as tricky as arriving. Once the manifests were completed and we all had tentative departure dates and times, the pressure decreased, and the excitement and anticipation increased. It was the little things most people don't think about that excited us: eating ice cream, period. Have you ever seen or tried to eat ice cream in a desert at 115 degrees? Cooking, driving, and doing things yourself without a convoy or 50 of your closest friends, without carrying weapons or chemical equipment, and without wearing a uniform 24/7. Of course, reuniting with family, seeing friends, and exercising your faith at church were all things I looked forward to. I did not, however, expect to have to walk through a minefield to get to the initial flight.

Bomblets-A-Plenty

There they were: a field of MH-47D Chinook helicopters waiting for us to board them. I was never a big fan of the 'flying buses '; however, those were a sight for sore eyes. The Shit Hook (as most of us referred to it) could seat 30 on webbed seats with all their equipment. We believed we were flying back to the Saudi Arabia port for out-processing before heading home. This was the good part.

As we left the buses and grabbed our bags, we realized the helicopters were on a makeshift airfield in the middle of a dimpled field. We discovered, to our horror, that the dimples on the ground contained the DPICM bomblets we discussed before, and they were everywhere!!! We had to walk across the minefield to reach the helicopters. I used the term 'minefield' because the bomblets were still active and could explode if enough pressure was applied.

We had just lost a Soldier a few days earlier and recalled the horror we felt when Doc said,

"There was nothing I could do."

Often, when Soldiers stepped on the bomblets and wore flak jackets, the upward force sat between the flak jacket and the body. This did not allow the shrapnel to go anywhere but into the body. This thought alone placed an additional mental strain on the process.

Photo 66. MH-47 Chinook Helicopters, likely in Saudi Arabia.
Photo provided by the Author.

This was one of the times that my weight and strength were valuable. Because of the bomblets, we could not drag our bags across the ground for fear of triggering an explosion. We also could not use a cart because the ground was soft sand. Loading our bags onto a vehicle was out because the weight of an HMMWV would indeed cause an explosion. None of those scenarios, however, helped us resolve our problem of getting ourselves and our bags across the field to the helicopter.

Since no one volunteered to go first and I was the senior-ranking person there, I offered to start the process. Trust me, this was not my first thought, but leadership has no luxuries, © 2022, and besides, that was the only way we were getting home. The flight chief said,

"Sir, just step where I stepped and walk where I walked, and you should be fine."

Strategizing in my mind, I knew that I needed to make two trips. I put the duffel bag on my back and cradled the rucksack in front of me. This was the best way to maintain stability and follow the flight chief's instructions. Also, if I had a misstep and triggered an explosion, the duffel and rucksack would shield me from most of the blast.

The thing about leadership is that once one person steps up, people begin to follow. Step by step, foot by foot, inch by inch, I walked across the minefield. Once I got to the plane, I realized we needed baggage handlers, not baggage loaders, and I was just a handler. I made my way back for my second bag and told the chief,

We needed to form a chain and load the bags first, then load the people. Everyone can carry their own carry-on bag, but it's too risky to have everyone carry their own duffel bags. If too many people walk on the same ground back and forth, we can't be fortunate enough not to trigger an explosion.

We required about five handlers and sent two of the larger Soldiers to load their bags. I became the #3 man, carrying my bag to the middle of the field and passing it on. We added two more Soldiers and pushed their bags through, forming the chain. We loaded 25% of the 100 bags, then rotated five new people in as handlers and loaders. I stood on the sidelines as our bags were loaded, and then the Soldiers. I went on the helicopter last, mostly because I was tired and stressed about the ordeal. With 30-35 of us on board and all our bags and equipment strapped down, it was time for the lift off.

The Third Storm Front

Even after the ceasefire, we were still briefed that incoming artillery, small arms fire, and, in our case, RPGs to shoot down helicopters could occur. We were about to fly the unfriendly skies, and I knew that from my previous 'recon' of the battlefield a few days earlier. Fortunately, the Chinook had two 7.62 mm machine guns, one forward of us and one or two to the rear of us. Seeing the machine guns was a welcome relief, as I had never seen a Chinook with weapons. I only recall a little about the flight after sitting down. There were no evasive maneuvers with quick turns and drops, and the machine guns never fired, so it appeared to be a smooth flight except for what we saw.

Seeing What War Looks Like

There were 10 of us in our advanced party; however, we were on different flights. You would think we would all be on the same flight, but the Army often does not work that way. Although I dozed here and there, and we were packed in like sardines, you could get a glimpse out of the small portholes. Imagining the carnage as we raced across the battlefield was one thing, but seeing it from above was quite another. We saw burnt-out enemy vehicle hulks of all types: Tanks, trucks, artillery pieces, etc., were everywhere. The phrase "the battlefield was littered" now made perfect sense.

I am uncertain how long the flight from where we were in Iraq to the port in Saudi Arabia was, but it was great to be leaving Iraq in one piece. Once we crossed the airspace into Saudi Arabia, there was a collective sigh of relief. I do not recall the Iraqi Army ever firing into Saudi Arabia, so there was a feeling of safety. As we continued flying, we could see the port with all the ships and equipment. The odd thing was that we were landing on a helipad at the port. Puzzled, I wondered what new adventure was about to begin.

Welcome To the Bedouin Inn

After we landed, we realized we weren't staying in the warehouse as we had when we arrived. Where were we staying? Four structures looked like apartment buildings, but why would we stay there? We disembarked the helicopter, and shortly after that, a man came out, welcomed us all, and told us to follow him. We did not move. Who was this strange little man, and why should we follow him? Then, a Master Sergeant (E8) came out and said,

"Let's go."

We followed him as he told us, *"Listen, this is where you will stay overnight, so when we unload the rucksacks, grab yours and then follow this gentleman."* As we were asked, we followed the odd little man to an elevator that took us to the second or third floor. There were eight of us, and the man said,

"Pick an apartment. All the apartments have four bedrooms."

As we began to pair off, we asked for the keys.

"Keys?" asked the man. *"Keys for what? There are no locks."*

As we looked at the doors, we discovered he was right. Boy, what a Twilight Zone moment!

Awake In a Dream

As we entered the apartments, we found them beautiful. Fully furnished with a living room, dining room, kitchen, and four bedrooms with two full bathrooms, I said,

"This just feels weird."

Why would we be staying in a place like this? We headed out to the hallway, and Soldiers must think alike because everyone else was also coming out. We walked around to see what was on the floor, peeked into each other's apartments, and suddenly, Mr. Welcome appeared.

"May I help you?" he asked.

"Ya, what's up with this place?" someone replied.

Mr. Welcome then told us the story of what I referred to as **The Bedouin Inn.**

"These apartments were built for the Bedouins to bring everyone out of the desert, but they never occupied them."

Someone asked, *"Why not?"*

"Because they never wanted the apartments in the first place, or to leave the desert," Mr. Welcome answered. He continued.

"There was a grand announcement about the plan, a groundbreaking ceremony, and construction began. After the apartments were completed, enough Bedouin families were visited to fill the buildings. The ribbon-cutting date was announced, and the finest chairs, food, and dignitaries were invited to open the buildings and honor the Bedouins, but not one of them showed up.

Looking puzzled, I'm sure this Rod Serling tale only got stranger and stranger, so I asked, "*Why not?*" Mr. Welcome began speaking again.

As I mentioned, they never asked for apartments. No one consulted them, asked what they wanted, or even if they wanted to leave the desert, so they assumed that the buildings were not really for them. Not one of them ever set foot in these buildings. They probably have never even seen the buildings.

That whole escapade made me feel like I was awake in a dream.

We Should Have Minded Our Own Business

When Soldiers hear about a problem, it is natural for us to want to solve it. As we continued asking questions and wargaming ways to get the Bedouins to the buildings, Mr. Welcome made a startling remark.

"You are the first and only ones to occupy these buildings in the 10 years since they were built."

I felt dizzy just hearing this, but we had not learned our lesson when someone asked, *"Why?"*

"*Because,*" said Mr. Welcome, "*If we had allowed the buildings to be occupied, the Bedouins would have claimed that the buildings were never built for them to begin with."* And it did not end there.

After 10 years of asking, begging, and pleading for them to at least look at the apartments, and they have not, someone figured that they were never going to. Someone else thought that if we allowed the US Soldiers to use them, the Bedouins could never accuse us of insincerity in building them.

"Enjoy your stay," said Mr. Welcome, and he disappeared again.

After hearing all of that, I thought, 'TMI. We should have minded our own business.' We went back to our rooms, and someone came upstairs and told us that the first assembly was at 0800, and that was all she wrote for me. I recall setting my alarm clock for 0600, getting undressed, and falling into slumberland. I had no dinner or shower, and my body and mind did not care because I was so exhausted. It is incredible what real sleep will do for your mind, body, and soul. No, not catnaps or sleeping upright in a vehicle of any kind, but real sleep in a real bed.

The Point of This Point

From mid-October 1990 through early March 1991, that is how we slept for one reason or another. Either sitting up in a moving vehicle, on the floor of a tracked vehicle, on the ground, or in a cot, none of which were comfortable. Now, imagine this happening for each deployment, field exercise, or practice alert over XX years (32 for me), and you will gain some insights into why Soldiers have such bad backs, necks, and sleep disorders. Ask your combat-patched, deployment-laden significant other if this is true, and then treat them to a massage. For all we had endured, the next leg of the journey would be a bus ride to the airport for the flight back home.

Chapter 20:
"The Heroes' Homecoming, Act I"

Was this real?

The flights back to the US were uneventful, especially since we avoided traveling through Egypt again. We were notified when we entered US airspace, and the cheering began! If you were asleep, you woke up, asked what was happening, and joined in the cheering! It was empty when we approached Robert Gray Airfield at Fort Hood, TX. No band, fanfare, or anything else. As we began to deplane, the Rear Detachment Commander, a retiring LTC, greeted us and explained what would happen next. We would turn in our weapons, classified information, COMSEC (Communications Security) information, and whatever else might be pertinent.

There were also preprinted Leave forms (PTO); we had to verify the information and sign on the dotted line. We had all accrued 15 days of Leave (PTO), so we could take up to two weeks! A baggage detail had already been selected, and they went to work, downloading the pallet on which our duffel bags and rucksacks were, and uploading it to a 5-ton truck as we loaded the buses. Once on the bus, we were instructed that we were returning to the gym from which we had deployed and debussed, and that we were to form up. As the NCOIC continued talking, I did not believe anyone was listening.

As soon as we entered Fort Hood proper, the roads were lined with people holding signs with,

WELCOME HOME!!! And WE MISSED YOU!!!

They were also screaming and shouting:

"WELCOME BACK!" "WELCOME HOME HEROES!" and
"WE LOVE YOU!"

Any thought that we were not coming home to a Hero's Welcome disappeared.

King David Would Have Been Proud

King David enjoyed a good parade. Between enjoying the pageantry of what we saw, we heard that we would debus, form two platoons, and march into the gym with our go-bags! In the army, a go-bag is a carry-on bag. As we got to the main road, we old Soldiers began to tear up when we saw yellow ribbons everywhere. The singing trio Tony Orlando and Dawn hit number one in 1973 with the song **Tie a Yellow Ribbon Round the Ole Oak Tree.** The key lyrics in the music were,

"And the whole damn bus was cheering,

"And I can't believe I see…

"A…hundred yellow ribbons round the ole oak tree." [16]

We heard on the radio that the song had a resurgence, but we did not expect this. There were yellow ribbons and bows on every lamp post between the main road and the gym! King David would have been proud of this reception.

Now, the moment of truth. We arrived at the gym, formed up, and heard, *"Right, FACE." "Forward, MARCH."* As we marched in, the crowd was immense and intense, and we attempted to maintain our soldierly bearing: head and eyes forward, with no expression on our faces. The following commands of *"Halt. Left FACE"* faced us towards the stage. Much to my surprise, who should walk out? Our DIVARTY Commander, COL G., was selected to lead the transition from Iraq to Fort Hood.

The Iraq I Knew...

COL G began speaking and was always an excellent, colorful speaker.

"Ladies and gentlemen, I present the heroes of Operations Desert Shield and Desert Storm. We are so proud of them and everything they sacrificed to help keep democracy safe. This is just the first wave, but they are YOUR first wave."

Everyone began clapping and cheering. It was awesome.
Then, COL G gave a command that none of us were ready for,

*"Soldiers of the First Cavalry Division, welcome back, and a job well done. **DISMISSED!**"*

You may not get the distinction if you are a civilian who never served. The command FALL OUT means 'Get back to work.' The command DISMISSED, however, means 'Go home' (or wherever you want). It was like graduation without throwing up your cap into the air. In this mass of people – women, children, husbands, wives, sons, daughters, parents, etc., we all managed to find our families. We greeted them with embraces and a bit of crying, then went outside to try to find our bags!

As I loaded the car and got in, Terry drove us home since I had not driven in six months. Besides, I wanted to enjoy the scenery and the quiet and see what had changed. Seeing reality and that so much had changed was like waking up from a dream, but in this case, a coma. Not only had Fort Hood and Killeen, TX, changed, but so had I, and this was only the beginning.

The Haunted Homecoming, Part I

Jet-lagged, dirty, and tired, I needed a hot shower, some real food, and time to unwind. My memories of what happened that evening are vague at best. I recall lying on the bed and sitting on the couch, but I am sure that I looked like a zombie. I remember waking up the next morning and not knowing where I was. Once I got my bearings, I went to the patio and smoked a cigarette. Startled, I heard something, and it was my wife.

"When did you start smoking?" she asked.

"*Just now*," I said.

The readjustment back to civilization was difficult. I was still jet-lagged, tired, and edgy. Days were likely filled with napping, while nights were filled with jumping out of bed and crouching into a fighting position at the slightest unfamiliar sound.

I had left the fight in Iraq, but the fight had not left me.

We had no debriefing or physical examination when the advanced party arrived home. Whatever state we were experiencing in our minds, bodies, or personal journey was where we were. Little did I know I would experience a similar phenomenon two more times in my career.

I knew then that the jury was still out on whether I would make the Army a career. I had not seen enough of it to make an informed decision. Except for smoking, my other behaviors went on for at least another week or two until I reported back to work, I think. I had not seen my family since July 1990, so we headed to Kansas City, MO. If anyone knew I was acting weird, it would be my parents and siblings. The 11–12-hour drive north was usually a big deal, but with all the riding I had experienced over the previous six months, this trip was a piece of cake. Once we arrived, my parents were glad to see us, but especially me in one piece. My Dad had fought cancer a couple of years earlier. Then, he was diagnosed with a different cancer in 1990, so I was anxious to see how he was doing.

As my mom began chatting with my wife, I spoke with my dad. I only recall some of the particulars of the conversation, other than asking him how he was doing and thanking him for writing to me in Iraq. Because my dad suffered from Parkinson's disease, my mom usually did all the writing, but, in this case, he made an exception. We did not stay long, just 4-5 days, but in that time, I saw all my siblings, some aunts and uncles, a few cousins, and a few neighbors. I did not ask my siblings or parents if I was acting strange; they never told me I was. I was odd anyway, so they probably did not see a difference. My personal hell was only a tiny part of what I would discover and experience. The haunted homecoming had just begun.

$700? THAT'S IT?

After we returned from Kansas City, I'm sure I just wanted to sleep and lounge around. I was still on leave from Iraq when my mid-month pay was deposited. As I sat on the couch watching TV and relaxing, my spouse came over with a grim look on her face.

"What's up?" I asked.

"We have a problem," she said in a foreboding tone.

"Well, what is it?" I said in a slightly raised voice.

She replied in an eerie voice, *"Your mid-month pay is only $700."*

I sat there for a moment, motionless, and then began to chuckle.

"Ya, right," I said. *"You're joking, right?"* I asked.

With a stern look, she replied, *"Do I look like I'm joking?"*

Remember, there was no internet in 1991, so she had to pick up my Leave and Earnings Statement (LES). She handed me the LES, and the amount was $700. There was no explanation because it was a mid-month LES; it was just the identifying information and the amount. I finally involuntarily spoke,

"$700, that's it?" I uttered.

We just looked at each other in silence. After what seemed like eternal quietness, she broke the ice and said,

"Don't look at me. I didn't do anything."

Rolling my eyes, I'm sure, telling me that did not account for where the rest of my paycheck was. I had no idea who to call at Fort Hood, but I did know how we were paid: Through the Defense Finance and Accounting System (DFAS pronounced - D-FAS). That was one telephone number every Soldier was given before we deployed, just in case of any pay problems back home. I took a deep breath and made the call. Once I finally got through to a financial analyst who was verifying my identity, I told her of my plight.

"I just returned from Iraq and received my mid-month pay. It was only $700," I said, trying to be as calm as possible. *"That can't be right,"* I continued.

"Sir, thank you for your service. Can I place you on hold while I investigate?" she said. What else could I say but *"Sure."*

When the financial analyst returned, what seemed like an eternity was only a few minutes. She said, *"Thank you for waiting, sir."* However, her next question was ominous: *"Are you sitting down, sir?"*

Yes, It Was Only $700, that's it!

My stomach immediately began to churn, and my head started aching. *"Sir, are you still there?"* I heard her say. I managed to squeak out a *"Yes"* in a mousey voice.

"Well, sir," she began. *"It looks like the federal income tax exemption for combat continued for two months. So, taxes were not being deducted from your pay. I'm sure you know that officers in a combat zone are only exempt from paying federal tax for the first month."*

She briefly paused and said, *"The IRS recouped the taxes for the two months they were not deducted from your pay."*

"Okay," I said. *"But that's not my fault, so why am I being penalized?"*

"Sir," she said in a sympathetic voice, *"I'm sure you know that when it comes to the IRS, it does not matter who's at fault; they ALWAYS get paid."*

All I could do was sigh and say, *"I know."* She asked me if there was anything else she could help me with, and instead of being my typical sarcastic self, I replied, *"No, thank you."* She apologized and wished me a good day, and I may have said, *"You too,"* unconvincedly, and we hung up.

"Well," I said, *"We got $700 for the next two weeks."*

Terry just looked at me, waiting for an explanation of some sort. She just shook her head after I explained what was clarified to me. I called Major B, the Advanced Party Commander, and told him about it, but he already had the same situation in his house. His response was what I expected,

"Well, suck it up, buttercup. Welcome home."

Easy for him to say because he was a major and earned a higher salary. Although that would logically result in higher taxes, he also had three additional deductions that lowered his tax bracket, so he likely only paid what I paid. I felt like, *'Oh my gosh, bend over, again, Gumby.'* This situation likely only made my night tremors and terrors worse, except with dollar signs chasing me, and there were incoming LES rounds with **NO PAY DUE**. It did not matter much because we had some money in the bank, and I was back to work in a week. By then, my attitude had changed to, 'I'm just lucky to be back,' until we began delving into the task ahead.

Broken Paychecks and Broken Barracks

We were directed to report to the HHB orderly room to begin redeployment and transition operations. Major B, the Brigade Fire Support Officer (BDE FSO), was the advanced party commander, and I was his trusty, dusty XO. MAJ B was a lean, mean, fighting machine that arrived from the 82nd Airborne Division stationed at Fort Bragg, NC. He was lean and a fighting machine, but not 'mean' if you were on point and did what you were supposed to. The HHB Orderly Room did not seem bad, so we expected the rest of the battalion to be the same. Boy, were we dumbasses.

We had our first planning session to prioritize what needed to be done. Before that, MAJ B and I had a sidebar.

"Shit, XO," he said. *"I couldn't tell those spouses what I told you when you called about the pay gap. After we talked, they were calling fast and furious, and I felt like I was in an artillery barrage."*

"So, what did you do, sir?" I said.

"Shit, the only thing I could do, XO," he replied. *"Kept my head down, threw in a shitload of 'Yes, Ma'am's' and curtsied over the phone.*

"So, it wasn't just us?" I said, knowing the answer.

"Oh, shit no," he said. *"Every officer in the battalion got hit. More than likely, every deployed officer in the Army. The entire Army has not been deployed in a long time, so trying to manage all of that was probably a nightmare."*

He continued, *"Hell, I got so many phone calls, I went into the battalion that night and called the Old Man in Iraq. That bad news would definitely not get better with time. He thanked me."*

Our HQ building remained open and manned 24 hours a day, but only in the lobby, where the Rear Detachment was assigned. Every battalion and above had a rear detachment to man the phones to help spouses and family members as needed. They also ran errands and were generally available if a Red Cross message or something significant needed to be communicated to Iraq. They issued LESs to authorized spouses at the middle and end of the month. Not every Soldier had authorized his spouse to pick up the LES, and there was heck to pay when they got back, but at the time, the Rear-D took the brunt of the anger.

I wrote this little vignette to illustrate that everything wasn't peaches-and-cream (or Peaches and Herb) when we returned. Let's face it: Most people have their paychecks already spent before they get them because they know how many bills they have. Imagine only getting paid half or a third of what you are accustomed to. And for the shit we were about to encounter, we still deserved combat pay!

Broken Barracks

Once everyone arrived, we went into the HHB training room for the meeting.

"'2', said MAJ B. *We need to retrieve our classified material and place it in our safe. We also need to look at getting the weapons."*

"Yes, sir," I said. The classified documents are no problem, but we do not have an active arms room for the weapons, so that might take a day or two."

"Okay," he said. "Just get it done and tell me who I need to jump on to make it happen."

In the remaining two years we worked together, MAJ B's attitude never changed: He was there to accomplish the mission and help where needed.

I was supposed to sign for the entire operations building to receive the keys to the HQ Operations section. Back then, I did not know that,

"Friends are better than money unless you can have both,"

but I was already applying the principle. The Key Control Officer for housing was my former LT, who worked with me in the S4 before we deployed. He was a non-deployable member of our unit because of a medical issue. The LT intimately knew about the comings and goings in the rear detachment, and we struck a deal.

"Sir, I'll <u>give</u> you the key without signing over the building, but you gotta get me outta here," he said. *"These supply weenies are driving me crazy! You know me, Sir!"*

"LT," I said, *"Deal, and I know just the man who can do it."*

The LT smiled from ear to ear and handed me the key, but with a warning: *"Sir, you can't <u>ever</u> let anyone see you going into the building. If one of those supply dogs sees you, they will report it and make you sign for the building to get it off their books."*

"Not a problem," I told him. *"Stealth is my middle name."*

My middle name is Wesley, but I used an undercover ID for that mission.

I managed to drive into the near-empty parking lot and parked my car away from the building. I scanned my surroundings before exiting my car and zigzagged across the parking lot. I casually walked right to one area, then left to another, and then to the front door. I quickly unlocked the door, ensuring I was not observed. Since the building had no windows on that side, I could turn on the lights without being seen. Once the lights were on and my eyes adjusted, I could not believe what I saw. The only thing I could say was the S3 officer's favorite line:

"You gotta be shittin me!"

The Fhit Was Going to Hit the Sham

I could not believe my eyes. In short, the room was trashed. All the furniture had been moved and piled in the middle of the room, as if whoever did it was building a barricade. The only thing that remained the same was the 1,000-pound four-drawer safe, which I saw from its top. I only signed for our classified documents once I had safely secured the key, and I was glad I did. I had to move just enough furniture to create a path to the safe. Although I was young and in decent shape, that little bit of moving tired me a bit. After a quick rest, I dialed the combination, and the safe opened on the first attempt.

"Thank you, Jesus," I uttered. *"I'm free at last."* Securing the classified would be a huge relief. I turned off the lights, peeked out the door, and saw no one. I made a beeline for my car and went to pick up the classified. After inventorying the documents to ensure they were all there, I returned to the OPS building. Using the same stealth techniques, I entered the building and placed the documents in the safe. I knew the safe and the locked building door met the requirements of double-barrier security, and I could check that off my list. I knew this was the easy part compared to what I had to tell MAJ B.

"What?" he said. *"You gotta be shittin' me!"*

Obviously, it's a popular phrase, but it's accurate. I knew 'the shit would hit the fan,' or 'the fhit would hit the sham.'
"Sir, we need to get into our buildings to see what they look like before we sign for them, " I recommended. He asked me how, and that is where I got a foot in the door with the lieutenant.

"I can get us the keys from an ally and fellow Red Dragon, but we need to have him reassigned back to our unit after he helps us."

Red Dragons was our unit motto, and how we referred to ourselves when we saluted. MAJ B told me to do it so, *"I can see this shit."*

BLUF (Bottom Line Up Front): The barracks were trashed more than the operations building. The skinny was that our buildings were used to house reservists awaiting deployment to Iraq. The sickening part was that the Soldiers were packed four to a room, yet the rooms were only designed for two.

Some of the stories we heard about the reservists' treatment were appalling. Four Soldiers to a room, limited contact with their families, and constantly training 12 to 14 hours a day were just some of what we heard. When they left, they left everything the way it was. This caused us to expedite our operations to restore the barracks and the battalion.

Operation Overdrive

All five of our barracks were in the same condition: Trashed. We needed to 'outfox' the supply guys before we signed for the buildings, and time was short. The Old Man had called MAJ B at least three times, wanting to know the status of reestablishing the battalion because they could redeploy *"any day now."* Our only recourse was to schedule building inspections and sign for the buildings once they were returned to their original condition. That meant all the excess equipment was moved out, and the rooms were spic-and-span. The housing and supply folks finally caved because many supply personnel were scheduled to depart Fort Hood once their mission of signing over the buildings was completed. And I knew just the man to supervise all this.

With one phone call, MAJ B got the ball rolling to get my old LT back. He was back by the next week, supervising the personnel restoring our buildings. While he did that, I reestablished all our logistics accounts, restored our arms room security systems, and slowly reclaimed each of our buildings after they met our reinspection standards. The Battalion S1 and S3 reps reestablished the operations building and accounts, then the headquarters building and accounts. We retrieved our weapons, placed them into the HHB arms room, and had them restore our motor pool. All of this occurred within a four-to-six-week period while coordinating with Iraq on the redeployment manifest.

This was done without the internet, Wi-Fi, or cell phones. We also retrieved one other item: Our AWOL (Absent Without Official Leave) Soldier. I did not know the Soldier, but I knew his section was hopping mad when he was 'No Showed' for deployment. Before his surrender at the orderly room, his new wife arrived with their new baby. Because he went AWOL, he stopped getting paid, which left his family high and dry. Now, MAJ B and I got mad. We got the AWOL Soldier back on the Army rolls ASAP so his family would have some semblance of a life. Although it was a shame, this was minor compared to what occurred next.

Cursing In My Head

We were less fortunate with the transition to the company office spaces in the barracks. In the Army, company office spaces are referred to as Orderly Rooms, and those were anything but orderly. The rooms looked like they had been used extensively in our absence, were littered with trash and men's magazines, and were generally pitiful. The housing folks hated cleaning these up, and I'm sure it was the same across Fort Hood. Even with the best intentions, you cannot account for the behavior of others. All I could do was shake my head in public and curse the perpetrators in private, neither of which resolved the problem.

Restoring the two office buildings was an oddity. All we could do was ensure the furniture was appropriately arranged and the debris was removed. The unpacking of office equipment and files was left to the returning occupants. And then there was the S4 building that housed my old office and the battalion motor pool. For some reason, the S4 building was in a different motor pool and separated from the remainder of the battalion. I felt no obligation to restore the S4 building because I would no longer be the occupant. Besides, the unit that owned the motor pool had not returned, and the facility was locked.

Our largest and arguably most expensive piece of real estate was the motor pool, which housed all our vehicles and the specialized equipment needed to maintain them. To envision the size of the motor pool, think of an NFL stadium, with at least half of the parking lot, 3-4 automotive bays, and a warehouse. Because of the motor pool's expansive layout, specialized equipment, and storage for Soldiers' privately owned vehicles (POVs), we inspected the area to ensure the POVs and buildings were undamaged. We reclaimed our spaces and their contents and locked them back up. All the buildings and acreage were considered 'real property' worth millions of dollars. I had signed for it all and could not wait to get this burden off my back, although having the property back in our possession provided safety, security, and stability. Once the battalion returned, we would need it.

Part V:
Here Come The "The Real Storms"

Homecomings should be simple, right?

We were finally home! We could not believe it! No more MREs, B rations, T-rations, and sometimes no rations. I soon discovered that many Soldiers were dreading the redeployment home, and with good reasons. Some spouses had moved families out of Texas and moved in with relatives. Others had moved and did not leave a forwarding address. Many families remained at Fort Hood, with several family bank accounts drained. We were told we were going home to a Hero's Welcome, but I can only imagine what some Soldiers were thinking.

We also had to address the elephant in the room: combat trauma. The entire deployment process might be considered traumatic, beginning with the alert, deployment announcement, and pre-deployment activities. Then there was the deployment, the waiting game, still dealing with problems at home and engaging the enemy in combat. Also, there were Iraqi soldiers and units unaware of the ceasefire, and those who did know were allowed to conduct a passage of lines through our ranks back to Baghdad. Finally, there was policing of the battlefield of enemy ammunition, equipment, and, in some cases, prisoners of war (POW) and bodies. Also, mourning our own KIAs.

Walking across a minefield to take the flight to the port did not help. We also had to wrap our minds around going home. Please do not read what I did not write: We were all happy to get home, but with anything new, there is a bit of trepidation about the unknown.

Chapter 21:
"The Heroes Homecoming, Act II"

"It was real!"

S ince the Advanced Party had returned home, six weeks passed. During that time, we accomplished all that 10 people could, expecting to welcome the 600+ Main body any day. We restored seven buildings to operational status – five barracks and two office buildings – the operations center and the Battalion Headquarters. The returning Soldiers who lived in the barracks would at least have clean rooms, a set of clean linen, and an inventory sheet to sign and return within 48 hours. In the Army, nothing is completed until the paperwork is done. All the showers and latrines were fully functional, and the dining facility began serving three hot meals a day two weeks ago. The Soldiers' living quarters were the priority, and we worked hard to ensure a smooth transition. We did the same with the orderly rooms.

Safety, Security, and Stability

MAJ B and I knew that safety, security, and stability would be vitally important with the entire division returning to Fort Hood. This meant ensuring that the barracks, orderly rooms, and office buildings were clean and restored, as well as some of the battalion's most essential rooms: the Arms Rooms. The Arms Rooms, where all small arms were secured, were part of the orderly room complex but offered distinct advantages. First, the Arms Rooms were secured with an IDS (Intrusion Detection System), and second, they did not appear to be used in our absence. IDS is a series of sensors and monitors activated once the armorer closes and locks the arms room with a three-inch-thick lock. If the room is breached by forced entry after being locked, an alarm is set off, and the military police (MP) are alerted and arrive, guns drawn, within minutes.

The armorer is trained and responsible for maintaining the arms room in accordance with the appropriate security regulations. All Army officers know this level of detail and more about arms rooms because weapons handling is the expertise of all Soldiers, and officers have typically been responsible for the Arms Room as junior officers. Also, the S2 was accountable for all security matters within the organization – physical, personnel (security clearances), classified documents, and information security. Operational Security, or OPSEC, however, was the responsibility of the S3.

Photo 67. IDS Warning Sign.

In 1991, we had no internet or cybersecurity to worry about. The warning sign outside the Arms Rooms is yellow and black, and it is much more impressive than the black-and-white shown in this photo. After our arrival, I only had one arms room activated, HHB, so we could store the weapons brought back with the advanced party. Overall, the barracks were a beast to restore, but taking care of the Soldiers was the most critical part.

Another Hero's Welcome, For A While

As the units began to return, it seemed like festivities were everywhere. Still, I only focused on our battalion, and it was like a blur. In mid-April 1991, our battalion began returning in waves, with about a battery a day, every other day, and two days for HHB because of its size and responsibilities. While the battalion was on two weeks' leave, we activated the arms rooms, retrieved the weapons and other sensitive items, and turned over the barracks rooms to each Soldier. Because the battalion returned over 10 days, it took three weeks for everyone to return to work. During that time, we heard rumblings of mischief, misbehaving, and misery, and the morning MP report began to confirm it. The report, titled The Blotter, listed offenses committed by Soldiers that 'blot' the Army's reputation. The hero's welcome was mingled with homecoming horrors.

A Haunted Homecoming, Part II

For the next three months, we dealt with all sorts of dangerous incidents to maintain good order and discipline. The other part of my job as the S2 officer was to review blotters to determine whether an offense affected the Soldier's security clearance. Unfortunately, many of the offenses did, ranging from domestic events because bank accounts were drained to drug addictions that were not present before deployment. In many instances, alcohol was involved in the incident, which had other ramifications for the Soldier, such as a suspended driver's license and/or suspension from driving on post. This created transportation issues, with Soldiers getting to work and, more importantly, doing their jobs. In our unit, even officers were licensed to drive all the equipment under their charge.

A Soldier without a license could inconvenience the section. Still, numerous Soldiers with suspended licenses could undermine unit readiness. Then there were the punishments for driving impaired, ranging from a Company Letter of Reprimand

(LOR) to a company- or field-grade Article 15, or, for higher ranks, even a General Officer Memorandum of Reprimand (GOMOR). The direst administrative punishment, GOMOR, could end the career of any senior NCO or officer of any rank, based on whether it is filed locally or in the Soldier's permanent record. The most helpful consequence of drug or alcohol-related incidents was enrollment in the ADAP – Army Drug and Alcohol Program (now referred to as the Army Substance Abuse Program or ASAP). Anything listed above requires suspending the Soldier's security clearance pending the outcome or adjudication of the offense. And then came the long-term effects many of us faced.

Drug and alcohol behaviors were more immediate manifestations of the deployment, and so were other behaviors. Throughout the cities of Killeen, Harker Heights, and Copperas Cove, there were thefts, robberies, and even armed robberies attributed to Soldiers. Arguments, fights, occurrences of disrespect, and even drug dealing within the unit were all parts of the haunted homecoming we endured while trying to return to normalcy.

Redeployment Physicals

The redeployment physicals were less like physical examinations and more like 'check-ups,' in my opinion. We were herded through the gym and the process like cattle, being examined physically, mentally, and emotionally. One young sergeant was injured and received the Purple Heart. He told me,

"Sir, the Army can have it back if it removes my injury."

His statement always stuck with me because it deglamorized what is always depicted in the movies and made it real. Many of our injuries were on the inside and would not be seen for months and, in many cases, years.

Some Soldiers had injuries that needed immediate attention, but others, like me, had minor aches and pains that would develop into something else later. For example, the ganglion cyst on my left wrist was not there before I deployed. Although the cyst shrank over the years, I developed a carpal tunnel syndrome in both wrists. My back pain began from carrying equipment on my back for several movements and wearing boots ill-suited for the desert because of their faulty design. And of course, the smoke from the oil fires and burn barrels, and numerous dust storms, all of which may have impacted my lungs. With most of the initial redeployment activities completed, the attention turned to recognition.

And The Award Goes To...

Before the leadership transition within the battalion, the Iraq awards ceremony was scheduled, with only the Command Group and the S1 knowing who was getting what awards. There was the pomp and circumstance of most award ceremonies, with the presentation of the colors, the national anthem, selected music, and speeches. Then, the awardees were presented. As they were marched out, it was apparent who was being showcased: The Bronze Star recipients. This consisted of the Battery Commanders and First Sergeants, selected platoon leaders and platoon sergeants, and selected Fire Support Officers. The personnel were aligned by rank, and I noticed what appeared to be a lone Specialist at the very end.

The crowd grew restless as the general descriptions for each award group were read. Some felt that their sacrifices were worthy of Bronze Stars. I must admit that I was feeling a little 'something—something. 'Considering that I was important enough to be cross-leveled across the battlefield from one vehicle to another to track the battle, that should count for something. As the names were read and they finally reached the last recipient, everyone else gasped, and I smiled.

That' lone Specialist' at the end of the formation was the mechanic who repaired our S2 vehicle under fire! Because I was sitting next to the Battalion XO, he leaned over and said with his thick Boston accent,

The Iraq I Knew…

"There's your Bronze Star."

Photo 68. Army Bronze Star Medal. Photo retrieved from https://en. wikipedia.org/wiki/Valorous_Unit_Award

I thanked Big Dave, and he told me, *"Don't thank me, you wrote the award and were willing to give it up for the Specialist."* He said that when he told the awards board my request, they said, *"Okay, he must have really earned it."* It felt good, however, to know that my work was recognized.

I did, however, receive the next most common combat award without valor, the Army Commendation Medal (ARCOM). That was my second ARCOM, earned a year earlier as the Bravo Battery Special Weapons Officer (SWO). In the end, our collective work was recognized by the Army.

And The Award Goes To... Everyone.

Although we did not know it at the time, our brigade, the 2nd Blackjack Brigade, 1st Cavalry Division, received an award no one saw coming: the Valorous Unit Award.

Photo 69. Valorous Unit Award.

Photo 70. Valorous Unit Award compared to the Silver Star Medal.

The Valorous Unit Award (VUA) is the second-highest U.S. Army unit award, following the Presidential Unit Citation (PUC). The award is presented to *"units of the United States Armed Forces or cobelligerent nations which display extraordinary heroism in action against an armed enemy of the United States on or after 3 August 1963. The unit degree of heroism required is considered the equivalent of the individual degree of heroism required for the Silver Star, which is awarded for gallantry in action."* [17]

I am uncertain if any of us expected the VUA and had to look up how it was earned. When a unit receives a Valorous Unit Award, although everyone in the brigade earns it, some pay the ultimate price more than others. Our award was for The Battle of Ruqi Pocket, which began the feint as the prelude to the ground invasion. Done with the parades and awards ceremonies, another part of normalcy was departures. Although those were everyday events, the separations were more complex after conducting combat training and serving together on the battlefield for over eight months.

Chapter 22:
"Reset – *"The Whirlwind Never Ends"*

"The merry-go-round from hell."

Reset was a term I became very familiar with in the 1990s and throughout what became the rest of my Army career. The most hectic part of the reset began with the departure of the Blackjack Brigade Commander. I happened to be the Staff Duty Officer (SDO) when the message came in during the wee-hours of the morning. Still groggy and not a tried-and-true coffee drinker yet, I thought I had misheard when I heard the message. I asked the DIVARTY SDO, *"Say again all after Brigade Change of Command."* It was only mid-May, and the main body had barely returned three weeks earlier. Our Brigade Commander, COL H, had not been in command for a year, but was selected as Brigadier General!

Of course, that set into motion the 1st Cav's way of endless parade practices to ensure everything was perfect. And the most challenging part: Changing command on horseback! The officers changing command, and the change-of-command official, conducted all their actions short of exchanging the unit colors (flags) on horseback. That meant the Commanding General and outgoing and incoming brigade commanders trooping the line (reviewing the units in formation) on horseback. This is important because horses will do what horses do, whether they're parading or not. Once the command was changed over and the speeches ended, we conducted a Pass in Review, which meant marching past the reviewing stand and saluting. It also meant dodging horse poop all over the field.

We had two more ceremonies when the DIVARTY Commander and our Battalion Commander changed command.

Lieutenant Colonels (LTC) and above were required to change command via horseback. And to add another wrinkle, those ceremonies were also conducted using bugle commands. Only a couple of people spoke, as the rest of us just reacted to the bugle commands. Although there were no lavish ceremonies, the entire Command Group did a Permanent Change of Station (PCS). The Battalion Change of Command was scheduled for June. We received a new Old Man in LTC B. Big Dave, the Battalion XO, departed and was replaced by MAJ Sig. The S3 left and was replaced by MAJ B, the Advanced Party Commander and Brigade FSO.

Although he was young, the Command Sergeant Major (CSM) retired, and many of the First Sergeants also left. The rest of the Battalion Staff were decimated with the departures of the S1 and S4 officers, Battalion Motor Officer (BMO), and possibly the Chemical Officer. We kept four of the five Battery Commanders, but most platoon leaders also rotated out. We were entering an entirely different world, and I felt somewhat alone.

The Lone Survivor

I remained in the battalion for another year, and all the changes left me as the sole surviving staff officer who had been deployed and was serving in that position. I had historical knowledge of how we functioned as the staff, which was helpful since I knew the Left Seat-Right Seat Ride requirements. Left-seat-right-seat rides are the civilian equivalent of onboarding, but they do not always occur. Because the entire Army was 'resetting,' everything appeared in flux, and we also received a new DIVARTY Commander and Assistant Division Commanders. With that much shuffling, the priorities quickly shifted from barracks to bombs. Those bombs differed from the type everyone could handle or had access to, and I was now responsible for the battalion program. This was my only job in the Army where errors could not occur.

The One Mission We Could Not 'Bomb'

Nuclear Recertification became the number one priority because we still had the tactical nuclear mission. However, ensuring that all sensitive items were properly secured felt like another mission. I will explain the recertification first because it was the one I had the most control over. The Personal Reliability Program (PRP) ensured that the personnel entrusted with delivering nuclear and chemical weapons were of the highest caliber and highly reliable. As a platoon leader, I served in that position for 14 months, went through an annual certification, and earned my first award in the Active Army, an Army Commendation Medal, or ARCOM. I was now the PRP Program Manager for our battalion, and with a new Command Group, I was starting from scratch. Fortunately for me, SFC P and SSG Ski were not scheduled to transfer out until late fall, so we still had their expertise.

In short, all PRP personnel were responsible for delivering tactical nukes if the need arose. Because of those duties and designations, special care was taken with those personnel and their records. Their records were designated as PRP, and their personnel, medical, dental, and personnel security records were segregated from everyone else's. Program personnel were required to act immediately if anything in those records needed updating. The S2 ensured that each member's security status was up to par. We were also responsible for training all officers (primarily platoon leaders) in handling Special Weapons and designating them as Special Weapons Officers (SWOs).

I only thought it was grueling at the battery level, but now, being responsible for the entire program could have been daunting. However, SSG Ski and I had worked together as SWO and SWNCOIC, so we had no problem administering the program and prepping for recertification in the fall. Now, back to security.

Security Took on A New Meaning

In early August, the new Assistant Division Commander for Maneuver (ADC-M) was assigned to ensure the division's sensitive items were secured correctly, and he did not play. We knew of the General's famous father, and I had worked directly with his younger brother, but knew nothing of him. Well, that quickly changed after he served notice that,

"The first unit I inspect and fail sensitive items security, I will relieve the company commander."

Sometimes people 'blow smoke,' but there is one thing I learned about General Officers (GOs): they don't blow smoke. Reports came in that one company commander within the division had been relieved of command, followed by another. The Battery Commanders knew them and confirmed the rumors better than I could. This presented us with a slight problem.

Since we had received our full complement of equipment, storage had become an issue. The biggest problem was not the weapons or communications security (COMSEC) equipment, but the night vision goggles (NVG). We had enough NVGs for everyone in the battalion, but they were stored in specialized cases that took up significant space. Also, they could not be stored in the arms rooms because they were not weapons. Truth-in-advertising, the NVGs were stored in our arms rooms until each Battery found suitable spaces within their units. Some Batteries used their chemical equipment rooms for NVG storage because they were windowless, secured with additional locks, and had double-barrier security. Others had chemical 'cages' that were good enough for chemical equipment but not NVGs at $6,000 apiece.

The fixes were to reinforce the cages with one-inch-thick plywood inside, secure them to the cage wire, and add locks at the top, bottom, and middle of each cage. SFC P was our security guru and hounded each Battery about proper security. He checked one Battery a day and submitted his report to me.

Everything was going well, but as the old saying goes, 'There's one in every crowd.'

Learning Things the Hard Way

Some people must learn things the hard way.

Why would a person complete a successful combat mission only to risk losing their career over a misplaced principle? That is what we were dealing with. To avoid discrimination, I conducted the next round of inspections within the battalion and spoke directly with the 'principled' Battery Commander.

"Dude," I said, *"He's relieving people left and right. What's the big deal?"* 'He' was the Assistant Division Commander for Maneuver (ADC-M).

The Battery Commander responded with, *"To make an example out of the system,"* and *"Be given the proper tools to do the job."*

"Dude," I said, *"You will be the only one made an example of, and you won't need the tools because you will be out of a job!"*

My arguments did not persuade the Battery Commander, so I did the only thing I could do: I failed his Battery on the security inspection and gave the results to the XO. The XO was not a happy camper.

"'2', did you really have to do that?" said MAJ Sig.

"Sir," I replied, *"It's either him or me, and I have no intention of being relieved."*

As fate would have it, the situation was OBE – Overcome by Events when the General arrived at our organization late the next afternoon to conduct his inspection. Since we would soon be in the training cycle, we would normally cease operations at 1630. SFC P shattered that when he said,

"Sir, the General is in the battalion and has already threatened to relieve a First Sergeant!"

'Oh crap,' I thought, we better get moving.

A Mad Dash

I made a mad dash to the wayward Battery and told the Battery Commander to put on his tap-dancing shoes because the General was on the way. Within 10 minutes, the General was there, demanding to know why the NVGs were improperly secured. The Battery Commander quickly replied with,

"Sir, we just got the plywood this afternoon, and everything will be secure by tomorrow."

'Good thinking,' I thought until it was my turn.

"What do you think '2'? Will he get it done?" said the General.

"Sir," I said, *"I'm certain he'll get it done."*

The General turned back to the Battery Commander and said, *"Don't make me come back here, because you won't like it!"* and strode off.

As we discussed the inspection the next day at our Command and Staff meeting, the offending First Sergeant said,

"He doesn't play. I found that out the hard way."

With that storm past us, we could focus on getting recertified. We had about six to eight weeks of field training to complete, and were conducting SWO training daily. We had a couple of drills from higher that 'enhanced' the seriousness of the task. All the security clearances had been returned clean, and all the records were tip-top. We had about three weeks of field training under our belt when I got a call from home. My dad was in the hospital, and it was not looking good.

Resetting My Life

It was one year later, and we had deployed and defeated Saddam Hussein and the Iraqi Army, driving them out of Kuwait. Dad's fight had not been so successful. It was Labor Day weekend, so we flew to Kansas City on Friday using the special military fares. We headed to the hospital, and my dad was angry about the amount of weight he had lost. He showed me by raising his arms. The skin was hanging there, but he otherwise looked good. Our dad was a big man from being a laborer, but not fat, so it showed in his arms when he lost weight.

He was scheduled to be released the next day (Saturday), so we were able to spend a bit of time before we had to leave on Monday. Although he looked good and was in good spirits, the severe weight loss concerned us all. We departed as scheduled on Monday afternoon, and I returned to work on Tuesday. I spent another couple of weeks preparing the battalion for recertification, an event I did not expect to be part of. About three weeks into September, I received the call to 'come home.' I had always kept significant leave since my dad first got sick in 1987, and now I was about to use it.

The End Was Near, But Not Quick

After I hung up the phone with Mom and explained to Terry what was going on, I called the airline to book flights to Kansas City, MO, with an unknown return date. I could estimate the return date and change it for free later, which is what I did. I then began writing down everything I needed my section to complete to lead the battalion through nuclear recertification successfully. I wrote down as much as I could and saved the rest for the next day. I arrived at the office early the following morning, completed my leave form, and dropped it on the XO's desk. I did not know he would be at appointments all morning and would not arrive at the office until noon. I was summoned at 12:01.

MAJ Sig was a quiet, polite, super-smart officer. After expressing his concerns, he got down to business.

"Why are you still here?" he asked. *"And why is your leave form for tomorrow and not today?"* he continued.

"Sir, I have instructions that I need to give my section and hand off everything I was working on for the recertification," I replied.

"You know those NCOs will do fine, right?" he said. *"You don't need to be here."*

"Yes, sir, I know," I said. *"Maybe I just need something to keep my mind occupied; plus, it's the right thing to do."*

MAJ Sig just nodded and signed my leave form. *"I'll let the Old Man know,"* he said.

I thanked him, took my leave form, and turned it in to the S1. I had already told SFC P and SSG Ski what was happening when they arrived at the office earlier. SFC P was not as 'gentile' as MAJ Sig.

"Sir, what the hell are you doing here? SSG Ski and I got this," he said.

"I know you do," I replied. *"But you know I wouldn't leave you hanging."*

"We know you wouldn't, sir," said SSG Ski. *"Let's just get started so you can get the hell out of here."*

Contrary to popular belief, officers *do* work, and this was an all-day affair. At least until the Old Man summoned me to his office.

LTC B expressed his concerns and told me, *"I know the XO already chewed your ass for being here, so go home. Now."*

I said, *"Roger, sir,"* went to my office, grabbed my stuff, said goodbye to my guys, and left to see the S1 about my leave form. We departed for KC on Friday morning and arrived in the afternoon. We went to my parents' house and dropped off our bags. There was not much to say as we departed for the hospital. Dad did not look much different from the way he did two weeks earlier, but was glad to see us.

Dad spent another week in the hospital, where I would visit twice daily: Once in the morning after my run, and then I would bring my mom and my wife in the afternoon. One day, Dad decided he wanted to leave the hospital and did the necessary things to make that happen. The detailed account is recorded in my other book, **Inspired, Not Retired**: *Leadership Lessons from Father to Son.*

The End Finally Came

My dad was out of the hospital in time for my birthday, but he didn't do much celebrating. We noticed his eating had significantly decreased, and he had been sleeping most of the time. The hospice nurses came by and briefed my mom on what to expect and what to do once Dad passed. My siblings visited daily, as my dad lived for another week after he was discharged from the hospital.

Burl Randolph, Sr., died peacefully at home on Monday, October 7, 1991, exactly seven months to the day I returned from Iraq. As you can imagine, we were all devastated, and the week was spent notifying his siblings and other family members, making the funeral arrangements, and preparing ourselves for the final goodbye. Those who follow biblical numerology would say that Dad dying seven months after my return from Iraq, on October 7, at the age of 77, would indicate perfection or completion. I believe Dad completed all the things that were important to him and passed the way he wanted to, at home surrounded by loved ones. Dad's funeral was on Saturday, October 12, 1991, the same day Redd Foxx died.

We departed for Texas the following Thursday. For some reason, I decided to call my mom from the airport to let her know we were back in Texas. I told myself it was because we would arrive back in Killeen from Austin so late. When I woke up the next morning and collected our newspapers, I was startled to learn about the Luby's cafeteria restaurant shooting, having eaten there almost weekly. Later in the day, when I called Staff Duty to report off leave, I was told to come into Battalion HQ on Saturday morning.

The Whirlwind Was Only Beginning

SFC P met me there and told me I had to deploy to the field on Monday morning. I chuckled and asked if it was a joke. SFC P was his direct self and said,

"Sir, this ain't no damn joke. I wish it was."

I went home seething. Fortunately, my bags were already packed because I would never be caught short again, and so began my obsessive-compulsive disorder with deployments. BTW, I was not diagnosed with OCD, but that was how I felt.

On Monday afternoon, I sat in the S3 vehicle with MAJ B and was angry, which I expressed to him. How could one person be so important that someone else wasn't sitting here? His answer was a simple one.

"Because," he said, *"You and I are the few who remain after the deployment. Especially you, since you are in the same position you were in during the war."*

MAJ B's answer did little to lessen my anger or appease my ego, and he knew it. So, he changed the subject and asked me about my dad and my family, how they were doing, and how I was doing.

We then exchanged stories about the funeral experience. I thought that it was very compassionate and helped to soothe my pain and grief a bit. MAJ B then said how great my guys did on the nuclear recertification and that I should be proud of them. I remarked that,

"Great NCOs make things happen." MAJ B replied,

The Iraq I Knew...

"Yes, but great NCOs are led by great leaders. It's what people do when the boss is not around, that's the mark of a great leader."

That was one of the most meaningful leadership conversations I had back then, and I took it to heart. People will typically do the right things when the boss is around, but how do you instill that excellence in mission accomplishment when you are not there? I needed to ponder that, and many other things related to my career. As I contemplated the meaning of the last 12-18 months, I also needed to discover how I would use my newfound skills. I believed that at least my Iraq deployment excursion was over, or so I thought.

Chapter 23:
"Using What I Learned, Part I"

Unfortunately, this was only the beginning.

I thought deploying to Iraq would be the longest six months of my life. Everything was done on a moment's notice: Alert for deployment, marriage, promotion, preparation for deployment, and deployment. No one could have told me that the redeployment, reset, and whirlwind of events that had occurred over such a short period would be replicated again-and-again.

Little did I know that it was only the beginning.

And, it was not the beginning of the end, but the beginning of the beginning. My life and career had changed, and I was moving on to my new branch of Military Intelligence. If nothing else, over the next eight months and the remainder of my career I would learn how to apply what I learned in Iraq.

Involuntarily Resetting My Career

During the eight months that I remained at Fort Hood, TX, as the Vice President for Intelligence and Security (S2 officer – Battalion Senior Intelligence Officer), the Army was reshaped by our actions in Desert Shield and Desert Storm. Our doctrine would be updated to include how we fought a conventional force in a desert and won. Our tactics, techniques, and procedures (TTP) for artillery, armor, infantry, and all the supporting branches would be taught differently at the qualification schools. However, the 1st Cavalry Division had other plans for me before I attended my MI qualification courses.

From October through December 1991, I stayed in the field because of one exercise or another to practice our new combat techniques. For one exercise, I was selected solely because I was the only Battalion S2 officer in the DIVARTY with the required security clearance. My response to MAJ B could have been more professional.

"Bullshit," I told MAJ B. *"How in the world could I be the only S2 in the entire DIVARTY with the required security clearance?"*

"Calm down, '2'," he said to me instead of chewing my ass out for my response.

"I said the same thing you did when we were tasked, 'Bullshit, not my S2. Show me the list." "And they did," he said. *"You're too damn good at your job, 2', and you do what you're supposed to. I think someone else told you this before that, 'No good deed goes unpunished.'"*

'No shit,' I thought, but when does the reward come?

The Reward Was in The Whirlwind

Once the new year arrived, we continued to test our new techniques with an HQ rotation to the NTC. The National Training Center (NTC) adapted its scenarios to what we *did* in combat, not what we <u>might</u> do. The Army realized that each campaign, battle, and engagement was unique in how the commanders utilized combat, coalition, and supporting forces. Those experiences translated into lessons learned that demanded sharing throughout our Army. Even with the extensive television footage, I can still only tell you what happened at the locations and battles I was in.

This was our first NTC rotation with the new Battalion Commander, all new Battery Commanders, and an entirely new C-level staff, except for me. I was by no means the *'go-to'* guy, but still, no one else could boast of deploying a 600-man battalion as a Battalion S4 and fighting as a Battalion S2 officer, in the same deployment. For that NTC rotation, I served as both the Battalion S4 and S2 officers simply because our commander applied the economy-of-force principle: Why use two people to do a job that one person can do? For the first time on active duty, I was confident that I knew my job.

Actions Spoke Louder

I do not recall who the new S4 was, but because our contingent was only deploying the headquarters, it was decided that *'Burl'* could do both. Of course, I did both jobs with proper support, but my primary focus was intelligence because that was my new branch. I was eager to learn what I was missing and to show what I knew. When Boris Yeltsin resigned as President of the Commonwealth of Independent States (CIS) in October 1991, I learned to track events and provide information to the commander.

At the time, I was unfamiliar with the Army intelligence PED system of processing, exploitation, and dissemination. As an artilleryman, my primary concern was the enemy, point-and-shoot, and I had little interest in where the targeting came from. However, as a future intelligence officer, I needed to be concerned about the source of all the information I received, so I could be crystal clear when I provided it to my team. That is where the hours of studying, poring over reports, scouring field manuals (FM), Army Regulations (AR), after-action review (AAR) reports, and, for the NTC, notes from the Opposing Forces (OPFOR) S2.

One OPFOR S2 had written very detailed notes on how OPFOR always beat the friendly forces, and it came down to one thing: S2s need to follow the basics. Because I only knew the basics, below is what seemed like the thing to do:

"When all else fails, try following directions."

Just like anyone else, I can follow directions when I want to, and this time, I wanted to. MAJ B and I were together again because we only deployed the TOC (Tactical Operations Center) and a few other staff members. After we arrived at NTC and the exercise began, we crushed the OPFOR, which rarely happens. My reward from the new DIVARTY Commander was an opportunity to command a battery, though I almost sabotaged myself.

Self-Inflicted Gunshot Wound, Metaphorically

I knew very little about COL B, but why would I know a Colonel well, as a new Captain? COL B had come out to visit us during the deployment, which, in my mind, spoke volumes about the caliber of the officer he was. He was only scheduled to be there for three days and came by the TOC three times. I briefed him on the enemy situation a couple of times, and on the third visit, he asked me to step outside the TOC. He asked about my plans, and I explained that I was about to PCS. He said that orders could be changed, and I could stay right at Fort Hood to command a battery.

I explained that I was switching to MI and leaving for the MI Advanced Course. Upon hearing that, his demeanor immediately changed. That was when MAJ B leaped outside the TOC to save my ass, unbeknownst to me.

"Sir, what CPT Randolph meant to say was that he is Branch Detailed to MI, so he doesn't have a choice," he said. *"Otherwise, he would have loved to command a battery in the DIVARTY."*

The DIVARTY Commander's stern expression changed, and he said, *"Too bad. Keep up the good work."* We saluted, and he left.

I was clueless as to what had occurred.

"'2', said MAJ B, *"Don't EVER tell a senior leader you are transferring out of their branch, especially when they're about to offer you a command, because they take that shit personally. He was ready to ream you a new one!"*

Standing there with my Little Orphan Annie bug eyes, all I could say was, *"Thanks, sir."* When the Battalion Commander came in later, MAJ B said, *"Sir, we almost lost the '2' today to friendly fire. He almost got an incoming O-6!"* The Old Man chuckled and shook his head.

Later, I asked MAJ B how the DIVARTY Commander knew anything about me.

"Reputation and credibility," he said. *"Just because someone does not know you, does not mean that they don't know **of** you. You impressed many people at the Division CPX. You never know whose watching you, '2'."*

That was the same exercise I complained about earlier, and I lost my military bearing with MAJ B. Ten years later, I would be advised again about *"Always being observed."*

Who knew that 15 years later, I would provide a young captain with the same advice MAJ B gave me? We closed the rotation without another nearly career-ending incident and headed back home. My last NTC rotation (Literally, for the rest of my career) and final act, or so I believed.

The Final Act

I received my orders to Fort Huachuca, Arizona, for the MI Officer Transition and Advanced Courses, and was excited. Sometime during the new year, SFC P transferred out, and we received Master Sergeant (MSG) D. A Master Sergeant is an E-8, the second-highest enlisted rank, and the rank my section was not authorized to hold. MSG D had been a First Sergeant and knew how to push Soldiers, but had never served on staff, so the learning curves were steep. That was okay because the last thing we did together needed someone with ingenuity and juice.

As the Army and the world changed, so did our mission. We received communications that required us to gather the team to check and countercheck the message for validity and authenticity, and we were all about shit-a-brick. I went into my boss's office and asked MAJ Sig to see him, the S3, and the Old

Man immediately, as in right now. He said something I had never heard before, but it was also noted by LTC B and the '3'.

"S2, you look pale," said MAJ Sig. *"Is everything alright?"*

It's The Final Countdown

I must have looked sick because MAJ B and the Old Man also told me so. *"Well, '2',* said the Old Man, *what is it?"* Like a zombie, I said,

"Sir, we're required to dismantle our entire nuclear weapons program within the next 30 days. More to follow."

It was so quiet, you could have heard a chigger scream, so guess who looked pale now? I do not recall the conversation after breaking the news; I only remember the flurry of Battery Commanders arriving at my office to verify what their lieutenants had told them. They were speechless and basically walked out.

Based on the INF (Intermediate Nuclear Forces) Treaty, the US and the Commonwealth of Independent States (CIS) (the country formerly known as Russia) had negotiated to end their tactical nuclear weapons programs. The timeline to implement the required treaty actions was short and even shorter for me. Did I mention I was leaving? Additional messages told us precisely what to do, and we got hot. We were done within two weeks, and I provided the Old Man with the final reports.

"It looks like you're finally done, '2,'" said the Old Man.

"Yes, sir," I sighed as MSG D came to get me with an odd look on his face.

The Real Final Act

What now? I thought. In short, we traded our nuclear mission for a chemical one. I was required to train myself, my section, and all battalion personnel involved in the new system within 30 days. The mission was accomplished within the allotted time, and exercises were conducted for two weeks afterward. I could not imagine that I would need and use this information again. With orders in hand, I began the dreaded task of 'clearing' (transitioning) the battalion, DIVARTY, the 1st Cavalry Division, and Fort Hood, TX. Clearing was dreaded because the Central Issue Facility (CIF) – where we requisitioned our personal field equipment from- expected the equipment to be returned in near-perfect condition. I managed to secure some 'used' but nearly new equipment, turned it in, and went about my business.

Departing was bittersweet because I served in that unit for four years and had done the most to that point in my life, personally and professionally. I knew, however, that all good things must come to an end. It was time not just to leave Fort Hood, TX, but to change my Branch (Officer specialty) and move into an almost entirely new area: Military Intelligence. We headed to Fort Huachuca, AZ, where I was enrolled in the MI Officer Transition Course and MI Advanced Course. We never returned to Fort Hood, but I used my new knowledge and experiences beginning in the MI Officer Advanced Course, in subsequent assignments, and until the Army returned to Iraq again. The next deployment was for reasons that none of us ever expected.

What I Learned

Over the past 18 months, I learned lessons that I would carry with me for the remainder of my career.

1. **Be Flexible**. The world was ever-changing as we entered an Era of Persistent Conflict. Desert Shield and Desert Storm were preceded by Operation Just Cause in Haiti, and there were so many operations after that I couldn't remember them all. What we accomplished in 60 days – deployment became the norm. The Army and its personnel would require adaptability to meet the challenges.

2. **Embrace Learning**. Most successful people may not be naturally gifted but are willing to learn new things. Most of the things I learned from this experience were new, and this book was one of the ways I used to understand them. Those operations also provided the blueprint for most Army, Joint Services, and Coalition primary operations afterward. By the next time I deployed on a significant Army Operation 13 years later, the Intellectual Capital – what people knew, had dissipated. Some people – like me - were still around to teach what they needed to learn about deployments.

3. **Be Innovative**. Many of the things we did during the pre-deployment, deployment, and redeployment phases had never been done that way. NCOs are known for their innovation, and it was put to the test. I did not put half of the things we created within these few pages
because I could not follow the results. I just knew what we did was new and groundbreaking, using equipment, doctrine, and personnel that would be incorporated into our Army DNA.

4. **Be Patient**. From August 1990 to January 1991 was a long time to pursue and wait for diplomatic solutions that never occurred; however, it was worth the wait. Never go into a fight ill-prepared if you can help it. Our patience and proper planning prevented poor performance, but what if we were impatient and deployed forces before we were truly prepared? Patience is sometimes the difference between success and failure, life and death.

5. **Always have Mentors**. Then and now, finding mentors has always been a task I never seem to accomplish. The lieutenants in the battalion held a farewell luncheon for me and presented me with 'The Mentor Award.' Eight officers thought enough of me to tell me how they appreciated me pouring into them. If I had a mentor back

then, who knows where I would be now? I may have remained in Field Artillery, commanded a battery or two, and kept moving up the chain of command. All those faux pas over the years could have been avoided with a mentor.

Those events dramatically changed the script of Army doctrine, training, and operations.

Photo 71. The Mentor's Award was provided to the author.

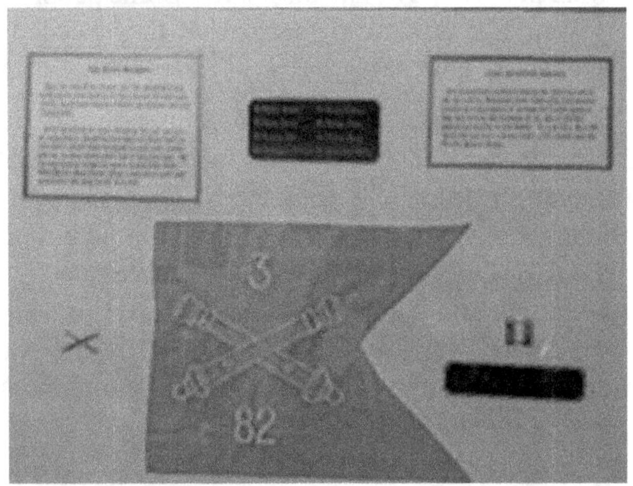

Photo provided by the Author.

I also realized that *nothing lasts forever*, no matter how good it is. I learned many things at my first duty station and my first deployment that no longer exist. The uniforms have changed three times, the equipment – at least four times, the doctrine and terminology countless times, and our ability to work in Joint Service and coalition environments has increased exponentially.

Fort Hood is no longer Fort Hood; it is now Fort Cavazos, and women are fully integrated into maneuver units as part of Brigade Combat Teams (BCT). The Army also has two distinctions where women have made history - the first woman four-star general in US military history and the second woman combatant commander in US military history.

Change is inevitable in life and *required* for growth. If we are adequately prepared, we can face any of life's storms with courage, dignity, and grace, allowing us to grow in the process. I went into this storm with my eyes wide open, carried these lessons into my next deployment, and helped flip the script again.

Photo 72. Captain Burl Randolph, Jr., in front of his M577 vehicle in Desert Storm. Photo provided by the Author.

Acknowledgements

First and foremost, I give thanks to God for providing me the skills, intellect, and courage to share my story, and the spirit to help others.

First, I would like to thank my family, friends, and fans who always support my work and push me to go further than I think I can.

Second, I would like to thank a fellow bestselling author and friend, Kelly 'Mack' McCoy, for challenging me to explore sharing my military combat deployments in detail so that nonmilitary people can share in my experiences.

Third, I would like to thank Jake Hines for providing the civilian perspective I sometimes lack, helping me better understand my nonmilitary audience.

Lastly, I would like to thank my previous clients who allowed me to hone my writing, editing, publishing, and promoting proficiencies by helping make their dreams come true.

Author's Biography

Dr. Burl W. Randolph, Jr., DM, is a retired US Army Military Intelligence Colonel with nearly 32 years of service. His career highlights included three combat tours in Iraq serving in intelligence officer positions, Inspector/Monitor duty in Russia enforcing the Strategic Arms Reduction Treaty (START), and commanding at every level, up to Colonel, with tours throughout the United States, Europe, and Russia. Dr. Burl last served as the Deputy Chief of Staff for Intelligence and Security at the Army Sustainment Command, Rock Island Arsenal, Rock Island, IL. After retirement in 2014, Dr. Burl remained inspired by founding and serving as the President and Chief Consultant for MyWingman, LLC, a Business Leadership and Management consulting company in Davenport, Iowa.

The competitive services offered by MyWingman, LLC include Leadership and Management Coaching, Organizational Planning, Corporate Training, Legacy Expression, and Government Contracting. Business highlights include helping form the Midwest Manufacturing Business Coalition (MMBC); training over 700 government civilians and military personnel on the Department of Defense (DoD) Performance Management and Appraisal Program (DPMAP); developing a 32-hour Diversity, Equity, Inclusion, and Belonging (DEIB) curriculum for ImpactLife Blood Center; and extensive coaching and writing projects.

Dr. Burl was conferred a Doctor of Management in Organizational Leadership (DM) from the University of Phoenix, with a doctoral dissertation titled "Mentoring and African American Army Captain Success: A Case Study." He also earned a Master of Strategic Studies from the US Army War College and a Master of Business Administration from Troy State University while on Active Duty. He has numerous publications, both academic and commercial. Peer-reviewed articles include Changing Steps: A Reflexive Journey in Transition, published in

The Journal of Global Health Care Systems, and Mentoring Leaders Across Racial and Gender Lines: Insight from US Army Officers, " published in *Global Business and Organizational Excellence*.

In 2015, Dr. Burl ventured into writing, editing, publishing, and promoting books for others. His first book was coauthored with the late Pastor Stanley Moore; the nonfiction work *Can God Trust You with Trouble?* He next forayed into editing with **No Disruptions**: *The Future of Mid-Market Manufacturing*. In 2023, he helped publish seven books: **Life Lines**: *A book of poetry and 'things' about my Life* in paperback and hardcover; **Sunshine for Your Soul**: *Love, Light, and Life Lessons*; **Prayer Time** *Calendar & Journal;* **Dragonflies & Orange Day Balloons:** *Embracing Your Resilient Spirit*; **Inspired, Not Retired** and **Can God Trust You with Trouble?** in hardcover. In 2024, he helped publish **Bible Light Snack:** *Learning the Scriptures Utilizing Visual 'Bites' of Knowledge.* Dr. Burl is the Author of the Amazon Bestselling book, " **Inspired, Not Retired:** *Leadership Lessons from Father to Son* available in paperback, eBook, audiobook, and hardcover. He is also the Author of **The Inspired, Not Retired Workbook**: *A Guide to Developing Your Leadership Lessons.*

Dr. Burl's community work includes serving on several nonprofit boards. These include serving as a co-founder and secretary of the Foreign Affairs Council; a Director of ImpactLife Blood Center, Vera French Community Mental Health Center, Lead(h)er, Inc., River Bend Food Bank, and the WVIK Community Advisory Board. He also serves as the Co-Chair of the Quad Cities Community Veterans Engagement Board (CVEB). He is a graduate, co-founder, facilitator, mentor, and Outreach Coordinator for Reboot Recovery of the Quad Cities. Dr. Burl also mentors doctoral students and military officers and edits doctoral dissertations. He is an Inducted Member of two prestigious organizations based on his doctoral studies: the International Honor Society in Business and the National Society of Leadership and Success (NSLS).

Additional Works by *Dr. Randolph*

Inspired, Not Retired: Leadership Lessons from Father to Son

Paperback, © 2019

eBook, © 2020

Audiobook, © 2022

Workbook, © 2022

Hardcover, © 2023

Can Trust You with Trouble, Co-Author

Paperback & eBook, © 2016

Hardcover, © 2023

No Disruptions: The Future of Mid-Market Manufacturing ©2016, paperback (Editor)

Prayer Time, © 2023   Bible Light Snack,   Lifelines, © 2023
© 2024

Dragonflies &
Orange Day Balloons
© 2023

Sunshine for Your Soul
© 2023

Peer-Reviewed Works

Randolph, Jr., B. W. (2010). Mentoring: A joint perspective from a deployed environment. (Master's Thesis). Retrieved from https://www.researchgate.net (235033149)

Randolph, Jr. B. W. (2015). Changing steps: A reflexive journey in transition. *Journal of Global Healthcare Systems,5*(2). Retrieved from https://www.researchgate.net/ publication/321444948_ Changing_Steps_A_ Reflexive_ Journey_in_Transition

Randolph, Jr., B. W. (2018). Mentoring and African American army captain success: A case study. (Doctoral Dissertation). Doi: 10.13140/RG.2.2.22343.19363

Randolph, Jr., B. W., & Nisbett, K. (2019, May-June). Mentoring leaders across race and gender lines: Insight from US Army officers. *Global Business and Organizational Excellence, 38*(5). Wiley Publications: New York. Doi: 10.1002/joe.21931

Business Information

Dr. Randolph also provides Business Leadership and Management Consulting through his company, **MyWingman, LLC**, where:

Helping Leaders Design Legacies That Last, ©2015 through:

➤ **Leader Coaching**. From Aspiring Leaders and Start-up Business Owners, through every management and leadership level, to President, CEO, and mature Business Owners.

➤ **Organizational Planning**. Strategy Formulation; Organizational Diagnosis; Strategic Planning Review.

➤ **Corporate Training**. Various leadership and management subjects from Diversity, Equity, and Inclusion (DEI) to Performance Management.

➤ **Legacy Expression**. Writing, editing, publishing, and promoting services for books, articles, peer-reviewed articles, and doctoral dissertations.

➤ **Government Contracting**. Registered in the System for Awards Management (SAM), a VA-verified Service-Disabled Veteran-Owned Small Business (SDVOSB).

➤ **Community Action**. Participation in various non-profit boards and causes that give back to and benefit the community.

Dr. Randolph can also be reached through social media at:

MyWingman, LLC website: www.mywingmanllc.com

Amazon.com Author page: amazon.com/author/drcolrandolph

LinkedIn page: www.linkedin.com/in/drburl

MyWingman, LLC Twitter page: https://twitter.com/mywingmanllc

Google My Business page: https://mywingman-llc.business.site/?m=tru

Alignable Page: https://www.alignable.com/davenport-ia/mywingman-llc

Facebook Business page: https://www.facebook.com/MyWingmanLLC/

Instagram Business page: https://www.instagram.com/mywingman.llc/

Abbreviations and acronyms are a way of life in America. U.S. versus United States is just one example. The military has its fair share, so I thought it wise to add an Abbreviations & Acronyms section at the beginning of the book. Not every abbreviation is an acronym because it does not spell a word, but every acronym is an abbreviation of a much longer phrase. I hope this section is helpful until you get your Army Jargon rhythm down and no longer need it. Also, known civilian acronyms will not be spelled out here under the belief that they are commonly known.

-A- AAR – After Action Review; **ADA** – Air Defense Artillery; AI – Artificial Intelligence; **ALICE** - All-Purpose Lightweight Individual Carrying Equipment; **AQI** – Al Qaeda in Iraq; **AR** – Army Regulation; **ASAP** – As Soon As Possible; **AT-4** – Antitank

-B- **BDA** – Battle Damage Assessment; **BDU** - Battle Dress Uniform; **BTRY** – Battery

-C- **CAA** – Class A Agent; **CCIR** – Commanders Critical Information Requirement; **CD** – Cavalry Division; **CIS** – Commonwealth of Independent States; **CO** – Contracting Officer; **C.O.** – Commanding Officer; **COL** – Colonel; **CONEX – Container Express; CPT** – Captain; **CRP** – Combat Reconnaissance Patrol; **CSM** - Command Sergeant Major; **CTC** – Combat Training Center

-D- **DBM** – Dominant Buying Motive; **DCU** – Desert Camouflage Uniform; **DIVARTY** – Division Artillery; **DJ** – Disc Jockey.

-E-   **EBDA** – Enemy Battle Damage Assessment; **EKIA** – Enemy Killed in Action; **EOD** – Explosive Ordinance Detachment; **EPW** – Enemy Prisoner(s) of War; **ERC** - Equipment Readiness Codes; **ETS** - Expiration Term of Service; **EXSUM** - Executive Summary

-F-   **FAASV** – Field Artillery Ammunition Support Vehicle; **FLIPL** – Financial Liability Investigation of Property Loss; **FM** – Field Manual; **FMS** – Foreign Military Sales; **FROG** – Free Rocket Over Ground; **FSG** – Family Support Group; **FSO** – Fire Support Officer

-G-   **GP** – General Purpose; **GPS** – Global Positioning Satellite

-H-   **HEMMT** – Heavy Expanded Mobility Tactical Transport; **HET** – Heavy Equipment Transport; **HHB** – Headquarters and Headquarters Battery; **HMMWV** – Heavy Mobility Multipurpose Wheeled Vehicle; **HQ** – Headquarters

-I-   **INF** – Intermediate Nuclear Forces; **INTREP** – Intelligence Report

-J-   **JOP** – Justice of the Peace

-K-   K – Kilometer; **KIA**- Killed in Action; **KKMC** – King Khalid Military City; **KSA** – Kingdom of Saudi Arabia

-L-   **LD** – Line of Departure; **LORAN** – Long Range Navigation; **LT** – Lieutenant; **LTC** – Lieutenant Colonel

-M-   **MAJ** – Major; **MASH** – Mobile Army Surgical Hospital; **MFE** – Maneuver, Fires, and Effects; **MI** – Military Intelligence; **MIA** – Missing in Action;

MILES – Multiple Integrated Laser Engagement System; **MLRS** – Multiple Launched Rocket System; **MOGAS** – Motor Gasoline; **MOPP** – Mission Oriented Protective Posture; **MOS** – Military Occupational Specialty; **MRE** – Meal Ready to Eat; **MSB** – Main Support Battalion; **MSG** – Master Sergeant

-N-   **NBC** – Nuclear, Biological, Chemical; **NCO** – Noncommissioned Officer; **NCOIC** – Noncommissioned   Officer in Charge; **NTC** – National Training Center; **NVG** – Night Vision Goggles

-O-   **OBE** – Overcome by Events; **OJT** – On the Job; **OPFOR** – Opposing Forces; **OPTEMPO** – Operational Tempo

-P-   **PBO** - Property Book Officer; **PCS** – Permanent Change of Station; **POW** – Prisoner(s) of War; **PT** – Physical Training; **PTO** – Paid Time Off

-Q-   **QRF** – Quick Reaction Force

-R-   **RDF** – Rapid Deployment Force; **R&R** – Rest and Relaxation; **Roger** – Okay; **RPG** – Rocket Propelled Grenade; **RRF** – Rapid Reaction Force

-S-   **SA** – Saudi Arabia; **SAM** – Surface to Air Missile; **SCIF** – Sensitive Compartmented Information Facility; **SITREP** – Situation Report; **SOL** – Shit-Out-of-Luck; **SWO** – Special Weapons Officer

-T-   **TA-50** – Tactical Assembly Gear; **TAA** – Tactical Assembly Area: **TEAMS** – Training, Education, Adventure, Money, Service to Country; **TF** – Task Force; **TOC** – Tactical Operations Center; **TTP** – Tactics, Techniques and Procedures

-U-   **UN** – United Nations; **UXO** – Unexploded Ordnance

-V-   **VCR** – Video Cassette Recorder; **VHS** – Video Home System

-W-   **WIA** – Wounded in Action; **WILCO** – Will Comply; **WMD** – Weapons of Mass Destruction

-X-   **XO** – Executive Officer

-Y-

-Z-

Notes

[1] Army Officer Career Fields: https://militaryscience.ucdavis.edu/career-fields

[2] SCUD Ranges: https://en.wikipedia.org/wiki/Scud_missile

[3] Summation of United Nations Proclamation on Iraq Invasion of Kuwait by 3/82nd Field Artillery Battalion Commander

[4] Photo of FAASV M90px Loader, M992

[5] Uzi reference. https://commons.wikimedia.org/wiki/File:Uzi_of_the_israeli_armed_forces.jpg

[6] Thobe Jubba Dishdasha. https://insidesaudi.com/the-common-sense-guide-to-how-non-saudi-men-should-dress-in-saudi-arabia/

[7] Five Muslim Daily Prayers and What They Mean. https://www.learnreligions.com/islamic-prayer-timings-2003811

[8] Burqa. https://en.wikipedia.org/wiki/Burqa

[9] Islamic Religious Holidays. https://en.wikipedia.org/wiki/Islamic_holidays

[10] Soldiers mixing orange juice and antifreeze. https://www.mynbc5.com/article/11-fort-bliss-soldiers-ill-after-ingesting-substance/35361743

[11] No good deed goes unpunished. https://en.wikipedia.org/wiki/ No_ good_ deed_goes_unpunished

[12] Universal Transversal Mercator coordinate system. https://en.wikipedia.org/wiki/Universal_Transverse_Mercator_coordinate_system

[13] Battle of Ruqi Pocket. https://en.wikipedia.org/wiki/2nd_Brigade_Combat_Team,_1st_Cavalry_Division_(United_States)

[14] Operational Map for Operation Iraqi Freedom Friendly Forces.

[15] Sun Tzu's The Art of War. Authors copy.

[16] Tony Orlando and Dawn. Tie a Yellow Ribbon Round the Ole Oak Tree. https://www.bing.com/search?q=tie+a+yellow+ribbon+song+lyrics&qs=LT&pq=tie+a+yellow+ribbon+song&sk=AS1&sc=9-24&cvid=19E777C1AC4 E4BAD9F08840B44AA1885&FORM=QBRE&sp=2&lq=0

[17] Valorous Unit Award Citation to 2nd Blackjack Brigade, 1st Cavalry Division, Operation Desert Storm. Operations DESERT SHIELD and DESERT STORM: Valorous Unit Award Citations | Unit Award Orders & Citations | U.S. Army Center of Military History